GENEALOGICAL ABSTRACTS FROM MISSOURI CHURCH RECORDS AND OTHER RELIGIOUS SOURCES

VOLUME 1

Sherida K. Eddlemon

HERITAGE BOOKS
2010

HERITAGE BOOKS
AN IMPRINT OF HERITAGE BOOKS, INC.

Books, CDs, and more—Worldwide

For our listing of thousands of titles see our website
at
www.HeritageBooks.com

Published 2010 by
HERITAGE BOOKS, INC.
Publishing Division
100 Railroad Ave. #104
Westminster, Maryland 21157

International Standard Book Numbers
Paperbound: 978-0-7884-0374-3
Clothbound: 978-0-7884-8559-6

DEDICATION

This book is dedicated to my paternal grandmother, Catherine Fay Campbell, b. 29 June 1911, Knoxville, TN, d. 12 April 1994, Memphis, TN. Grandma "Cat" was a descendant of Alexander Campbell of Scotland, William Campbell of Scotland and Ireland, Robert Campbell of Virginia and "Elder" David Campbell, Revolutionary War soldier who fought at the battle of King's Mountain and was a co-founder of Campbell's Station in Knox County, Tennessee. David Campbell married Janet Lockhart in 1785 in Greene County, Tennessee.

On 13 January 1934, Catherine Fay Campbell married Paul Nelson Eddlemon at the Church street Methodist Church in Knoxville, TN. Paul was a descendant of John Eddlemon who was in Maury County, Tennessee in the early 1800's. Catherine was the mother of four children.

She was a religious woman and was a member of the Bellevue Baptist Church at the time of her death, so that it is particularly fitting that this book on church records be dedicated to Grandma "Cat."

TABLE OF CONTENTS

Antioch Baptist Church, Chesterfield, St. Louis County............................ 154
Antioch Meeting House, Dade County........... 2
Baptist Ministers, Listing in Marshall Democrat, Covers Cass, Linn, Randolph, St. Louis, Jackson, Marion, Boone, Clinton, Macon, Livingston, Saline, Callaway, Daviess, Mercer, Cooper, Mississippi, St. Clair, Moniteau, Morgan, Platte, Lincoln, Ray, Bollinger, Cape Girardeau, Pike, Howard, Ralls, Shelby, Johnson, Carroll, Cole, Dekald, Perry, Audrain, Henry, Lewis, St. Francois, Montgomery, Warren, Chariton, Gasconade, Stoddard, Gentry, Hickory, St. Charles, Knox, Pettis, Grundy, Macon, Caldwell Counties........................ 104
Bethel United Baptist Association Meeting, St. Louis Free Press, Oct. 17, 1833, St. Francois County......................... 102
Bethel United Baptist Association Meeting, St. Louis Free Press, Oct. 24, 1833...... 132
Big Buffalo United Baptist Church, Benton County.................................... 101
Big Creek Baptist Church, Big Creek, Carroll County.................................... 107
Christ Episcopal Church, Lafayette County... 119
Concord Christian Church, Concord, Saline County.................................... 21
Crooked Creek Cumberland Presbyterian Church, Keysville, Crawford County............... 78
Ely-Union Valley Cumberland Presbyterian Church, Ely, Marion County............... 30
Evangelical Protestant Church of the Holy Ghost, St. Louis County................. 3
First Baptist Church, Miami, Saline County... 96
Huntsville Cumberland Presbyterian Church, Huntsville, Randolph County............. 19
Jacksonville Union Chapel, Randolph County... 85
Indian Grove Christian Church or Powell Church, Chariton County.................. 1
Kidd's Chapel Church, St. Clair County....... 18
Liberty Tribune, Baptist References, Clay County.................................... 88
Macedonia Methodist Church, Ripley County.... 133
Manchester Methodist Church, Manchester, St. Louis County............................ 114
Maramec Iron Worker's Cemetery, St. James,

Phelps County.......................... 156
Missouri Methodist Episcopal Church, Covers
    parts of Missouri, Arkansas and the
    Shawnee, Delaware, Peori, Cherokee, Creek,
    Kickapoo, Kings River Missions............. 157
Mount Hope Cumberland Presbyterian Church,
    Huntsville, Randolph County.............. 57
New Hope Baptist Church, West Union, Cass
    County.................................. 92
Platte River Baptist Assoication Delegates,
    St. Joseph Gazette, Buchanan County....... 100
Rochester Cumberland Presbyterian Church,
    Helena Andrew County..................... 82
Salt River Baptist Association, Bowling Green
    Radical, Pike County..................... 103
Shawnee Mound Cumberland Presbyterian Church,
    Chilhowee, Johnson County................ 4
Slater Christian Church, Salter, Saline
    County.................................. 39
St. Pauls' Episcopal Church, Iron County
    Register, Iron County.................... 119
State Census, 1883, Pettis County, Minister
    A. J. Van Wagner......................... 57
Suprise Cumberland Presbyterian Church,
    Clinton, Lafayette County................ 73
United Blue River Association, Twenty-Third
    Annual Session Minutes................... 86
Watson Cumberland Presbyterian Church,
    Watson, Atchison County.................. 62
West Fork Baptist Church, Raytown, Jackson
    County.................................. 99
Zoar Baptist Church, Napton, Saline County... 131

ACKNOWLEDGEMENTS

Thanks to my parents, Nelson and Amelia Eddlemon, for their continued support and encouragement.

PREFACE

Church records are a rich source of information on individual birth, death, baptism and marriage dates, that may not be recorded on the county level. In Missouri full compliance for the state registration of births and deaths was not until 1911.

In addition to basic vital information about an individual, there are clues as to where people moved to or when they left the area. It is possible to gain insight as to the character of an individual as it was possible to be suspended from attending church for such reasons as dancing, drinking and fighting. In many of the records women have an additional name recorded in parentheses. It is unknown whether this is their maiden or married name.

Ministers often rode a circuit in the earlier days covering a wide territory with a spread out congregation. Many times they never recorded the marriages they performed or the births and deaths of members of their congregations.

Included with the church records are articles in various newspapers, census and cemetery records with a religious reference. These were included to make this a more complete source.

Good luck in your search for your ancestor and hopefully, he is listed within these pages.

A B B R E V I A T I O N S

B	....	Birth Date
BD	....	Baptism Date
OF	....	Offical
MD	....	Marriage Date
MG	....	Minister
JP	....	Justice of Peace
PRTS	....	Parents
D	....	Death Date
DIS	....	Dismissed
ADM	....	Admission
SUS	....	Suspended
Y	....	Year
M	....	Month
D	....	Day
I	....	Issue
SP	....	Sponsor
R	....	Recorder

SELECTED LIST OF REPOSITORIES AND ARCHIVES

Baptist

Missouri Baptist Historical Society
William Jewell College Library
Liberty, MO 64068

Southern Baptist Theoloigcal Seminary
Louisville, KY 40206

Historical Commission of the Southern
Baptist Convention
127 Ninth Ave. North
Nashville, NC 37234

Baptist Historical Collection
Z. Smith Reynolds Library
Wake Forest University
Winston-Salem, NC 27109

Southwestern Baptist Theological Seminary
Fort Worth, TX 76122

Church of Christ

Harding Graduate School of Religion Library
1000 Cherry Rd.
Memphis, TN 38117

Cumberland Presbyterian

Historical Foundation of the
Cumberland Presbyterian Church
1978 Union Ave.
Memphis, TN 38104

Disciples of Christ

Disciples of Christ Historical Society
1101 Nineteeth Ave. South
Nashville, TN 37212

Lexington Theological Seminary
631 So. Limestone
Lexington, KY 40508

Jewish

American Jewish Archives
3101 Clifton Ave.
Cincinnati, OH 45220

Lutheran

Concordia Historical Institute
Lutheran Church - Missouri Synod
801 De Mun Ave.
St. Louis, MO 63103

Lutheran Church - Virginia Synod
317 Washington Ave. SW
Roanoke, VA 24016

Luthern Southern Seminary
4201 North Main St.
Columbia, SC 29203

Methodist

William R. Perkins Library
Manuscript Department
Duke University
Durham, NC 27706

Roman Catholic

St. Louis University
St. Louis, MO 63103

Catholic Archives of America
Notre Dame University
South Bend, IN 46624

United Church of Christ

Eden Archives
475 East Lockwood Ave.
Webster Grove, MO 63119

Chariton County, Missouri, Indian Grove Christian
Church or Powell Church.
Baptismal Register
Carter DeWeese: (B) Dec. 26, 1840, (BD) Feb.,
1862, (OF) Eld. J. Pavy.
Nancy E. DeWeese: (B) Dec. 23, 1843, (BD) Feb.,
1862, (OF) Eld. J. Pavy.
William DeWeese: (B) Dec. 31, 1837, (BD) Jul.,
1862, (OF) Eld. Jonathan Martin.
Sarah A. DeWeese: (B) Apr. 13, 1840, (BD) Jul.,
1862, (OF) Eld. J. Martin.
Milton Powell: (B) Sep. 9, 1847, (BD) Mar.,
1866, (OF) Eld. Martin.
Margaret A. Powell: (BD) Mar., 1866, (OF) Eld.
J. Martin.
Mary E. Ashley: (BD) Mar., 1866, (OF) Eld. J.
Martin.
Hiram McClure and Estella McClure: Names listed
only.
Charles E. Powell: (B) Oct. 18, 1816, (BD) Jun.
1833, (OF) Eld. Peter Haugn.
Sarah B. Powell: (B) Jul. 20, 1829, (BD) 1857,
(OF) A. Pauly.
Francis E. May: (B) Jul. 10, 1844, (BD) Oct. 13,
1872, (OF) S. C. Hutton.
Susan May: (B) Jul. 30, 1849, (BD) May 1868,
(OF) F. E. Hersenflow.
William H. May: (B) Mar. 20, 1853, (BD) Jul. 25,
1876, (OF) Eld. O. P. Wheeler.
Charles W. Bashaw and Sarah Bashaw: Names only
listed.
James Padgett: (B) Dec. 10, 1847, (OF) Alvin
Dooley.
Martha E. Padgett: (B) Feb. 4, 1854, (OF)
Jonathan Martin.
Clarissa A. Deweese: (B) Sep. 26, 1860, (BD)
Jul. 25, 1876, (OF) O. P. Wheeler.
Nancy J. May: (B) Nov. 26, 1860, (BD) Jul. 25,
1876, (OF) O. P. Wheeler.
John E. Jenkins: (B) Aug 23, 1851, (OF) F. E.
Hessenflow.
Charles L. DeWeese: (B) Oct., 1858, (BD) Jul.
25, 1876, (OF) O. P. Wheeler.
Tabitha E. Powell: (BD) ?, (OF) Jonathan Martin.
Willis G. Powell: (B) Mar. 1, 1846, (OF)
Jonathan Martin.
Margaret C. McLane: Name only listed.
Mary McLane: (BD) Aug. 4, 1878, (OF) C. DeWeese.
Eliza J. Allen: (B) Apr. 12, 1842.

1

Lydia A. Allen: Name only listed.
Sarah J. DeWeese: (B) Sep. 17, 1864, (BD) JUl.
7, 1878, (OP) O. P. Wheeler.
Mary J. Allen: (BD) Jul. 7, 1878, (OF) O. P.
Wheeler.
James W. Ashley: (BD) Aug. 4, 1878, (OF) C.
DeWeese.
John Mitchel: (BD) Sep. 6, 1841, (OF) C.
DeWeese.
Isaac Allen: (BD) Aug. 4, 1878, (OF) C. DeWeese.
Sarah Allen: (BD) Aug. 4, 1878, (OF) O. DeWeese.
James A. May: (B) Oct. 20, 1848, (BD) Jul. 31,
1881, (OF) C. DeWeese.

Dade County, Missouri, Antioch Meeting House, Marriage Records.

Walter S. Mitchell and America Heath, (MD) May
5, 1841.
William Turpen and Emily P. Pellin, (MD) May 6,
1841.
Robert M. Ward and Luvenia Bowles, (MD) Jun. 4,
1841,
Andrew Morris and Catherine Hudspeth, (MD) Jan.
26, 1842.
Jacob B. Parris and Mary E. Faires, (MD) Jan.
11, 1844.
John L. Berryman and Mirande Bowles, (MD) Mar.
14, 1844.
William Pell and Elizabeth Scott, (MD) Sep. 14,
1845.
Woodford Scott and Rebecca Jones, (MD) Dec. 18,
1845.
Benjamin Priddy and Nancy J. Scott, (MD) Feb.
14, 1846.
Radford Scott and Highly B. Hudspeth, (MD) Apr.
19, 1846.
Wm. K. Spilman and Mary E. Still, (MD) May 21,
1846.
Rufus Hudspeth and Frances Scott, (MD) Aug. 12,
1846.
Newell Cates and Mary Snadon, (MD) Aug. 13,
1846.
James F. Scott and Sarrah (sic) Poindexter, (MD)
Mar. 7, 1847.
Pleasant Spear and Emily Hays, (MD) Apr. 8,
1847.
Matthias Speers and Almirry Hudspeth, (MD) May
30, 1847.
Samuueal (sic) Harris and Martha Ann Carr, (MD)

Jun. 6, 1847.
Joseph T. Johns and Martha L. Duston, (MD) Aug. 1, 1847.
Charles W. Gates and Nancy Cox, (MD) Sep. 9, 1847.
Phillip Scott and Malzina Hall, (MD) Oct. 21, 1847.
Wm. Poindexter and Margaret Pellin, (MD) Jan. 13, 1848.
Joseph Williams and Miranda Penn, (MD) Feb. 10, 1848.
Mayfield Hinshaw and Mildred Brown, (MD) Sep. 14, 1851.
Andrew Hudspeth and Amanda Mallory, (MD) Dec, 10, 1852.
Owen W. Bates and Emillin Mills, (MD) Mar. 15, 1854.
D. P. Randolph and Julia Ann Brooks, (MD) Jun. 30, 1855.
James Simms and Nancy J. Lanton, (MD) Sep. 23, 1855.
Benjamin F. Moore and Mary R. Davis, (MD) Aug. 27, 1868.
Lewis Renfrow and Mary Finly, (MD) Sep. 24, 1868.
Joseph H. Renfrow and Jarlee Merrick, (MD) Oct. 18, 1868.
Absalum Spears and Lucy Springer, (MD) Feb. 21, 1869.
William F. Gates and Lucy Scott, (MD) Apr. 25, 1869.
Joseph Priddy and Jane Hoover, (MD) Jan. 2, 1870.

St. Louis County, Missouri, Confirmation List, Evangelical Protestant Church of the Holy Ghost, Apr. 4, 1869, St. Louis.
John Ruckert, Bernhard T. Spelbrink, Federick Wilhelm Keiser, Franz H. Krenning, Heinrich Mers, Julius Heitmeir, Franz Helage, Eduard F. Kayser, Julius Herm von Senden, Eduard Fritachle, Georg H. E. Schaburg, Wilhelm Ed. Mestemacher, Georg H. E. Schaberg, Eduard Fritschle, John Reckewag, Heinrich G. Sachleben, Heinrich Michel, Hermann Michel, Eduard Stossberg, Carl Kuehner, August Pepe, Friedrich Ferie, Christian Ingold, Heinrich Berger, Georg S. Reinhard, Wilhelm Banklage, Wilhelm Nolte, Otto Spannagel, John D. Frye, Christian H. Thies, Franz A. Mohrhardt, Johann Hensick, Carl H.

Buschmann, Otto Theo Zeng, Eduard Dickhoener, Heinrich Sander, Heinr. Rud. Frye, Sophie Suppe, Regula Simmen, Christine Weber, Marie Lindemann, Sophie Helene Scwenker, Julia Wilshusen, Minna Wrieden, Selma Louise Reinhard, Kate Marie Scwenker, Auguste Wagner, Emma Wilkens, Maria Helfenstein, Catharina Maria Sopp, Louise Marie Mueller, Angelica Braut, Ella Kapelle, Anna Helene O. M. Strauss, Emmma Marie Picker, Maria Emilie Temme, Louise Nies, Anna Ochterback, Catharine Brunner, Lina Suessdorf, Anna Friedr. Ehlich, Minna Aug. Sichting, Elise Kling, Louise Christine Benz, Maria Elise Haun, Anna C. A. Tiekemeyer, Louise Marie Stegemann, Mathilda E. Hoecker, Julie Hammel, Henriette Frank, Christine Deibel, Caroline A. Meskendorf, Dorette C. Behrens, Bertha Hirt, Louise M. Martin, Mathilde Doergea, Anna Schollmeyer, Caroline Cathr. Helmrichs, Emma Bergesch, Elise M. Eckert, Minna Schrader, Auguste Friedrika Thias.

Chilhowee, Johnson County, Missouri, Shawnee Mound Cumberland Presbyterian Church
Register of Adult Baptisms

Name	Date	Reverend
Mary Moore	Aug. 20, 1869	B. F. Thomas
Mary Jane Guian	Aug. 20, 1869	B. F. Thomas
Peter Smiley	Aug. 20, 1869	B. F. Thomas
Ferdinan W. Crooks	Aug. 23, 1869	B. F. Thomas
Ellen Thresher	Aug. 23, 1869	B. F. Thomas
William P. Moore	Nov. 19, 1869	B. F. Thomas
Daniel Grey	Nov. 19, 1869	B. F. Thomas
Marg. Jane Wade	May 22, 1870	B. F. Thomas
Margaret Gowens	Aug. 21, 1870	B. F. Thomas
Martha J. Hays	Aug. 22, 1870	B. F. Thomas
Julie F. Glasgow	Aug. 22, 1870	B F. Thomas
Joseph Mays	Aug. 22, 1870	B. F. Thomas
Martha Grey	Aug. 22, 1870	B. F. Thomas
Carry Powers	Aug. 18, 1870	B. F. Thomas
Jacob Wiseman	Aug. 22, 1870	B. F. Thomas
Anna Wiseman	Aug. 22, 1870	B. F. Thomas
Andrew Russell	Aug. 22, 1870	B. F. Thomas
Amanda Cassy	Aug. 22, 1870	B. F. Thomas
Robert B. Smith	Aug. 22, 1870	B. F. Thomas
Marg. E. Smith	Aug. 22, 1870	B. F. Thomas
Susan J. Crabtree	Aug. 22, 1870	B. F. Thomas
Susan Kimsey	Aug. 22, 1873	B. F. Thomas
Geo. W. Maze	Aug. 22, 1870	B. F. Thomas

Name	Date			Reverend
Josie Burgess	Dec.	23,	1874	B. F. Thomas
Alphonso Hickinson	Dec.	27,	1874	B. F. Thomas
Frank S. Sharp	Sep.	--,	1874	B. F. Thomas
Tho. P. Clagett	Sep.	--,	1874	B. F. Thomas
Mrs. Jennie Semson	Sep.	--,	1874	B. F. Thomas
Mrs. Emma Wolf	Sep.	--,	1874	B. F. Thomas
Sarah R. R. Frelden	Dec.	20,	1875	B. F. Thomas
Noah Hickerson	Aug.	8,	1877	S. H. McKlane
Robt. C. Frelden	Aug.	8,	1877	S. H. McKlane
A. F. McCall	Aug.	8,	1877	S. H. McKlane
J. C. Hubbard	Aug.	8,	1877	S. H. McKlane
Joseph Orkins	Aug.	12,	1877	G. L. Moad
Mrs. Fannie Orkins	Aug.	12,	1877	G. L. Moad
F. A. Whitenack	Aug.	12,	1877	G. L. Moad
Miss M. F. Moore	Jul.	29,	1877	S. H. McElvain
Mary F. Maize	Nov.	17,	1878	Y. W. Whitsett
George W. Brown	Nov.	17,	1878	Y. W. Whitsett
Mr. C. R. Rice	Nov.	24,	1878	Y. W. Whitsett
Miss Virginia Winehope	Nov.	24,	1878	Y. W. Whitsett
William Hinton	Nov.	20,	1879	J. Cal. Littrell
Mr. M. R. Glasgow	Nov.	20,	1879	J. Cal. Littrell
Mrs. Sarah A. Hinkle	Nov.	20,	1879	J. Cal. Littrell
Walter Nickelson	Nov.	20,	1879	J. Cal. Littrell
John R. Hinkle	Nov.	20,	1879	J. Cal. Littrell
James Hinkle	Nov.	20,	1879	J. Cal. Littrell
John L. Moore	Nov.	20,	1879	J. Cal. Littrell
Sarah H. Jones	Nov.	20,	1879	J. Cal. Littrell
Della Hickerson	Nov.	20,	1879	J. Cal. Littrell
Belle Hickerson	Nov.	20,	1879	J. Cal. Littrell
Bettie Moore	Dec.	7,	1879	J. Cal. Littrell
Mary J. Boling	Dec.	7,	1879	J. Cal. Littrell
Katie Guion	Jan.	2,	1881	J. H. Houx
Ida V. Mills	Nov.	4,	1881	J. H. Houx
Luie Casey	Nov.	14,	1881	J. H. Houx
Sarah O. Elliott	Nov.	14,	1881	J. H. Houx
Minnie Lee Casey	Nov.	14,	1881	J. H. Houx
Minnie A. Eagleson	Nov.	14,	1881	J. H. Houx
Lottie M. Mills	Nov.	14,	1881	J. H. Houx
Mary E. Smith	Nov.	14,	1881	J. H. Houx
Mattie A.	Nov.	14,	1881	J. H. Houx

Name	Date	Reverend
Eagleson		
Eugene Wolff	Nov. 14, 1881	J. H. Houx
Thomas W. Moore	Nov. 14, 1881	J. H. Houx
Llewellyn G. Wolff	Nov. 14, 1881	J. H. Houx
John S. Casey	Nov. 14, 1881	J. H. Houx
Sarah Holt	Dec. 4, 1881	J. H. Houx
John W. Bond	Nov. 5, 1882	J. H. Houx
Francis E. Comer	Sep. 11, 1885	J. B. Fly
H. J. Cook	Sep. 11, 1885	J. B. Fly
Elmo Maize	Sep. 11, 1885	J. B. Fly
Jasper N. Cale	Sep. 11, 1885	J. B. Fly
Anna Zarragar	Sep. 11, 1885	J. B. Fly
Andrew M. Comer	Sep. 13, 1885	Z. T. Orr
Clarrance McCann	Sep. 13, 1885	Z. T. Orr
Jennie Bemis	Sep. 13, 1885	Z. T. Orr
Robert Hawkins	Aug. 29, 1886	Z. T. Orr
Walter Runner	Aug. 29, 1886	Z. T. Orr
Moses E. Watkins	Aug. 29, 1886	Z. T. Orr
Jas. M. Barrager	Aug. 29, 1886	Z. T. Orr
Daniel Barrager	Aug. 29, 1886	Z. T. Orr
Sarah E. Watkins	Aug. 29, 1886	Z. T. Orr
Carrie L. McCann	Aug. 29, 1886	Z. T. Orr
Zerelda Barrager	Sep. 1, 1886	Z. T. Orr
James H. Roser	Sep. 1, 1886	Z. T. Orr
Maggie S. Whittaker	Sep. 2, 1886	Z. T. Orr
Ida Whittaker	Sep. 2, 1886	Z. T. Orr
John W. Hood	Sep. 5, 1886	Z. T. Orr
Della Hood	Sep. 5, 1886	Z. T. Orr
Georgia E. Whitside	Sep. 12, 1886	Z. T. Orr
Cynthia N. Bailey	Sep. 12, 1886	Z. T. Orr
Della M. Bailey	Sep. 12, 1886	Z. T. Orr
James Bailey	Sep. 12, 1886	Z. T. Orr
Allice Moore	Sep. 11, 1887	Z. T. Orr
Effa Casey	Sep. 11, 1887	Z. T. Orr
Clara A. Wade	Sep. 11, 1887	Z. T. Orr
Bertha Watkins	Sep. 11, 1887	Z. T. Orr
Lulia Watkins	Sep. 11, 1887	Z. T. Orr
Ella Wolff	Sep. 11, 1887	Z. T. Orr
Samuel T. Lycook	Sep. 11, 1887	Z. T. Orr
Thomas Hincher	Sep. 11, 1887	Z. T. Orr
Geo. W. Elliott	Sep. 11, 1887	Z. T. Orr
Luella Murray	Sep. 7, 1888	Z. T. Orr
Ada G. Smith	Sep. 7, 1888	Z. T. Orr
Anna M. Tilman	Sep. 7, 1888	Z. T. Orr

Name	Date	Reverend
Eli D. Bradshaw	Sep. 9, 1888	Z. T. Orr
Melissa C. Webb	Sep. 9, 1888	Z. T. Orr
Clara V. Hicks	Sep. 9, 1888	Z. T. Orr
M. C. Dunn	Sep. 10, 1888	Z. T. Orr
Wm. R. Hicks	Sep. 11, 1888	Z. T. Orr
Lucy M. Casey	Nov. 24, 1890	Z. T. Orr
Lullie Moore	Nov. 24, 1890	Z. T. Orr
Annie Lee Casey	Nov. 24, 1890	Z. T. Orr
Cliff H. Kensinger	Nov. 24, 1890	Z. T. Orr
George Barker	Nov. 24, 1890	Z. T. Orr
Frank Trissemiter	Nov. 27, 1890	Z. T. Orr
Laura Trissemiter	Nov. 27, 1890	Z. T. Orr
Mattie E. Andrew	Nov. 27, 1890	Z. T. Orr
Clara E. Bradshaw	Nov. 27, 1890	Z. T. Orr
Etta M. Bradshaw	Nov. 27, 1890	Z. T. Orr
Minnie Wade	Nov. 27, 1890	Z. T. Orr
Merodith Wade	Nov. 27, 1890	Z. T. Orr
Lena Tilman	Nov. 30, 1890	Z. T. Orr
Warren Wickham	Nov. 30, 1890	Z. T. Orr
James Heckter	Dec. 20, 1891	Z. T. Orr
Allice Bailey	Nov. 20, 1892	Z. T. Orr
Dora Snodgrass	Nov. 20, 1892	Z. T. Orr
Della Wade	Nov. 20, 1892	Z. T. Orr
Miss Lise Gains	Aug. 8, 1894	Z. T. Orr
Etta M. Powers	Nov. 2, 1894	L. R. Nichols
George F. Crooks	Nov. 2, 1894	L. R. Nichols
James C. Commer	Nov. 2, 1894	L. R. Nichols
George W. Comer	Nov. 2, 1894	L. R. Nichols
John H. E. Elliott	Nov. 2, 1894	L. R. Nichols
Henry C. Descombs	Dec. 23, 1894	L. R. Nichols
John W. Woolf	Dec. 23, 1894	L. R. Nichols
Albert Scott	Sep. 20, 1894	B. Margeson
Lewis F. Waldridge	Sep. 20, 1894	B. Margeson
John C. Whiteman	Sep. 22, 1895	B. Margeson
Lela J. H. Elliott	Sep. 23, 1895	B. Margeson
Mary Hathaway	Sep. 23, 1895	B. Margeson
Wm. W. Bailey	Sep. 23, 1895	B. Margeson
Roy Whitesides	Jul. --, 1895	L. R. Nichols
Edward Bailey	Jul. --, 1895	L. R. Nichols

Name	Date	Reverend
J. G. Beaty	Sep. 30, 1895	L. R. Nichols
Miss Hattie Lewis	Sep. 30, 1895	L. R. Nichols
Lewis Bradley	Jun. 21, 1896	Y.W. Whitsett

Register of Deaths

Name (Deceased)	Death Date	Reverend
James Kimsey	Jul. 9, 1870	---
Mrs. Martha J. Hays	Feb. 23, 1872	---
Mrs. Cary Baker	Aug. 17, 1876	B. F. Thomas
Mrs. Nancy Murray	Feb. 12, 1879	Y. W. Whitsett
Marietta Whitworth	Mar. 27, 1888	Z. T. Orr
Jane Morgart	Feb. 12, 1887	J. A. Murphey

Register of Marriages

Cary Allen Eager and Margaret Jane Wade, (MD) July 31, 1870, (JP) J. H. McCan.

Ferdinan Crooks and Mary DaComb, (MD) November 27, 1872, (MG) B. F. Thomas.

Frank S. Sharp and Nancy E. Evans, (MD) December 3, 1874, (MG) B. F. Thomas.

George W. Maize and Sallie W. Martin, (MD) December 17, 1874, (MG) B. F. Thomas.

W. L. Roy and Mary A. Davis, (MD) December 31, 1874, (MG) B. F. Thomas.

John B. Barker and Carrie L. Powers, (MD) May 6, 1875, (MG) B. F. Thomas.

Henry Hinton and Susan Kimsey, (MD) October 17, 1875, (MG) B. F. Thomas.

Wm. Tuttle and Mrs. Jemina Darling, (MD) July 20, 1875, (MG) B. F. Thomas.

Wm. Whitworth and Mrs. Marideth Crooks, (MD) Not given, (MG) J. H. Gillespie.

J. R. Maize and Mary Neal, (MD) Not Given, (MG) B. F. Thomas.

John R. Barker and Amanda E. Casey, (MD) November 27, 1879, (MG) B. F. Thomas.

Thomas Zarnes and Mattie A. Eagleson, (MD) Not given, (MG) S. Finis King.

David Williamson and Elizabeth Sharp, (MG) Z. T. Orr.

C. H. Kensinger and Minnie Eagleson, (MD) January 28, 1891, (MG) Z. T. Orr.

Johnson Kensinger and Clara A. Wade, (MD) Mar. -, 1892, (MG) Z. T. Orr.

Register of Elders

Name	Ceased to Act	Ordained
P. W. Moore	---	1850
Daniel Grey	Sep. --, 1876	Feb. 20, 1876
Mosses (sic) E. Watkins	---	---

8

Name	Ceased to Act	Ordained
--- Fitzwater	Mar. --, 1873	---
Saml. H. Elliott	---	Sep. 20, 1874
Geo. W. Maize	Mar. 9, 1878	Sep. 20, 1874
John W. Brouagh	---	Mar. 5, 1882
Robert Sharp	---	Mar. 5, 1882
G. W. Watkins	---	Feb. 22, 1894
Frank S. Sharp	May 18, 1878	Mar. 12, 1876
Llewellyn Woolff	---	Feb. 22, 1891
Dr. J. G. Beaty	---	Nov. 8, 1897
Wm. Hinton	---	Nov. 8, 1897
C. L. Crooks	---	Nov. 8, 1897

Register of Deacons

Name	Ceased to Act	Ordained
Geo. M. Casey	---	Sep. 20, 1874
Ferdinan Crooks	---	Sep. 20, 1874
Andrew Russell	d.Mar. 11, 1877	Sep. 20, 1874
Jacob Wolf	---	Mar. 12, 1876
James Eagleson	Mar. 1, 1895	Mar. 5, 1882
Wm. Hinton	Nov. 8, 1897	Mar. 5, 1882
Mrs. Wm. Hinton	---	Nov. 8, 1897
Alice Powers	---	Nov. 8, 1897

Register of Infant Baptisms

Sallie A. Whitsett, (PRTS) Mr. and Mrs. Y. W. Whitsett, (BD) November 19, 1878, (MG) W. W. Brannum.

Olive B. Maize, (PRTS) Mr. and Mrs. J. R. Maize, (BD) November 19, 1878, (MG) W. W. Brannum.

Charles L. Crooks, (PRTS) Mr. and Mrs. F. M. Crooks, (BD) November 19, 1878, (MG) W. W. Brannum.

George F. Crooks, (PRTS) Mr. and Mrs. F. M. Crooks, (BD) November 19, 1878, (MG) W. W. Brannum.

Delia A. Crooks, (PRTS) Mr. and Mrs. F. M. Crooks, (BD) November 19, 1878, (MG) W. W. Brannum.

William S. Sharp, (PRS) Robert and Alice Sharp, (BD) February 28, 1888, (MG) Z. T. Orr.

Joseph Sharp, (PRTS) Robert and Alice Sharp, (BD) February 28, 1888, (MG) Z. T. Orr.

Ava Lee Hinton, (PRTS) Wm. and Lizzie L. Hinton, (BD) November 24, 1890, (MG) Z. T. Orr.

Emeline Hinton, (PRTS) Wm. and Lizzie L. Hinton, (BD) November 24, 1890, (MG) Z. T. Orr.

Fannie S. Nichols, (PRTS) Rev. L. R. and Hattie M. Nichols, (BD) August 8, 1894, (MG) Z. T. Orr,

Edna Isabella Kensinger, (PRTS) Mr. and Mrs. Johnson Kensinger, (BD) September 7, 1897, (MG) J. A. Murphy.

Building Fund Pledges, March 23, 1871

G. M. Casey, Philip W. Moore, Wm. Adair, John R.

Powers, F. W. Crooks, Joseph Sharp, J. H. McCann,
Wm. Tuttle, Danl. Grey, George W. Murray, F. W.
Bleil, W. T. Wilson, D. B. Whidbee, C. E. Powers,
Geo. Arnold, Wm. Paul, Wm. Hinton, John Woolfolk
Wm. P. Moore, Bedford Tuttle, Frank Crooks, Frank
Kemp, Charles DesCombs, Joseph Williams, Jane
Stone, William J. Ferel, William Freeland, D. B.
Lambert, Isaac Adair, N. B. Moore, Robert Harwood,
David Snodgrass, Rebecca Neil, V. J. Moore, Jacob
Thrasher, Jacob Fingle, Sarah Kimsay, Robert Sharp,
sr., P. DesCombs, Max McCann, Mary F. Moore, H.
Caldwell, Frank Caldwell, D. P. Kimsey, M. E.
Watkins, Joseph Cole, Jas. H. Carter, John Coppage,
Willis Helm, Joseph Berger, W. D. Wash, Elias
Tuttle, W. J. Butler, G. Townsler, R. C. Ceicil,
Emma Wolff, A. Judge, W. A. Bryson, E. C. Gillam,
N. H. Fitzwater, B. F. Thomas, W. E. Foster, P. R.
Webster, J. D. Wiseman, Alexr. Miller, John J.
Mason, A. J. Bailey, J. W. Harriger, G. Y. Salmon,
Philip Land, D. C. Stone, F. H. Land, Jacob Wolff,
John Curtis, A. C. Comer, Robt. Allen, Herkett &
Brother, John Ragland, Ed Curtis, H. Riehl, N. D.
Land, Haysler & Brother, B. L. Quarrels, E. A.
Covington, Geo. Barker, Salmon & Stone, S. D.
Garth, F. W. McFarland, W. G. Rogers, ---
McCollins, R. W. Cressy, Wm. S. Stone, B. G. Boone,
Roberts & Bro., Jas. Webb, Robert Lewis, Jacob
Goldsmith, Andrew Russell, R. B. Smith, R. T.
Lindsey, Robt. Gilbert, Miles Weeks, R. B. Casey,
John A. Townsend, Sarah Jane Holt, Y. G. Culley,
Jack Johnson, John C. Culley, G. D. Wright, T. J.
Wright, J. D. Farr, E. H. Askew, W. R. Culley, P.
P. Embrey, Saml. R. Brown, John R. Johnson, W. P.
Huff, Arthur Hand, W. J. McFarland, J. D.
Willaimson, N. W. Norris, J. F. Loyd, S. V. Turner,
D. W. Bennzette, Myron Wallace, T. N. Carpenter, R.
R. Walls, Jas. G. Turk, W. S. Wantland.

Register of Communicants

Name	Admission Date	Dismissed Date
Mary Moore	Sep. 1869	---
Jane Kimsey	Sep. 1869	Jul. 7, 1870
Mary Jane Guion (Lamar)	Sep. 1869	Sep. 2, 1886
Elizabeth Sharp (Williamson)	Sep. 1869	---
Jane Ann Sharp	Sep. 1869	Dec. 12, 1890
Maryette Jane Wade	Sep. 1869	Mar. 1872
Ferdinan W.	Sep. 1869	---

Name	Admission Date	Dismissed Date
Crooks		
Jesse Sharp	Sep. 1869	Dec, 12, 1890
George M. Casey	Sep. 1869	---
Philip W. Moore	Sep. 1869	---
Arminta Moore	Sep. 1869	1881 - died 1884
Laneclin Fieland	Sep. 1869	---
Nancy Murray	Nov. 1869	Feb. 12, 1879 died
Wm. Pleasant Moore	Nov. 1869	Sep. 1870 moved
Daniel Grey	Nov. 1869	Oct. 7, 1876 moved
Margrett Goings	Aug. 1870	Dec. 1873 moved in Aug., 1873
Martha J. Hays	Aug. 1870	Feb. 27, 1872 died
Julia T. Glasgow	Aug. 1870	Jan. 26, 1870
Jacop Goings	Aug. 1870	Dec. 1877 moved in Aug. 1877
Joseph Maize	Aug. 1870	May 9, 1885
Martha Grey	Aug. 1870	Dec. 5, 1884
Barlow Eskern	Aug. 1870	Oct. 31, 1870
*D. H. Fitzwater * (Moved March 1873)	Aug. 2872	Jan. 8, 1876
*E. H. Fitzwater * (Moved March 1873)	Aug. 1872	Jan. 8, 1876
Susan Kimsey (Hinton)	Aug. 1872	Oct. 7, 1875
Eliz. C. Gillam	Aug. 1872	---
Cara Powers (Barker)	Aug. 1872	---
Joseph D. Wiseman	Aug. 1872	Aug. 1873 moved
Ann Wiseman	Aug. 1872	Aug. 1873 moved
*Andrew Russell * (Died, Age: 72Y 7M 11D)	Aug. 1872	*Mar. 11, 1877
Amanda Casey (Barker)	Aug. 1872	---
*Robert B. Smith * (Repeated immoral conduct)	Aug. 1872	Nov. 23, 1872
Margrett E. Smith	Aug. 1872	Nov. 23, 1872
Susan Crabtree	Aug. 1872	1875
Martha J. Ely	Aug. 1872	Mar. 1876
Moses E. Watkins	Aug. 1872	---

Name	Admission Date	Dismissed Date
Nancy Jane Watkins	Aug. 1872	---
Mrs. David Prosser	---	---
Mary Caldwell (Stone)	---	Non-resident
Mary J. Crooks	Mar. 1873	---
Willis Helm	Jul. 1873	1873
Martha Helm	Jul. 1873	---
Francis M. Kimsey	Jul. 1873	1879
Susan Kimsey	Jul. 1873	1879
Mary P. McMahan	Aug. 1873	---
Lucy H. Casey	Aug. 1873	---
George Maize	Aug. 1873	1878
*Wm. M. Whitworth *(Expelled)	Aug. 1873	Jun. 7, 1890
Anson A. Whitaker	Aug. 1873	Mar. 29, 1877
Mary C. Whitaker	Aug. 1873	Mar. 29, 1877
Cary E. Davis	Aug. 1873	Mar. 1875
Mary A. Davis	Aug. 1873	1874
Cary Watkins (Brooks)	Aug. 1873	May 1886
Niel Tuttle	Sep. 11, 1874	Mar. 1876
Saml. H. Elliott	Sep. 11, 1874	---
Jacob Wolff	Sep. 11, 1874	---
Addiline Eagleson	Sep. 11, 1874	---
Elias Wolf	Sep. 11, 1874	---
Jeannie Simpson	Sep. 11, 1874	1879 moved in Mar. 1875
Elias Tuttle	Sep. 11, 1874	---
Francis Sharp	Sep. 11, 1874	1878
Thomas J. Clagett	Sep. 11, 1874	May 15, 1891
Mrs. Eliza Jane Johnson	Dec. 22, 1874	Oct. 28, 1881
George W. Glasgow	Dec. 23, 1874	Jan. 25, 1876
*Josie Burges *(Found guilty of violation)	Dec. 23, 1874	Jun. 16, 1877
Alphonso Hickerson	Dec. 27, 1874	1881
Sarah R. Fielden	Dec. 30, 1874	Aug. 1876 moved Feb. 1876
Robert C. Fielden	Dec. 30, 1874	Aug. 1876 movedin Feb. 1876
Nancy E. Sharp	Dec. 16, 1875	---
Elizabeth Elder	Dec. 16, 1875	---
Syntha Kate Smith	Dec. 14, 1876	1877 moved in Sep. 1876

Name	Admission Date	Dismissed Date
Mrs. Marcella Tingle	Aug. 18, 1876	Jun. 2, 1883
Carrie Y. Elliott	Aug. 18, 1876	---
Rev. Y. W. Whitsett	Jul. 29, 1877	Jun. 30, 1883
Mattie Moore (Robins)	Jul. 29, 1877	Feb. 24, 1895
*Mrs. Mary Smith *(Died, Age: 75 y)	Jul. 30, 1877	Jul. 9, 1880
Mr. J. C. Hubbard	Aug. 8, 1877	1878
F. McCall	Aug. 8, 1877	Nov. 28, 1875
Noah Hickerson	Aug. 1877	1879
Jennie Whitsett	Aug. 1877	Jun. 30, 1883
*Joseph Oskins *(Died, Transferred to Tebo Congregation)	Aug. 13, 1877	Dec. 19, 1898
Mrs. Fannie Oskins	Aug. 13, 1877	Transferred to Tebo Congre.
Mrs. Whitmack	Aug. 13, 1877	Oct. 1, 1881
Mrs. Lydia Tingler	Aug. 13, 1877	1880
Mr. L. B. Lambert	Aug. 20, 1877	Nov. 23, 1878
Mrs. Mary F. Maize	Nov. 17, 1878	May 1885
Robert Sharp	Nov. 17, 1878	Feb. 27, 1888
George W. Brown	Nov. 17, 1878	1880
Mrs. C. R. Rice	Nov. 23, 1878	1879
Mr. J. M. Thompson	Nov. 23, 1877	---
Mrs. P. Y. Rice	Nov. 23, 1878	---
Virginia Wineholfe	Nov. 24, 1878	1881
James Eagleson	Nov. 20, 1879	---
Major Brown	Nov. 20, 1878	1885
Francis M. Land	Nov. 20, 1878	Dec. 15, 1893
Mrs. M. R. Glasgow	Nov. 20, 1879	1888 left the county
Mrs. S. F. Glasgow	Nov. 20, 1879	1893 moved
Sarah A. Hinkle	Nov. 20, 1879	1894 moved
John R. Hinkle	Nov. 20, 1879	1894 moved
*Frank Crooks *(Suspended for unchristian conduct)	Nov. 20, 1879	Nov. 6, 1880
*Walter Nickelson *(Moved on Oct. 20, 1880, died 1881)	Nov. 20, 1879	Nov. 19, 1880
James Hinkle	Nov. 20, 1879	---
John L. Linstone	Nov. 20, 1879	Feb. 8, 1889 moved 1885
J. T. Jones	Nov. 20, 1879	1882 moved
Sarah A. Jones	Nov. 20, 1879	moved
Amanda Hickerson	Nov. 20, 1879	moved
Della Hickerson	Nov. 20, 1879	moved
Bella Hickerson	Nov. 20, 1879	moved
Amanda E. Moore	Dec. 7, 1879	(Wolff)

13

Name	Admission Date	Dismissed Date
Mary J. Boling	Dec. 7, 1879	*Feb. 1, 1888
		*(died)
Margaret E. Smith	May 1, 1880	Mar. 8, 1889
*Robert B. Smith	May 1, 1880	Mar. 12, 1887
*(Suspended)		
*Sarah D. Elliott	Nov. 7, 1880	Jun. 8, 1883
*(Died Jul. 14, 1886)		
Leonia Eager	Jan. 1, 1881	Jun. 30, 1883
Dr. J. W. Bronaugh	Jun. 25, 1881	Feb. 19, 1884
Katie Guion	Jun. 2, 1881	Joined
		Baptists
Miss Ida V. Miller	Nov. 4, 1881	Feb. 19, 1894
Sallie McCann	Nov. 6, 1881	---
Julia Casey	Nov. 14, 1881	(Kingsberry)
Minnie Lee Casey	Aug. 14, 1881	Jun. 21, 1877
(Hughes)		
*John C. Casey	Aug. 14, 1881	Sep. 1886
*(Expelled)		
*Sarah O. Elthel	Aug. 14, 1881	Apr. 1893
*(Descombs)		
Minnie H. Eagleson	Aug. 14, 1881	---
*(Kensinger)		
*Mollie A. Eagleson	Aug. 14, 1881	---
*(Zarnes)		
Lottie M. Mills	Aug. 14, 1881	Jun. 2, 1883
Millie A. Mills	Nov. 15, 1881	---
*Mary E. Smith	Nov. 15, 1881	(Atchison)
Eugene Wolf	Nov. 15, 1881	Aug. 12, 1887
Llwellyn G. Wolf	Nov. 15, 1881	---
Thomas W. Moore	Nov. 15, 1881	Aug. 12, 1887
Abner E. Adair	Nov. 15, 1881	Dec. 22, 1888
*Sarah Holt	Dec, 4, 1881	Aug. 4, 1883
*(Suspended for immoral conduct)		
Mary Allice (sic)	Dec. 4, 1881	---
Eagleson (Powers)		
John W. Bond	Nov. 5, 1882	Aug. 8, 1885
Joseph Nash	Dec. 9, 1883	1885
Mary E. Nash	Dec. 9, 1883	1885
Francis E. Comer	Sep. 11, 1885	Aug. 8, 1890
H. J. Cook	Sep. 11, 1885	Oct. 1886
Jasper N. Cale	Sep. 11, 1885	May 8, 1886
Elmo Maizo	Sep. 11, 1885	1894
Anna Barrager	Sep. 11, 1885	1894 (Reid)
Andrew M. Commer	Sep. 13, 1885	Aug. 8, 1890
Clarance McCann	Sep. 13, 1885	Jan. 15, 1892
Jennie Bemis	Sep. 13, 1885	1885
Allice Kinsinger	Mar. 14, 1886	---
W. F. Guion	May 9, 1886	1887

14

Name	Admission Date	Dismissed Date
*Nellie U. Clark	May 9, 1886	May 12, 1894
*(Moved in 1889)		
Jane Morgart	May 9, 1886	*Feb. 12, 1897
*(Died)		
A. Morris	Aug. 29, 1886	1889
Walter Runner	Aug. 29, 1886	Feb. 1887
Robert Hankins	Aug. 29, 1886	Joined the Methodists
*Moses E. Watkins, Jr.	Aug. 29, 1886	Sep. 9, 1897
*(Suspended for immoral conduct)		
James M. Barragar	Aug. 29, 1886	1894
Daniel Barragar	Aug. 29, 1886	Dec. 12, 1890
Sarah E. Watkins	Aug. 29, 1886	Oct. 4, 1894
Carrie L. McCann	Aug. 29, 1886	---
Zerelda Barrager	Sep. 1, 1886	---
James H. Roser	Sep. 1, 1886	Aug. 12, 1887
*Miss B. A. Orr	Sep. 1, 1886	*Dec. 29, 1890
*(Died, wife of Rev. Z. T. Orr)		
Maggie S. Whittaker	Sep. 2, 1886	Aug. 1883
*Ida Whittaker	Sep. 2, 1886	Dec. 6, 1896
*(Joined the Methodists)		
Cyntha N. Bailey	Sep. 5, 1886	---
Ellia S. Hammons	Sep. 5, 1886	---
John W. Hood	Sep. 5, 1886	---
Della Hood	Sep. 5, 1886	Oct. 12, 1896
Anna H. Tilman	Sep. 8, 1886	Feb. 3, 1888 died
Geo. W. Whitsides	Sep. 8, 1886	---
Della M. Bailey	Sep. 8, 1886	---
James Bailey	Sep. 8, 1886	---
Eliz. A. Watkins	Sep. 8, 1886	---
Marietta Whitworth	Sep. 8, 1886	Mar. 26, 1888 died
William H. Hammons	Oct. 9, 1886	---
Lottie Main	Nov. 14, 1886	1888
George W. Rondel	Nov. 28, 1886	---
Harriett Rondel	Nov. 28, 1886	Apr. 1898
John L. Descombs	Dec. 12, 1896	Jan. 6, 1893 died
James Webb	Jun. 26, 1887	---
Elizabeth Webb	Jul. 24, 1887	---
Allice (sic) Moore	Sep. 8, 1887	---
Effa Casey	Sep. 8, 1887	---
Clara A. Wade *	Sep. 8, 1887	*(Kensinger)
Bertha Whitsides	Sep. 8, 1887	---
Lula Watkins	Sep. 8, 1887	Oct. 4, 1894

Name	Admission Date	Dismissed Date
Effa Wolff	Sep. 8, 1887	---
Samuel T. Laycock	Sep. 8, 1887	Mar. 6, 1894
Charles Crooks	Sep. 8, 1887	---
Thomas Hincher	Sep. 8, 1887	Jan. 10, 1890
George W. Elliott	Sep. 8, 1887	Mar. 2, 1894
Martha A. Wade	Sep. 8, 1887	---
L. D. Wade	Sep. 8, 1887	---
Mary L. Orr	Sep. 8, 1887	May 12, 1894
Ella Whitsides (Crow)	Sep. 8, 1887	Aug. 8, 1888
Jones A. Orr	Sep. 8, 1887	May 12, 1894
Emily Whitsides	Sep. 8, 1887	Aug. 12, 1891 died
Rusinlee Dunaway	Sep. 25, 1887	1890
Mary E. Webb (Orr)	Nov. 13, 1887	May 12, 1894
Cora J. Webb (Ragland)	Nov. 13, 1887	Aug. 1893
Luella Murray (Baker)	Sep. 7, 1888	Aug. 1883
Ada F. Smith	Sep. 7, 1888	Sep. 11, 1901 moved in 1890
Anna M. Tilman	Sep. 7, 1888	---
Bridget Powers	Sep. 8, 1888	---
Manerva E. Evans	Sep. 8, 1888	Dec. 22, 1888
Matilda E. Smith	Sep. 8, 1888	1890 moved to Warrensburg
Wm. H. Bradshaw	Sep. 9, 1888	1889 moved
Melissa C. Webb	Sep. 9, 1888	(McQuitten)
Clara V. Hicks	Sep. 9, 1888	---
M. C. Dunn	Sep. 10, 1888	Oct. 17, 1891
Sarah Ford	Sep. 11, 1888	1889
Lucy Bailey	Sep. 11, 1888	1890 moved
Sarah E. Bailey	Sep. 11, 1888	Nov. 13, 1891 moved in 1890
Lucy Bailey	Sep. 11, 1888	1890 moved
Frank H. Ford	Sep. 11, 1888	1890 moved
Wm. R. Hicks	Sep. 11, 1888	Moved out of bounds
J. W. Wright	Mar. 23, 1889	---
Martha F. Wright	Mar. 23, 1889	---
Mrs. Wilhemia F. Redford	Mar. 23, 1889	---
Lizza L. Hinton	Apr. 28, 1889	---
Miss Emma McDorman	Dec. 22, 1889	Nov. 18, 1893
Eugene Wolff	Dec. 22, 1889	May 12, 1894
Lucy M. Casey	Nov. 24, 1890	May 12, 1894
Annie Lee Casey	Nov. 24, 1890	---
Lullie Moore	Nov. 24, 1890	---

Name	Admission Date	Dismissed Date
Lizzie A. Hinton	Nov. 24, 1890	(Moore)
Y. N. Watkins	Nov. 24, 1890	---
Cliff H. Kinsinger	Nov. 24, 1890	Dec. 15, 1893
George Barker	Nov. 24, 1890	1892
Charles H. Cameron	Nov. 27, 1890	Nov. 16, 1894
Lewis H. Kinsinger	Nov. 27, 1890	Jul. 7, 1893 died
Frank Tressinriter	Nov. 27, 1890	---
Laura Tressinriter	Nov. 27, 1890	---
Mattie E. Andrew	Nov. 27, 1890	---
Clara E. Bradshaw	Nov. 27, 1890	---
Etta M. Bradshaw	Nov. 27, 1890	---
Minnie Wade	Nov. 27, 1890	---
Merredith Wade	Nov. 27, 1890	---
Lena E. Orr	Nov. 27, 1890	May 12, 1894
James Tilman	Nov. 30, 1890	1892 moved
Warren Wickham	Nov. 30, 1890	1891
A. M. Tilman	Dec. 14, 1890	1893
G. L. Ball	Sep. 26, 1891	Oct. 17, 1891
Ann E. Ball	Sep. 26, 1891	Oct. 17, 1891
Lizzie M. Ball	Sep. 26, 1891	Oct. 17, 1891
Jennie Holton	Sep. 26, 1891	1892
Thomas B. Holton	Sep. 26, 1891	Oct. 1894 joined the Methodists
Dora A. Hammar	Dec. 11, 1891	---
James Heckter	Dec. 11, 1891	1892
Mary Hecktor	Dec. 11, 1891	1892
Annie Fenley	Dec. 20, 1891	1892
Una B. Watkins	Sep. 26, 1892	---
Cora E. Comer	Sep. 26, 1892	Dec. 15, 1893
Nora Wade	Sep. 26, 1892	1892 moved
Ola Smith	Sep. 26, 1892	---
Allice Bailey	Sep. 30, 1892	---
Della Crooks	Sep. 30, 1892	---
Della Wade	Oct. 4, 1892	Dec. 15, 1893
Dora Snodgrass	Oct. 16, 1892	(Bailey)
Mrs. Georgie Bronaugh	Sep. 2, 1893	Feb. 18, 1894
Miss Lue Gains	Nov. 13, 1893	Oct. 4, 1894
Mrs. Hattie M. Nichols	Aug. 8, 1894	Jul. 5, 1896
F. E. Comer	Nov. 1, 1894	---
Etta M. Wolff (Powers)	Nov. 2, 1894	Nov. 1876
Lula Wade	Nov. 2, 1894	---
George F. Crooks	Nov. 2, 1894	---
John H. C. Elliott	Nov. 2, 1894	---

Name	Admission Date	Dismissed Date
James C. Comer	Nov. 2, 1894	Feb. 24, 1895
George W. Comer	Nov. 2, 1894	Feb. 24, 1895
Johnathan Morgart	Dec. 23, 1894	---
Henry C. Descombs	Dec. 23, 1894	---
Roy Whitsides	Dec. 23, 1894	---
George W. Elliott	Dec. 23, 1894	---
John W. Woolf	Dec. 23, 1894	---
George Hathaway	Mar. 3, 1895	---
Huffman Landon	Sep. 20, 1895	---
Amanda Landon	Sep. 20, 1895	---
Olive Effie Landon	Sep. 20, 1895	---
Lewis G. Waldridge	Sep. 20, 1895	---
Albert Scott	Sep. 20, 1895	---
John C. Whiteman	Sep. 22, 1895	---
Miss Hattie Lewis	Sep. 23, 1895	---
Miss Mary Hattaway	Sep. 23, 1895	---
William W. Bailey	Sep. 23, 1895	---
Samuel T. Laycock	Sep. 23, 1895	---
Lela J. H. Elliott	Sep. 23, 1895	---
Mrs. Allice H. Mogart	Sep. 23, 1895	---
J. G. Beaty	Sep. 23, 1895	---
C. C. Bradley	Oct. 13, 1895	---
John W. Clark	Aug. 16, 1896	---
Ida M. Clark	Aug. 16, 1896	---
Mrs. John Dunaway	Unknown	

Kidd's Chapel Church, southeast of Appleton City, MO, 100th Anniversary Article, "St. Clair County Courier," Oscelo, Oct. 11, 1984.

On February 28, 1951 the church burned. The church was rebuilt and dedicated on October 6, 1952.

Mentioned were: Rev. Bob Fenwock, Liberal, MO; Ester Lou Breon; Susanne Johannigmeier; Rev. C. H. Crandall, Sarcoxie, MO.

Rev. George Penn, native of Virginia, helped with the formation of the church.

Daniel Kidd died 1907 and is buried at Kidd's Chapel Cemetery.

Caleb T. Barr, organizer of the Cumberland Presbyterian Church at Chalk Level; Dr. R. W. Garnett, Chas. Higgins, and Rev. Gay Shoemaker are also buried there.

Alma Bieser, Appleton City, and Myrtle Moree, Ottawa, KS, both age 90, were the oldest present at the celebration.

Huntsville   Cumberland   Presbyterian   Church,
Huntsville, Randolph County, Missouri

Register of Deacons

Name	Date Ordained
J. W. Hammett	Jul. 27, 1890

Register of Elders

Name	Date Ordained	Ceased to Act
M. Hammett	Jul. 27, 1890	---
W. Malone	---	---
W. Craven	Jul. 27, 1890	Jan. 10, 1893
Owen Craven	Apr. 23, 1893	Jan. 10, 1893
W. Manning	Feb. 24, 1895	Aug. --, 1899
A. Wood	Feb. 24, 1895	---

Register of Adult Baptisms

Name	Date	Reverend
Mrs. Sarah A. McLaughlin	Oct. 5, 1890	J. S. Howard
Garvin Jack	Dec. 7, 1890	J. S. Howard
Mrs. Stonie Ferrell	Feb. 22, 1891	J. S. Howard
Joseph M. Prior	Dec. 24, 1893	S. A. McPherson
Alice F. Prior	Dec. 24, 1893	S. A. McPherson
Lizie Williams	Mar. 23, 1895	J. T. Bacon
Perry Hartman	Dec. 13, 1896	T. S. Love
Miss Hattie Burgstresser	May 15, 1898	C. L. Hiskett

Register of Deaths

Name	Died	Reverend
Mrs. Susan F. Malone	Sep. 8, 1890	J. S. Howard
G. H. Lowry	Jan. 22, 1898	E. B. Surface

Register of Communicants

Name	Admission Date
Owen Craven	Jul. 27, 1890
Mrs. Owen Craven (d. Feb. 14, 1910)	Jul. 27, 1890
J. K. Craven (d. May 14, 1910)	Jul. 27, 1890
J. W. Craven	Jul. 27, 1890
Mrs. Ida A. Craven	Jul. 27, 1890
J. W. Hammett	Jul. 27, 1890
Mrs. J. W. Hammett	Jul. 27, 1890
F. M. Hammett	Jul. 27, 1890
Mrs. Susan Hammett	Jul. 27, 1890
Miss Rebecca Hammett	Jul. 27, 1890
Mrs. Kate Kirkpatrick	Jul. 27, 1890
B. W. Malone	Jul. 27, 1890
Mrs. Susan Malone	Jul. 27, 1890

19

Name	Admission Date
(d. Sep. 8, 1890)	
Mrs. Smith	Jul. 27, 1890
Mrs. Thomas (Dis. May, 1896)	Jul. 27, 1890
J.S. Howard (Dis. Jul. 27, 1891)	Jul. 27, 1890
Mrs. L. A. Howard	Jul. 27, 1890
(Dis. Jul. 27, 1891)	
John Jack	Sep. 28, 1890
Mrs. Mary Jack	Sep. 28, 1890
Mrs. Stonie Terrell	Sep. 28, 1890
James McLauhlin	Oct. 5, 1890
Sarah A. McLaughlin	Oct. 5, 1890
Mrs. Lucy E. Williams	Nov. 2, 1890
Gavin Jack (Sus. Aug. 8, 1896)	Dec. 7, 1890
J. B. Carney (Dis. May 23, 1892)	Oct. 19, 1890
Mrs. Fannie Carney	Oct. 19, 1890
(Dis. May 23, 1892)	
Mrs. Lutie Malone	Apr. 25, 1892
*Miss Fannie Smith	Jun. 26, 1892
*(Pastor would not emerse so she joined the Baptists.)	
Rev. S. A. McPherson	Nov. 13, 1892
(Dis. Apr., 1894)	
Sister Addie McPherson	Nov. 13, 1892
(Dis. Apr.,1894)	
Peter Walker	May 28, 1893
Mrs. Mary Walker	May 28, 1893
Mary A. McPherson	Aug. 13, 1893
(Dis. Apr., 1894)	
*Maggie Walker	Dec. 24, 1893
*(Joined the Christian Church, Dis. Aug. 8, 1896)	
Joseph M. Prior	Dec. 24, 1893
Alice F. Prior	Dec. 24, 1896
W. A. Wood	Nov., 1894
Mrs. Lillie H. Wood	Nov., 1894
Miss Jennie Bradney	Dec., 1894
John W. Manning	Feb. 24, 1895
Mrs. John W. Manning	Feb. 24, 1895
*Miss Elizabeth William	Mar. 23, 1895
*(Joined the M. E. Church)	
*Mary Jane Walker	Apr. 21, 1895
*(Joined the Christian Church, Dis. Aug. 8, 1896)	
Miss Maggie Jack	Apr. 21, 1895
Mrs. Allie Lowry	Jun. 2, 1895
(Dis. Oct. 12, 1896)	
Charles M. Tradway	Jun. 16, 1895
(Dis. Jun., 1896)	

Name	Admission Date
Perry Hartman	Dec. 13, 1896
Mrs. Eva Hartman	Dec. 13, 1896
G. H. Lowry (d. Jan. 11, 1898)	Jan. 10, 1897
Mrs. Alle H. Lowry	Jan. 10, 1897
Miss Hattie Burgstusser	May 15, 1898
B. W. Malone (d. 1906)	---
Lutie Malone (d. June, 1903)	Apr. 25, 1892

Revised Register of Communicants, December 19, 1898

J. W. Hammett, Mrs. Mary A. Hammett, F. M. Hammett (Married & moved), Mrs. Susan Hammett, Mrs. Kate Kirkpatrick (Moved to Yaes), Mrs. Calvin Smith (Moved to LaPlata, Mo), John Jack (Moved to Columbia, Mo), Mrs. Mary Jack, Mrs. Lillie H. Wood, Mrs. Stonie Jack, Mrs. Lucis E. Williams, Peter Walker, W. A. Wood, Miss Jennie Bradney, J. W. Manning, Mrs. J. W. Manning, Miss Maggie Jack, Mrs. Allie Lowry, Miss Hattie Burgstressor, Miss B. Slankard, J. H. Slankard, J. K. Craven, Mrs. Owen Craven, Owen Craven.

Concord Christian Church, Concord, Saline County, Missouri.
Membership Register, November 19, 1873
John Thornton, Sarah Thornton, I. I. Davidson, S. B. Davidson, Zachariah Roland, Louisa Roland, Mary E. Roland, Elizabeth Roland, Lavisa Roland, Wm. Roland, Anna Roland, Mary Thornton, Henietta Bigelow, E. Johnson, J. E. Johnson, F. Evans, Eliza M. Evans, Mary Evans, Samuel Shaw, Mrs. Shaw, Sarah Jackson, Wilder Jackson, Moore Casey, Bettie Casey, Liddia Haley, Isaac Neff, Polly Neff, Geo. Neff, Julia Thomas, Albert Thomas, Clay Thomas, Amelia Jones Price, Laura Thornton, M. C. Keeton, Sarah J. Thornton, M. A. Burnett, Louis Burnett, Elizabeth Burnett, Mary Cowan, Franics Cowan, Bettie Cowan, Mahala Davidson, Verline Thornton, Richard Ballard, Robert Casey, Matilda Evermann, Judith Eversmann, Mary Eversmann, James Thronton, Benjamin Pierce, Sallie Wood, James T. Davidson, Nannie Davidson, Maggie Judy, Sharlott Pierce, Matt Piper, Hugh Craig, Stephen Craig, William S. Craig, Isaac Thornton, Rachel Thornton, David Emerson, Mary Emerson, John E. Collins, Laura H. Collins.
Membership Register, January, 1891.
T. J. Allen, Mrs. N. A. Allen, Millard Allen, Mrs. Fanny Allen, James Allen, Mrs. Novella Allen, Mrs. Betti Allen, T. J. Burton, John Atterbury

(Reclaimed Aug., 1891), Miss Kate Atterbury (Reclaimed Aug. 1891), Richard Atterbury, Mrs. Dovie Amsbery, Miss Florence Anderson (Dis. Oct., 1896), Mrs. Mattie Brown, Mrs. Sallie M. Brown, Harrison Burton, Mrs. Livona Bobbett, Mrs. Mahala C. Burton, John Burton, Miss Mary S. C. Burton, W. B. Ballard, William Burnett, Henry C. Burdell (Letter granted Dec. 27, 1891), Eddie Brockway, Miss Sophronia Burdell (Letter granted Dec. 27, 1891), Richard Brown, Mrs. Sarah E. Bocting (Letter granted Aug. 18, 1894), Miss Rosa Bird, Doc. Burton (Reclaimed 1893), George W. Baker (United Oct. 4, 1896, Dis. Mar. 19, 1899), Hugh Craig, P. S. Craig, Mrs. Kate Craig, Mrs. Nancy E. Craig, Miss Sarah Cook (Married Prittchett Marshall, d. Apr. 25, 1923), Mrs. Margaret Craig, Mrs. Mary C. Cowan, Mrs. Mary Cowan, G. W. Cowan, Howard Cowan, Mrs. Sallie P. Cowan, Mrs. Hannah Chandler, Will Cowan (Adm. Oct., 1896), Anna Cowan (Adm. Oct., 1896), Robert Cowan (Reclaimed Aug., 189?, d. Mar. 1, 1923), Miss Mary Cowan (Reclaimed Oct., 1896), J. P. Davis, Mrs. E. A. Davis, Wm. Davis, Miss Laura J. Davis (Letter granted Oct., 1892), Ada Lee Davis (Mrs. Duncan), J. J. Davis (Letter granted Oct., 1892, Letter rec. Jun., 1892 from Grand Pass), T. H. D. Dixon, Mrs. Nancy J. Dixon, John Dixon, James Dixon, D. D. Davidson, Mrs. S. B. Davidson, Miss Ora Davidson, J. F. Figgins, Murray Davidson, Mrs. J. Mahala Davidson, Mrs. Julia Drumeller, Miss Ida Dixon (Mrs. Ida Taylor), Mrs. Jennie Dixon, Miss Bettie Davis (Adm. Oct., 1896), Miss Jennie Everman (Stone), William Eversman, Mrs. Margaret E. Figgins, Miss Viginia Garnett Frazier, Miss Sallie Figgins (Neff, Reclaimd from the Baptist, Oct., 1896), Claud Fraizer, Will Figgins (Adm. Oct., 1896), Mrs. Fannie Gergory, Mrs. Minerva Gregory, Peyton Glenn, Mrs. Martha Glenn, Mrs. Sallie Garrett, Miss Anna Grooms (Junkerman), William Garius, George Geisler, Wm. Highbarger, Mrs. Adeline Highbarger, Bettie Highbarger (Glenn), Miss Annie Highbarger, Miss Nancy Highbarger (Sims), Miss Lucy Highbarger (Reclaimed 1893 as Mrs. Cross), Simon Highbarger, Mrs. A. D. Hudson (d. Feb. 12, 1907), W. B. Harring, Mrs. Melissa A, Haring, Miss Nettie Haley, John Heuman, Miss Hattie Hays, Lee Howell (Mrs. Fowler), Mrs. Caroline Haggard, Dink Highbarger (Reclaimed Aug. 11, 1891), Logue Hartley, William Hubard, Peter Haggard, Miss Lizzie Haggard, Mrs. Lena Harding (Letter granted from the Baptists, Apr. 24, 1892), Minnie Highbarger (Mrs. G. O. ?, Restored Mar. 15, 1896), Amelia Jones (Mrs. Price), Thomas Highbarger, Barbara Highbarger (Mrs. Cross), James Harring (Adm. Oct., 1896), Miss Jenny Harring (Adm. Oct., 1896), George Harring (Adm. Oct., 1896), Mrs. Bell Hensick, J. F. Jarvis (Letter granted Jul. 10, 1892), Everett Howell (Confession Feb., 1897), Mrs. Mary Jackson, George Kinkead, Mrs. Margaret Kinkead, W. B. Kinkead, Miss Mary Kinkead, Miss Manie King (Adm. Oct., 1896), Mrs. Ida May King (United Oct., 1896), Miss Lulu Loudy, Mrs. Thurza Liggett (Letter granted Sep. 10, 1892), Mrs. Oscar Liggett, Miss Ellen Laforce, Mrs. Sallie Lee, John Amos Laughlin (By Letter Aug. 16, 1891), C. H. Moore (St. Charles), Mrs. Samantha Laughlin (Statement Nov., 1903), John McCabe, Caroline McAfee (Letter granted Aug. 18, 1894), Miss Margaret McCabe (Reclaimed, 1893), Miss Maude Mosley (Adm. Oct., 1896), Miss Ollie McCarty (Adm. Oct., 1896), Miss Mary Mattox (Adm. Oct., 1896), Anna McCarty (Adm. Oct., 1896), Mrs. Bettie Neff, Isaac Neff, Mrs. Judy Neff, Mrs. Mary Neff, Miss Luty Neff (Stivers), Miss Fannie Neff, Miss Laura Neff, Mrs. Mattie M. Piper, Miss Lula Piper, G. F. Pearson, Mrs. Mary A. Pearson, Mrs. Mary J. Pearson, Henry C. Pearson, Miss Roxie Pearson, Mrs. Matilda Prewitt, Daly Prewitt, William Prewitt, Roy Piper, Mrs. Emma Piper, Miss Ola Piper, Miss Myrtle Poindexter (Adm. Oct., 1896), Abram Romines, Mrs. Bettie Romines, E. G. F. Ross, Charles Ross, Lawson Roberts, Mrs. ALice Roberts, Miss Woody Rummons (Reclaimed Aug. 11, 1891), Miss Mamie Rummons, Richard Ross, David M. Soper, Mrs. Laura B. Soper, Mrs. Nancy Scott, Miss Lee Stapp, Joseph Stapp, Townsend Scott, Miss Maud Scott (Adm. Oct., 1896), Mrs. S?? Scott (Adm. Oct., 1896), Robert Simms (Reclaimed Oct., 1896), E. E. Thornton, Mrs. Emiline Thornto, Miss Perlula Thornton, Miss Annie Lee Thornton, Mrs. Arretta Thornton, Henry Thornton, James M. Thornton, Mrs. Eliza Thornton, Clay Thornton (Letter granted Feb. 8, 1891), Mrs. Vilena Thornton, Robert W. Taylor (Reclaimed Aug., 1891), Mrs. Genevieve Taylor, C. E. Taylor (Dis. Jun. 14, 1891, Reclaimed Oct., 1895), George Thornton, William H. Thornton, Miss Clara L. Thornton, Mrs. Mina Thornton, Mrs. Ada Thornton, Miss Luellen Thornton, Miss Nora Taylor, Ben Taylor, Miss Rebecca Thornton (Adm. Oct., 1896),

Miss Clara Thornton (Adm. Oct., 1896), Miss Sallie
Thornton (Adm. Oct., 1896), Miss Mollie Utterback,
Miss Lida Utterback, Millard Wiley, Mrs. Frances A.
Wiley, Mrs. Sallie A. Wood, John West, Mrs. Sarah
West, Mrs. Alice Walker, Mrs. Lena M. Wilhite, S.
D. Wilkerson, Mrs. Nellie Wilkerson, Charles
Woodruff (Letter granted Oct., 1896), James Welch,
Mrs. Welch, John Henry Wilson, R. A. Wilhite,
William Wood.

Membership Register, 1909

Name	Comments
T. J. Allen	Dismissed to Berea
Mrs. Donie Amsberry	Dis. by letter Nov. 14, 1913
Glen Amsberry	Dis. by letter Nov., 1915
Mrs. Florence Asselmeyer	---
Miss Josie Amsberry	(Odell)
Theodore Alspaw	---
Frank Allen	BD. Sep., 1916, Dis. to Berea
Lee Asselmeyer	BD. Oct. 7, 1917
Nellie Burton (Teckmeyer)	BD. Sep. 7, 1919
Luther Burks	BD. Oct. 7, 1917
Tracy Burks (Thomas)	BD. Oct. 13, 1917
Georgia Benbow	BD. Oct. 8, 1916
Mary Burton (Purvius)	BD. Sep., 1916
Mrs. Mattie Brown	---
T. J. Burton	---
Harrison Burton	---
Mrs. Mahala Burton	d. Sep. 17, 1915
Mrs. Cyntha Burton	---
Miss Inez Brown (Amrine)	---
Linwood Brown	---
F. H. Brockway	---
Mary Mildreth Brockway	---
Jennie Kate Brockway	(Mosley)
Eugene Brockway	---
Preston Brockway	---
Mrs. Rosa Brockway	---
Miss Sunie P. Brown	---
Houston Brockway	Adm. Oct. 13, 1912, d. Sep. 3, 1919
Carl Burton	Adm. Oct. 13, 1912, d. Jul. 9, ????
A. Jennings Brown	BD. Sep. 10, 1916
Edgar E. Brown	BD. Sep. 10, 1916
Sallie C. Brown	BD. Sep. 10, 1916
Hugh Craig	---

Name	Comments
Miss Gracie Craig	---
Miss Florence Craig	---
Norman Craig	---
Stephen Craig	d. Apr. 5, 1917
Otis Craig	---
Miss Ruby F. Craig	---
Vena Craig	Dis. Jan. 25, 1914, Moved to Electria, TX
Miss Anna Craig (Lucas)	---
Clifton Craig	---
Miss Janet Craig	---
Miss Jane Craig	---
Miss Alma Bird Craig	---
Miss Cecil Craig	---
J. Harden Cook	d. Aug. 13, 1919
Mrs. Willie E. Cook	---
Archie Craig	Adm. Oct. 13, 1919
John Craig	Adm. Oct. 13, 1919, Died at sea Oct. 27, 1918
Mrs. Cora Craig	Left the Methodist Dec. 27, 1914
Cecil Craig	BD. Sep., 1916
Etta Craig	---
Bennie Craig	BD. Oct. 2, 1917
Dorothy Craig	BD. Sep. 6, 1919
T. H. B. Dickson	---
Miss Nancy Dickson	d. Feb. 20, 1922
D. D. Davidson	Dis. Dec. 13, 1914
Mrs. Sallie B. Davidson	Dis. Dec. 13, 1914
Mrs. Ora Davidson	Dis. Dec. 13, 1914
Mrs. Jenny Dickson	---
Harry Dickson	---
Ray Dickson	Dis. Apr. 25, 1915
Miss Annie May Dickson	Dis. Apr. 25, 1915
Miss Ruth Dickson	Dis. Jan. 25, 1914
Miss Effie Dickson (Neff)	Dis. Jan. 25, 1914
R. H. Davidson	d. Aug., 1911
Abram Davis	---
Jack Dysart	---
Miss Reberta Dysart	---
Miss Eulalia Dysart	Joined the Lutherans
Willie Dysart	---
Arthur N. Dickson	---
Lester Dickson	--
Miss Vena Davis (Lafaiver)	Letter granted to Salem
Ray Dysart	Adm. Oct. 13, 1912

Name	Comments
Howard Dysart	Adm. Oct. 13, 1912
William M. Davis	BD. Aug. 29, 1915
Estelle Dysart	BD. Sep., 1916
Mrs. Jane Duncan	BD. Oct. 2, 1917, d. May 17, 1976
Joe F. Figgins	d. Aug. 12, 1914
Mrs. Margaret E. Figgins	d. Aug. 15, 1922
Miss Virginia Frazier	---
Edgar Fenwick	---
Mrs. Lena Fenwick	---
Edith Fenwick	BD. Sep., 1916
Mary Fenwick	BD. Sep., 1916
William Lee Fenwick	BD. Sep. 23, 1917
Henry Fenwick	BD. Nov. 15, 1917
Mildred Fenwick	BD. Sep., 1918
George Giesler	---
Mrs. Sarah Giesler	---
Mrs. Susannah Gibson	---
James Gibson	---
George Haring	d. May 10, 1911
James M. Haring	---
John Heuman	---
Wm. Haring	---
Mrs. Melissa Haring	---
Lester Haring	---
Miss Jenny Haring	---
Mrs. Cora Howel	d. Jan. 10, 1912
Hattie Frances Haring	---
Miss Stella Haring	---
Jessee Hensick	---
Mrs. Laura Hensick	---
Mrs. Bettie Hudson	---
Willard Hall	Adm. Oct. 13, 1912
Austin H. Hudson	---
Austin L. Hudson	---
Earnest Harvey	---
Lura Harvey	---
Mrs. Emma Howel	---
Mrs. Nellie Hall	Adm. Oct. 1, 1912, Dis. Apr. 9, 1916
Gold Howel	---
Jewel Howel	---
Pearl Howel (Houchin)	---
John Howel	---
Miss Nora Howel (Martin)	---
Wilson Hall	---
Woodie Hall	Adm. Oct. 1, 1912
John Hall	Adm. Oct. 1, 1912

Name	Comments
Lindsay Hall	Adm. Oct. 13, 1912
Edgar Hall	Adm. Oct. 13, 1912
Russell Haring	Adm. Oct. 13, 1912
Miss Mabel Hueman	Adm. Oct. 13, 1912, Dis. Aug.,1916, Joined the Baptists.
Bryan Howel	BD. Sep., 1916, Dis. to the Presbyterians, Nov., 1917
Mrs. Minnie Hay	Dis. May 26, 1918
Mrs. Maud Haring	BD. Sep. 7, 1919
Homer Iman	BD. Oct. 2, 1917
Howard Iman	BD. Oct. 7, 1917
Mildred Iman	BD. Oct. 7, 1917
Minnie Iman	BD. Oct. 7, 1917
Miss Elizabeth H. Johnson	---
Miss Ollie Johnson	(Loyd)
Miss Virgie Johnson	(Thornton)
Scott Johnson	---
Mrs. Bessie M. Jonson	---
Mrs. Mary Johnson	Adm. Sep., 1916
Mrs. Mollie Johnson	Came from the Baptists Sep., 1916
Richard Johnson	BD. Sep., 1916
Eva Johnson	BD. Oct. 2, 1917
Emmet Johnson	BD. Oct. 7, 1924
Forest Keyton	BD. Oct. 7, 1917
Carrol Keith	BD. Jun. 8, 1924
Amos J. Laughlin	---
Mrs. Samantha Laughlin	d. Mar. 23, 1920, 11:50pm
Cecil Liemkueler	BD. Sep., 1916
Ester Liemkueler	BD. Sep., 1916
Herman Liemkueler	BD. Sep., 1916
Mrs. T. J. Lakin	Dis. May 26, 1918
Alonzo Liemkueler	BD. Sep., 1919
Anita Liemkueler	BD. Sep., 1919
Mrs. Minnie Leimkueler	BD. Sep., 1919
James Leimkueler	Adm. Sep. 7, 1919
Miss Anna Lee Mattix	---
Henry Mattix	---
J. W. Moore	Dis. Aug., 1916, Joined the Baptists.
Mrs. Ida Moore	Dis. Aug., 1916, Joined the Baptists.
Artie E. Morris	---
Mrs. Annie A. Morris	---
Miss Zella Mattix	Dis. Oct. 13, 1912

27

Name	Comments
(Johnson)	
Tom Murdock	BD. Sep., 1916
Mrs. Tom Murdock	Adm. Sep., 1916
Lawrence Miller	BD. Jun. 10, 1917
Alpha Murdock	BD. Oct. 2, 1917
Marie McClain (Edson)?	BD. Sep. 7, 1919
Edson Merrell	BD. Sep. 7, 1919. Came from the Presbyterians, Letter granted Mr. and Mrs. Merrell Jan. 24, 1923
Mrs. Sallie Neff	Letter to Salem
Miss Bessie Odell	(McCurdy). Dis. Mar. 2, 1919
Miss Mary Odell (Amick)	---
Mrs. Josie Odell	Dis. Nov. 14, 1915
Ruth Piper	(Mrs. Wilson Hall)
Mrs. Mattie M. Piper	---
Miss Lula Piper	---
Miss Ola Piper	Dis. Sep. 10, 1912 to Fayette, MO.
Ollie Piper	---
Edgar L. Piper	---
Mrs. Bettie Piper	---
Ham Piper	---
Geo. F. Pearson	d. Apr. 14, 1916
Mrs. Mary A. Pearson	---
Miss Mabel Pearson	---
Henry C. Pearson	---
Miss Roxie Pearson	d. Dec. 13, 1917
Mrs. Eliza Piper	---
Miss Sallie Piper (Flyn)	---
Edgar Piper	---
Miss Alma Piper	---
Miss Ruth Piper (Smyth)	---
Roy Piper	d. May 20, 1922
Mrs. Amelia Price	---
Miss Mollie Piper	(Spencer), Adm. Oct. 13, 1912.
Russell Pickerine	Adm. Oct. 13, 1912
Ruby Poindexter	Adm. Oct. 13, 1912, Dis. Jan. 11, 1914
Loraine Piper	BD. Sep., 1916
Mrs. Lizzie Quigg	Moved membership to Marshall
Mrs. Myrtle Ritter	Dis. Oct. 10, 1915
Mrs. Sallie Reynolds	--

Name	Comments
Mrs. Alice Roberts	---
Mrs. Woodie Rearidon	Restored Sep. 24, 1912
Oscar Purvis	BD. Jun. 8, 1924
Mrs. Lutie Stivers	---
J. F. Spense	d. 1916
Mrs. Annie Scott	---
Miss Ethelene Scott	(Durrett)
Miss Lillian Scott	(Brown)
Miss Stella Scott	(Geo. Allison)
Miss Willie Stafford	(Morris)
Mabel Scott (Harvey)	Dis. Mar. 9, 1924
Connell Sappington	---
Myrtle Shope	BD. Sep., 1916
Bertha Shope (Allen)	BD. Sep., 1916, Dis. to Berea
Mamie Shepherd	BD. Oct. 8, 1916, Dis. Aug. 3, 1919
Morene Stepp	BD. Oct. 7, 1917
Mrs. Nellie Skinner	---
E. E. Thornton	d. Jun. 22, 1920
Mrs. Emeline Thornton	---
Miss Rebbeca Tornton	(Eubanks), Dis. Dec. 8, 1912
James Thornton	---
Eliza Thornton	d. Jan. 19, 1915
George Thornton	---
Charley Taylor	Reclaimed Sep., 1916
Mrs. Ida Taylor	---
Robert W. Taylor	---
Mrs. Nora Tornton	---
Mrs. Perlula Thomas	---
Lon Taylor	---
Ben Taylor	---
Mrs. Annie Taylor	---
Mrs. Kizzie Thornton	d. Aug. 5, 1921
Mrs. Caroline Thornton	Confession Aug. 9, 1914
Wm. Thornton	Restored Sep. 29, 1912
Mrs. Mollie Thornton	Restored Sep. 28, 1912
Miss Phoebe Thornton	---
Miss Jesse Thornton	Adm. Oct. 13, 1912
Miss Mable Townsend	(Brown), Adm. Oct. 13, 1912
*Miss Neva Townsend	d. Apr. 21, 1923
*(Mrs. Robert L. Thompson)	
Alonzo D. Taylor	BD. Sep. 12, 1915
Jane Katie Taylor	BD. Sep. 12, 1915
James Thornton	BD. Sep. 12, 1915

Name	Comments
Kizzie Thornton (Martin)	BD. Sep., 1916
Mrs. Sarah West	d. Dec. 21, 1919
S. W. Wilkerson	Dis. Dec. 14, 1913
Mrs. Nellie Wilkerson	Dis. Dec. 14, 1913
Miss Nanny Wilkerson	Dis. Dec. 14, 1913
Miss Eva Wilkerson	Dis. Dec. 14, 1913
Wm. Wood	---
James C. Wood	---
Mrs. Myrtle Wood	---
Mrs. Pheobe Webb	---
Jas. W. Webb	---
Miss Elsie Webb	(Spencer)
Miss May Webb	(Thomas)
Miss Rosie Webb	(Hickman)
J. W. White	---
Mrs. Sarah Ellen West	---
Sallie Pearl Wood (Craig)	BD. Sep., 1916
Ray Taylor	BD. Sep., 1916
Elmore Taylor	BD. Sep., 1916
Mrs. Ada Thornton	BD. Sep., 1916
Paul Thompson	BD. Sep. 23, 1917
Sallie Taylor	BD. Oct. 2, 1917
Henry Taylor	BD. Oct. 2, 1917
John Thornton	BD. Oct. 2, 1917
Joe Thornton	BD. Oct. 2, 1917
Loraine Thornton	BD. Oct. 2, 1917
Bessie Thomas (Jones)	BD. Oct. 2, 1917
Jaunita Thomas	BD. Oct. 2, 1917
Sallie Thomas (Greene)	BD. Oct. 7, 1917
Georgia Thomas	BD. Oct. 7, 1917
Liney Thornton	BD. Oct. 14, 1917
Emmett C. Thompson	BD. Nov. 15, 1917, d. March, 1920
Mildred Thornton (Smith)	BD. Sep. 7, 1919
Mrs. Addie Townsend	BD. Sep. 7, 1919

Ely-Union Valley Cumberland Presbyterian Church, Ely, Marion County, Missouri

Register of Elders

Name	Ordained	Ceased to Act
William Moss	1855	d. Feb. 20, 1886
John A. Moss	1858	Mar. 21, 1870
Darius Browning	1864	d. Mar. 17, 1879
Joseph Crim	Aug. 22, 1870	Nov. 10, 1888
John Maston	Aug. 5, 1872	Apr. 9, 1887
Wm. H. Wadsworth	May 5, 1878	---
Henry A. Potterfield	May 1, 1887	Feb. 12, 1892

Name	Ordained	Ceased to Act
Robert S. Hayden	May 1, 1887	May 29, 1899
Jos. W. Crim	Feb. 12, 1892	---
Vincent S. Corder	Aug. 13, 1899	---
Perry Maxwell	Aug. 13, 1899	---

Register of Deacons

Name	Ordained
Francis T. Wadsworth	May 1, 1887

Register of Infant Baptisms

Mary Emaline Caldwell, (PRTS) D. C. and E. R. Caldwell, (BD) December 24, 1871, (MG) James W. Devall

Henry F. Potterfield, (PRTS) H. A. and M. A. Potterfield, (BD) September 15, 1872.

Sterling E. Tuley, (PRTS) E. M. and E. L. Tuley, (BD) Oc- tober 29, 1889, (MG) J. N. Lowrance.

Mable Clare Tuley, (PRTS) E. M. and E. L. Tuley, (BD) Oc- tober 29, 1889, (MG) J. B. Lowrance.

Effie F. Wadsworth, (PRTS) F. T. and C. Wadsworth, (BD) August 5, 1883, (MG) J. B. Lowrance.

Clara B. Wadsworth, (PRTS) F. T. and C. Wadsworth, (BD) April 10, 1883, (MG) David Armstrong.

Mary C. Wadsworth, (PRTS) F. T. and C. Wadsworth, (BD) January 10, 1892, (MG) W. H. Jones.

Maud Luvenia Tuley, (PRTS) Elisha M. and Emma L. Tuley, (BD) January 14, 1894, (MG) W. Brooks.

Mary Lela Tuley, (PRTS) Elisha M. and Emma L. Tuley, (MG) W. Brooks.

Register of Adult Baptisms

Name	Date	Reverend
Margaret F. Crim	Sep. 24, 1871	James W. Duvall
Miss Manerva Knox	Sep. 24, 1871	James W. Duvall
Edwin C. Hayden	Sep. 24, 1871	James W. Duvall
David C. Caldwell	Dec. 24, 1871	James W. Duvall
George Simpkins	Dec. 24, 1871	James W. Duvall
Mrs. Mary Roach	Nov. 5, 1876	James W. Duvall
Miss Lou Browning	Jan. 31, 1876	James W. Duvall
Mrs. Eudora Lear	Aug. 12, 1877	T. G. Pool
Lulla Stephens	Sep. 2, 1877	T. G. Pool
Robert Hayden	Sep. 2, 1877	T. G. Pool
Rosa E. Forman	Nov. 8, 1878	T. G. Pool
Miss Bessie Payne	Nov. 10, 1878	T. G. Pool
Miss Ella Payne	Nov. 10, 1878	T. G. Pool
Newton A. Moss	Nov. 10, 1878	T. G. Pool
Daniel F. Payne	Nov. 10, 1878	T. G. Pool
John Payne	Nov. 10, 1878	T. G. Pool
Lewell H. Griffin	Nov. 10, 1878	T. G. Pool

Name	Date	Reverend
George J. McIntye	Nov. 10, 1878	T. G. Pool
John E. Griffin	Nov. 10, 1878	T. G. Pool
John Timmons	Nov. 10, 1878	T. G. Pool
James Tuley	Nov. 10, 1878	T. G. Pool
Alexander Clark	Nov. 12, 1878	T. G. Pool
Thomas Hayden	Nov. 12, 1878	T. G. Pool
Elisha M. Tuley	Nov. 12, 1878	T. G. Pool
Chas. E. Stephens	Nov. 15, 1878	T. G. Pool
Frederick Humble	Oct. 14, 1883	A. M. Buchanan
Wm. L. Edmunds	Oct. 14, 1883	A. M. Buchanan
Amos E. Ravenscroft	Oct. 14, 1883	A. M. Buchanan
Cordelia Wadsworth	Apr. 3, 1887	D. Armstrong
Theodore W. Smith	Apr. 3, 1887	D. Armstrong
Mamie Guinn	Jan. 10, 1893	H. H. Jones
Robert Corder	Jan. 10, 1893	H. H. Jones
Venie Corder	Jan. 10, 1893	H. H. Jones
J. D. Culbertson	Jan. 10, 1893	H. H. Jones
J. W. Crim	Jan. 10, 1893	H. H. Jones
Thomas Moss	Jan. 10, 1893	M. Brook
William Emery	Jan. 10, 1893	M. Brook
Annie McIntre	Jan. 10, 1893	M. Brook
Ella S. Daulton	Jul. 29, 1893	M. Brook
Miss Pearl Lear	Dec. 25, 1893	M. Brook
James H. Brooks	Feb. 11, 1894	M. Brook
James Corder	Mar. 17, 1895	M. Brook
Matilda Ellen Harris	Oct. 24, 1895	M. Brook
Isaac McIntire	Nov. 2, 1895	M. Brook
Sarah McIntire	Nov. 2, 1895	M. Brook
Vincent S. Corder	Nov. 2, 1895	M. Brook
Willis Campbell	Nov. 2, 1895	M. Brook

Register of Marriages

John Hitch and Hester F. McCloud, (MD) April --, 1866, (MG) M. Rhodes.

H. A. Potterfield and Margaret A. Woodsworth, (MD) June 22, 1865, (MG) M. Rhodes.

J. W. Moss and --- Miload, (MD) December --, 1866, (MG) M. Corban.

James W. Gentry and Mary D. Moss, (MD) January 2, 1866, (MG) --- Firman.

David Caldwell and Ellen R. Wadsworth, (MD) March 25, 1869, (MG) --- Faubian.

John Horn and Martha F. Moss, (MD) October 28, 1869, (MG) --- Faubian.

Joseph Hotchkiss and Naomi Dalton, (MD) September 11, 1870, (MG) John Leighton.

Saml. M. Crim and Mary D. Moss, (MD) April 6, 1869, (MG) --- Faubian.
Wm. C. Moss and Elizabeth E. Dreshee, (MD) December 27, 1869, (MG) Mim. Bell.
Albert Dilliner and Eliza J. Wilcoxen, (MD) April 1, 1869, (MG) --- Faubian.
James W. Moss and Geneva J. Wadsworth, (MD) October 3, 1869, (MG) J. R. Taylor.
James W. Lear and Millie A. Tuley, (MD) ?, (MG) J. R. Taylor.
John W. Stephens and Harriet Payne, (MD) October 15, 1873, (MG) J. R. Taylor.
Edwin Hayden and Miss America J. Moss, (MD) October 1, 1874, (MG) J. R. Taylor.
Benjamin Walker and Miss Mary Browning, (MD) ?, (MG) J. R. Taylor.
Thomas Haiser and Miss Annie Thomas, (MD) 1874, (MG) J. R. Taylor.
Wm. Payne and Miss Emma Walker, (MD) 1874, (MG) J. R. Taylor.
Elisha M. Tuley and Miss Emma Wadsworth, (MD) December 3, 1878, (MG) T. G. Pool.
John Willis and Miss Eva Moss, (MD) February 2, 1879, (MG) T. G. Pool.
F. J. Wadsworth and Cordelia Cassady, (MD) March 30, 1880, (MG) T. G. Pool.
C. V. Hammes and Venie Potterfield, (MD) Jul. 3, 1890, (MG) T. G. Pool.
D. F. Payne and Rosa Forman, (MD) November 20, 1881, (MG) T. G. Pool.
David Payne and Lousia J. Browning, (MD) November 20, 1881, (MG) T. G. Pool.
R. L. Hayden and Maggie Crim, (MD) September 1, 1881, (MG) T. G. Pool.
Jerry Harris and Julie Frogg, (MD) February 10, 1992, (MG) --- Youngman.
John W. Crim and Abbie Mitchell, (MD) September 13, 1893, (MG) M. Brook.
Thomas Moss and Annie McIntire, (MD) November 28, 1893, (MG) M. Brook.

Register of Deaths

Name	Date
Mathew Moss	March 1, 1878
Mrs. Margaret A. Browning	April 8, 1878
Darius Browning	March 17, 1878
Mrs. Jane Moss	February 5, 1880
Mrs. Margaret Moss	February 19, 1880
Mrs. Mary A. Wadsworth	September 16, 1882
William Moss	February 20, 1896

Name	Date
Mrs. Abbie Crim	August 11, 1896

These persons were listed without dates: H. A. Potterfield, Bessie McIntire, Ellen R. Caldwell, Francis T. Wadsworth, J. W. Crim, Fanny Crim, Mary Crim, Mary J. Lee, Matha F. Warren, Jenuva J. Moss.

Register of Communicants

Name	Comments
William Moss	d. February 20, 1896
Mrs. Louisa Moss	Dis. November 10, 1888
Mrs. Jane Moss	d. February 5, 1880
Mrs. Mary Ann Stephens	Dis. January 8, 1883
Mathew Moss	d. March 1, 1878
Mrs. Winford Howel	d. January 6, 1888
John T. Dalton	Dis. July 17, 1871, misconduct
Mrs. Hester A. Moss	Dis. by letter
John McCloud	Dis. July 17, 1871, misconduct
Mrs. Mary E. Dalton	Dis. April 9, 1887
Margaret A. Wadsworth	---
William H. Wadsworth	AD. February, 1858
William O. Forman	Removed
John A. Moss	Dis. March 21, 1870
John W. Wilcoxen	Dropped
Mrs. Eliza A. Wilcoxen	Dropped
Mary Ann Wadsworth	d. September 16, 1882
Darius Browning	d. March 17, 1879
Margaret A. Browning	d. April 8, 1878
Francis Wadsworth	---
Catharine Hayden	Dis. July 7, 1876, d. 1887
Thomas Hayden	Suspended Sep. 14, 1872
William A. Moss	Suspended
Benjamin C. Moss	Dis. February 17, 1871
Susan M. Wadsworth	---
Miss Ellen Wadsworth	---
Miss Margaret Melond	---
Mrs. Mary E. Dolton	AD. November 1, 1863, Dis. April 9, 1887
Mrs. Alice Clark	---
Mrs. Cynthia Upton	AD. January, 1869, Dis. May 17, 1874
Miss Emma Walker (Payne)	d. 1886
Miss Eliza J. Wilcoxen	d. Nov. (?) 12, 1869
William A. Williams	AD. February 28, 1865
Miss Mary D. Moss	AD. March 1, 1865, d. July 21, 1869
Hayden L. Moss	AD. March 1, 1865

Name	Comments
Miss Sarah C. Moss	AD. March 2, 1865, Dis. September 21, 1881
Mrs. Parthenia Williams	AD. March 3, 1865
Miss Martha F. Moss	AD. March 3, 1865, Dis. July 15, 1870
Mrs. Leah Richeson	AD. August 27, 1865, d. July 22, 1875
Miss Naomi Dalton	AD. August 28, 1865
Thomas Hunter	AD. September 24, 1865, d. November 5, 1870
Samuel Clark	AD. April 22, 1866, Dis. August 22, 1870
Mrs. Susan J. Horn	AD. April 22, 1866, Dis. July 10, 1870
Mrs. Elizabeth Grafford	AD. June 24, 1866
Mrs. Margaret Moss	AD. November 24, 1866, Dis. February 17, 1880
Joseph W. Crim	AD. November 24, 1866, Dis. November 10, 1888
Mrs. Leah F. Crim	AD. November 24, 1866, Dis. July 15, 1870
John Horn	AD. November 24, 1866, Dis. 1869
Mrs. Laura A. Dalton	AD. November 27, 1865
Miss Jenieva Wadsworth	AD. November 27, 1865, Dis. 1869
George Dalton	AD. November 27, 1865
Miss Mary Moss (Crim)	AD. November 27, 1865, Dis. November 10, 1888
Miss Sarah Wilcoxen	Suspended Nov. 27, 1866
William C. Moss	AD. November 27, 1866, Dis. October 15, 1873
Joseph Stephens	AD. November 27, 1866
James D. Shaw	AD. November 27, 1866, Dis. September 26, 1881
Harrison W. Moss	AD. November 27, 1866, Dis. Oct., 1872, d. 1872
Mrs. Mary Forman	AD. November 27, 1866, Joined M. E. Church
Mrs. Ann E. Howell	AD. August 23, 1868
Mrs. Elizabeth E. Moss	Dis. October 13, 1873, AD. 1870
America J. Moss (Hayden)	AD. August 22, 1870, d. March 5, 1888
John Maston	AD. August 22, 1870
Martha F. Wadsworth	AD. December 29, 1870
Miss Mary M. Browning	AD. August 22, 1870

Name	Comments
Mary M. Browning (Walker)	AD. August 22, 1879, Joined Christian Church
Miss Margaret F. Crim (Hayden)	AD. December 29, 1870
David C. Caldwell	Ad. November 24, 1871
Miss Minerva Knox	AD. December 29, 1870, Dis. September 25, 1871
Edwin C. Hayden	AD. December 29, 1870, Dis. February 23, 1889
Milliy A. Tuley (Lear)	AD. December 27, 1871
George W. Simpkins	AD. December 28, 1871
Miss Mary J. Tuley	AD. July 27, 1873
Miss Emma L. Wadsworth	AD. August 25, 1873
Hattie Payne (Stephen)	AD. August 25, 1873, Dis. January 8, 1883
Eva L. Moss (Willis)	AD. August 25, 1873, Dis. September 2, 1889
Annie Thomas (Kiser)	AD. August 25, 1873, Sus. Nov. 10, 1897, Reinstated Aug. 26, 1898
Mistress Eudora Lear	AD. November 5, 1875
Mistress Mollie Roach	AD. November 5, 1875
Miss Lou J. Browning	AD. January 30, 1876, Dis. July 8, 1883
Henry H. Potterfield	AD. August 13, 1877, Dis. January 8, 1883
Miss Luella Stephens	AD. August 13, 1877, Dis. January 8, 1883
Robert Hayden	AD. August 13, 1877
Rosa E. Forman (Payne)	AD. November 8m 1878, Dis. July 7, 1887
Miss Bessie Payne	AD. November 20, 1878, Dis. October 9, 1883
Miss Ella Payne	AD. November 10, 1878, Dis. October 9, 1883
Newton A. Moss	AD. November 10, 1878
Daniel F. Payne	AD. November 10, 1878, Dis. July 7, 1884
John Payne	AD. November 10, 1878
Lewell H. Griffin	AD. November 10, 1878, Misconduct
George J. McIntyre	AD. November 10, 1878
John E. Griffin	AD. November 10, 1878, Dis. August 21, 1882
John Timmons	AD. November 10, 1878
James Tinley	AD. November 10, 1878, Dis. February 2, 1880

36

Name	Comments
Alexander Clark	AD. November 12, 1878, Dis. March 8, 1880
Thomas Hayden	AD. November 12, 1878
Elisha Tinley	AD. November 12, 1878, Dis. Apr. 12, 1880
Edward Griffin	AD. April 6, 1879
Mrs. Mary Griffin	AD. April 6, 1879
Miss Vernie Potterfield	AD. December 3, 1882
Frederick Humble	AD. October 14, 1883
Wm. L. Edmunds	AD. October 14, 1883, Dis. June 8, 1885
Amos E. Ravenscraft	Ad. October 14, 1883, Suspended Apr. 9, 1887
Margaretta A. Wadsworth	---
William H. Wadsworth	---
Francis Wadsworth	d. April 11, 1913
Susan M. Wadsworth	---
Miss Ellen Wadworth	d. January 9, 1912
Elizabeth Grafford	AD. June 24, 1861
Leah F. Crim	AD. November 24, 1861
Martha F. Wadsworth	AD. December 29, 1870
Margarette F. Crim	AD. December 29, 1870
David C. Caldwill	AD. December 24, 1871, d. October 25, 1903
Mary J. Tuley	AD. July 27, 1873, d. January 15, 1914
Emma L. Wadsworth	AD. August 25, 1873
Robert Hayden	AD. August 13, 1877
Edwin Griffin	AD. April 6, 1879
Mary Griffin	AD. April 6, 1879
Emma L. Potterfield	AD. December 3, 1882
Cornelia Wadsworth	AD. April 8, 1887
Annie W. Daulton	AD. April 8, 1887
Chas. E. Stephens	AD. April 8, 1887
Jacob Humble	AD. April 7, 1887, Joined the Methodists
Ida Crim	AD. January 10, 1892
Jem (sic) Harris	AD. August 5, 1890, Dis. November 15, 1910
Elisla Tuley	AD. January 10, 1892, Joined the Methodists
Mamie Crim	AD. January 10, 1892, Dis. November 5, 1910
Robert Corder	AD. January 10, 1892, Dis. December 13, 1893
Venie Corder	AD. January 10, 1892, Dis. December 13, 1893
Abbie Mitchell	AD. August 17, 1893,

Name	Comments
	d. August 11, 1896
Miss Cordelia Wadsworth	AD. April 3, 1887
Theodore W. Smith	AD. April 3, 1887,
	Dis. November 10, 1888
Annie Wakeman Daulton	AD. April 3, 1887
Charles E. Stephens	AD. April 3, 1887
Mrs. Mary A. Stephens	AD. April 3, 1887,
	d. October 16, 1888
Mrs. Leella Smith	AD. April 3, 1887,
	d. October 16, 1888
Jacob Humble	AD. April 10, 1887
Miss Ida Crim	AD. October 16, 1887
Wm. L. Edmonds (d. 1888)	AD. October 16, 1887,
Jerry Harris	AD. August 3, 1890
Clem Hamner	AD. September 14, 1890
Miss Mamie Crim	AD. January 10, 1892
Elisa Tuley	AD. January 10, 1892
Robert Corder	AD. January 12, 1892
Mrs. Vernie Corder	AD. January 12, 1892
Willie C. Potterfield	AD. January 10, 1892
	Dis. August 13, 1894
J. D. Culbertson	AD. January 10, 1892
J. H. Crim	AD. January 10, 1892
Xenia Boulding	AD. January 10, 1892
William Emery	AD. January 10, 1892,
	Joined Baptists
Thomas Moss	AD. January 10, 1892
Annie McIntire	AD. January 10, 1892
Ella S. Daulton	AD. July 29, 1893,
	Dis. October 18, 1899
Mrs. James Lear	AD. December 13, 1898
Miss Pearl Lear	AD. December 13, 1893
Newton A. Moss	AD. December 15, 1893,
	Dis. January 29, 1887
James H. Brooks	AD. February 11, 1894
Matilda Ellen Harris	AD. October 24, 1895
Isaac McIntyre	AD. November 2, 1895
Vincent S. Corder	AD. November 2, 1895
Miss Amelia Corder	AD. November 2, 1895
H. A. Potterfield	AD. September 15, 1896
Rev. Hiter W. James	AD. August 9, 1896
Perry Maxwell	AD. August 21, 1896
Clem Hainer	AD. September 14, 1890

The following names were listed with no dates or other information: Low. Patterson, Mrs. Patterson, Henry G. Hayden, Mrs. Hayden, Wm. Corder, Miss Stella McFortune, Delbert Lear, Homer Corder, Pearl Corder, Miss Clara Wadsworth, Lela Tuley, Miss Cleo

Crim, Mrs. Mary Kiser, Jas. Wadsworth.

Slater Christian Church, Slater, Saline County, Missouri.

Membership Register

Name	Comments
John H. Allen	Adm. 1872
Mrs. Sally Allen	Adm. 1872
Claude Allen	Adm. 1897, Confessed
Miss Ina Allen (Schultz)	Adm. 1900
Mrs. Fanny Allen	Adm. 1899
M. F. Allen	Adm. 1899
Mrs. Louise Avitt	Adm. 1887
Miss Etta Atterbury	Moved
Nona Anderson	Moved
Mr. J. H. Armstrong	Adm. 1916
Mrs. J. H. Armstong	Adm. 1916
Norwin Armstrong	Adm. 1916
Mrs. Norwin Armstrong	Adm. 1916
Miss May Alexander	Adm. 1916
Casey Adams	Adm. 1917
Mrs. O. W. Adams	Adm. 1917
F. E. Alsup	---
Mrs. F. E. Alsup	---
*Miss Julia Arnold	Adm. 1921,
*(Mar. J. Miller)	Letter rec. from Moberly Central
B. D. Allen	Adm. 1921
Mrs. Ethel Allen	Adm. 1921
Mrs. Price Aulger	---
Mrs. John Price	Adm. 1922
W. W. Austin	Adm. 1922
Dudley Allen	Adm. 1921
Wilbur Austin	Adm. 1928
Mrs. China Beverly	---
R. J. Brown	Adm. 1872
Mrs. Alice Brown	---
Wm. H. Brown	---
Mrs. Lillie Brown	---
Mrs. Geo. Brown	---
James G. Bellamy	Adm. 1890
Mrs. Edith Bellamy	Adm. 1889
Mrs. Vera Bellamy	---
John Booting	Adm. 1895
Mrs. Sarah Booting	Adm. 1894
Mrs. C. L. Benedict	Adm. 1908
Mrs. Mollie Baker	---
Mrs. Musie Baker	---

39

Name	Comments
Mrs. Everett Baker	---
Hubert Brown	Joined the Baptists
Marvin L. Brown	Adm. 1909
Lovis Brown	Adm. 1911
Mrs. Guy Bradley	Adm. 1912
Arline Benedict	Adm. 1911, d. Mar., (McMahan)
Vera Benedict	Adm. 1911
Mrs. Geo. Bryson	Adm. 1912
Guy Bradley	Adm. 1912
Mrs. Odessa Butler	---
Dwight Bidwell	Adm. 1911
Clifford Blackburn	---
Mrs. N. Byrd	---
Miss Ora Byrd	---
J. W. Boulton	Adm. 1920, Dis. 1924
Lucile (sic) Byrd	---
Mrs. Ella Bridges	---
Mrs. J. E. Butler	---
J. E. Butler	---
Miss Clara Brown	Adm. 1920, Dis. 1924
Chester Bellamy	---
Mrs. Jesse Boulton	Adm. 1920, Dis. 1924
Mrs. Lewis Brown	---
Grace Blanchard	---
Horace Blanchard	---
Mrs. Bushnell	---
Carl Bellamy	Adm. 1917
A. R. Bybee, Jr.	Adm. 1917
S. F. Bennett	Adm. 1917
Mrs. S. F. Bennett	Adm. 1917
Jinks Barksdale	Adm. 1917
Mrs. Minnie Black	---
A. R. Bybee, Sr.	---
C. L. Benedict	Adm. 1919
Fred Berry	Adm. 1919
Mrs. F. Berry	Adm. 1919
Miss Alma Blevins	Adm. 1919
Miss Florence Blevins	Adm. 1919
Forest Blevins	Adm. 1919
Allen Blevins	Adm. 1919
Mrs. B. E. Bertram	Adm. 1920
Mrs. Marie Officer Brown	---
Mrs. John Brown, Jr.	---

Name	Comments
Mrs. Mary Baker	---
Opal Marie Black	Adm. 1922
Mrs. Jack Bushman	Adm. 1922
Doris Bellamy	Adm. 1922
Mrs. Martha Baker	Adm. 1922
Mrs. Anna Bushman	Adm. 1924
Louise Boulton Barnaby	Adm. 1924, Letter issued 1924
Allen Boulton	Adm. 1924, Letter issued 1924
Wendall Berry	Adm. 1925
Kenneth Berry	Adm. 1925
David Byers	Adm. 1926
J. E. Ball	Adm. 1926
Mrs. J. E. Ball	Adm. 1926
Mrs. Nancy Cameron	---
Mrs. Leona Cameron	---
Charles Cameron	---
Mrs. Charles Cameron	---
Bryson Crawford	Adm. 1903
Mrs. Bryson Crawford	---
Mrs. Jas. Cogswell	Adm. 1901
Mrs. P. H. Clifford	Letter for the Baptists, Removed 1918
Mary Cameron	Adm. 1911
Alta Coons	Adm. 1911
Mrs. Bessie Crawford	Adm. 1911
Carlisle Cooper	Adm. 1912
Mrs. Georgia Cook	Adm. 1913
Gibson Cameron	Adm. 1913
P. H. Clifford	Adm. 1913
Mrs. Chas. Crawford	---
R. W. Compton	Adm. 1914
Jas. Cogswell	Adm. 1914
Delores Collins	Adm. 1915
Mrs. William Collins	Adm. 1915
Vernon Carroll	Adm. 1917
Della May Carroll (Callahan)	Adm. 1917
Douglas Carroll	Adm. 1917
Robert Cameron	Adm. 1917
Mrs. Carlisle Cooper	Adm. 1909
Edna Campbell	Adm. 1917, Married E. D. Brown
Cecil Cole	Adm. 1919

Name	Comments
Carl Cameron	Adm. Jul. 20, ????
Oscar Carrol	---
Mrs. Harry Christ	---
Harry Christ	Adm. Jan. 20, ????
Jno. Cameron	Adm. Mar. 24, ????
Mrs. John Cameron	Adm. Mar. 24, ????, Letter the Baptists.
Effie Crawford	Adm. 1923
Roger Carroll	Adm. 1923
Stella Cody	Adm. 1927
Mrs. Alice Carter	Adm. 1921
Mrs. Hattie Cramer	Adm. 1920
Mr. and Mrs. Childs	Adm. 1928
Jno. Callahan	Adm. 1928
W. P. Dulaney	Adm. 1889
Mrs. W. P. Dulaney	Adm. 1889
Miss Dean Dulaney	---
Miss Grace Dulaney	Adm. 1907, Married Cotton Becker
Stewart Dulaney	Adm. 1911, Moved to Iowa
Mary Helen Dulaney	Adm. 1911
W. L. Decker	---
Mrs. W. L. Decker	d. 1925
Miss Ella Decker	---
Lula Decker	Adm. 1907
Miss Inez Decker (Sharp)	Adm. 1907
Miss Marian Decker	Adm. 1911, Married W. Baker
Jessie Donohue	Adm. 1911
Verta Driscoll	Adm. 1911, Moved to Mexico, MO
Mrs. Nell Dysart	Adm. 1911, Moved to Colorado
Roy Decker	Adm. 1911
Leo Donohue	Adm. 1913
Mrs. A. J. Dixon	---
Mrs. A. M. Dickerson	---
A. M. Dickerson	---
Mrs. W. S. Dillard	---
Mrs. F. M. Day	Adm. 1910
Raymond Day	Adm. 1910
Mrs. A. Donohue	---

Name	Comments
Mrs. Mary Deis	---
Mrs. D. J. Dickson	---
S. J. Duncan	Adm. 1919, Letter granted to Marshall, MO
Carrie Duncan	Adm. 1919
Mrs. Birdie Dobbins	Adm. 1921
Ed N. Dobson	Adm. 1921
Mrs. Ed N. Dobson	Adm. 1921
Mrs. Homer Delong	Adm. 1922
Herschel Delong	---
Wm. Donohoe	Adm. 1924
Geral (sic) Donohoe	Adm. 1923
Jack Donohoe	Adm. 1923
Mrs. Ed Donohoe	Adm. 1923
June Dobbins	Adm. 1923, Moved to Kansas City
Allen Deis	Adm. 1925
Geo. Dodson	Adm. 1925
Mrs. M. A. Edwards	Adm. 1881
E. E. Elmore	Adm. 1897, Returned to the Presbyterians
Mrs. E. E. Elmore	Adm. 1897
Lilliam Elgin (Smith)	Adm. 1911
Russell Elgin	Adm. 1911
Miss Georgia Edwards	Adm. 1912
Mrs. E. L. Eubanks	Adm. 1913, Moved to Kansas City
E. L. Eubanks	Adm. 1913, Moved to Kansas City
Roy Eubanks	Adm. 1913
Mrs. Roy Eubanks	Adm. 1913
P. L. Eubanks	Adm. 1913
Mrs. P. L. Eubanks	Adm. 1913
Mrs. Eva Elder	Adm. 1915
Vernon Elliott	Adm. 1917
Mrs. Jno. Elder	Adm. 1915
Virgil Elgin	Adm. 1917
Geo. Eubanks	Adm. 1918
Margaret Eubanks	Adm. 1918
Mrs. Fred Eichman	---
John Elgin, Jr.	Adm. 1922
Mrs. Oliver Entrickin	---
Mrs. Cris Fishbeck	Adm. 1895
Miss Millie Fishbeck	Adm. 1902

43

Name	Comments
Harold Fishbeck	Adm. 1911
Maud Fox	Adm. 1902
Mrs. Ina Feis	Adm. 1904
Mrs. Frank Featherston	Adm. 1907
Halbert Featherston	Adm. 1912
George Fishbeck	Adm. 1913
Oliver Fishebeck	Adm. 1913
Frank Featherston	Adm. 1913
Charles Feis	Adm. 1915
Morrell Featherston	Adm. 1916
Robt. Fields	Adm. 1917
Mrs. Robt. Fields	Adm. 1917
Mrs. P. H. Freil	Adm. 1920
J. J. Funk	Adm. 1920
Mrs. Funk	Adm. 1920
J. G. Francis	Adm. 1921
Mrs. Francis	Adm. 1921
Mrs. Harold Fishbeck	Adm. 1922
Viola Fritsch	Adm. 1922
Gordon Featherstone (sic)	Adm. 1922
Herbert B. Francis	Adm. 1922
Maxin Featherstone (sic)	Adm. 1922
Mary Cathyrn Eubank	Adm. 1927
Antimesse Francis	Adm. 1928
R. P. Gwinn	Adm. 1873, from the Baptists
Mrs. R. P. Gwinn	Adm. 1873, from the Baptists
Walter Gwinn	Adm. 1895
Mrs. Walter Gwinn	Adm. 1909
E. P. Gwinn	Adm. 1883
Mrs. E. P. Gwinn	Adm. 1883
Rufus Gwinn	Adm. 1897
Ira Gruber	Adm. 1908, Moved to California
Mrs. Ira Gruber	Adm. 1908, Moved to California
Arthur Gorker	Adm. 1902
Harry Gorker	Adm. 1902
John George	Adm. 1907
Mrs. John George	Adm. 1897
Winnie George	Adm. 1904
Willie George	Adm. 1904
Cleo Groce	Adm. 1902
Esco Groce	Adm. 1902
Mrs. Carry Gilliam	Adm. 1911
Mrs. T. E. Gibbs	Adm. 1909
Roy Gwinn	---

44

Name	Comments
Evelyn Grant	Adm. 1915, Married J. Dysart
Mrs. Geo. Grant	Adm. 1916
John Guimple	Adm. 1917, Moved to Kansas City
Lera Groce	---
Mrs. A. Gorker	---
Dewey Gorker	---
Georgia Grant	Adm. 1918
Mrs. Sarah Groce	Adm. 1920
H. B. Gwinn	Adm. Jan., 1921, Gone to the Baptists.
R. A. Guile	Adm. Feb., 1921, From Broadway Church at Sedalia. Moved to Mexico
Mrs. R. A. Guile	---
Jasper Gilbert	Adm. 1921
Mrs. E. A. Grimsley	---
Mrs. B. P. Goodson	---
Ethel Gwinn	Adm. 1922
B. P. Goodson	Adm. 1922
Mrs. Roy Gwinn	Adm. 1922
Mrs. L. M. Gwinn	Adm. 1922
L. M. Gwinn	Adm. 1923
Mrs. Minnie Griffin	Adm. 1923
Mrs. J. H. Gilbert	Adm. 1921, Moved to Iowa in 1922
Dulaney Gwinn	Adm. 1925
Mrs. Alice Goodson	---
Velma Goodson	Adm. 1928
Robert Ham	---
Jesse Ham	---
R. W. Hickman	---
James L. Hickman	---
C. H. Hickman	---
T. R. Haynie	Adm. 1893
Mrs. T. R. Haynie	Adm. 1887
Jessie Haynie	Adm. 1910
Nora May Haynie	Adm. 1910, Moved to Sapulpa, OK, Mar. S. P. O'Neal
Harry Herider	Adm. 1911
Maysie Herider (Bridges)	Adm. 1911
Mrs. May Herider	Adm. 1895

Name	Comments
Mrs. Ed Hawley	---
Mrs. Harper	Adm. 1891
Dan V. Herider	Adm. 1910
Lilliam Ham	Adm. 1911
Daisy Ham	Adm. 1911
W. I. Hockaday	Adm. 1911
Mrs. W. I. Hockaday	Adm. 1911
William Hickman	Adm. 1911
Jerome Hill	Adm. 1912
Harry Holman	Adm. 1913
Dan Herider, Jr.	Adm. 1912
Mrs. Adam Ham	Adm. 1914
Roger Haynie	Adm. 1922
Mrs. Wm. Hains	Adm. 1914
C. H. Hitchborn	Adm. 1914
Mrs. C. H. Hitchborn	Adm. 1914
Edith Hitchborn	Adm. 1915
Wilbur Hitchborn	Adm. 1915
Zora Howell	Adm. 1916
Cyrus Hall	Adm. 1916
Olie Hall	Adm. 1916
Thomas Hall	Adm. 1916
Mrs. Nellie Hall	Adm. 1916
Wood Hall	Adm. 1917
Mrs. Ophelia Hall	---
Mrs. Charlotte Hamilton	---
Jerry Hobson	Adm. 1918
Mrs. Hattie Harrison	Adm. 1918
George Harrison	Adm. 1918
Anna Hand	Adm. 1918
Mr. Holmes	Adm. 1918
Cora Holmes	Adm. 1918
F. W. Hutchinson	Adm. 1919
Mrs. F. W. Hutchinson	Adm. 1919
Velma Hutchinson	Adm. 1919
Mrs. Minnie Hood	Adm. 1919
Adam Ham	Adm. 1919
Miss Sue Hockaday	Adm. 1919
Mrs. Ruth Hockaday	Formerly Ruth Scipes
Minnie Harper	Adm. 1919
D. L. Hutchinson	Adm. 1921
Mrs. D. L. Hutchinson	Adm. 1921
Christine Hall	Adm. 1924
Mrs. E. E. Hopson	Adm. 1924
Geo. Hardin	Adm. 1923
Helen Herider	Adm. 1923
Irwin Hockaday	Adm. 1923

Name	Comments
Weller Hockaday	Adm. 1923
--- Hamby	Adm. 1922
Victor Hutchinson	Adm. 1922
Chas. D. Hutchinson	Adm. 1922
Mrs. John Herider	Adm. 1921
Harold Hutchinson	Adm. 1921
Mrs. Frank Hinton	Adm. 1921
Marjorie Heibner	Adm. 1921
Jno. Herider	Adm. 1921
Louise Haynie	Adm. 1920
Wm. Harper	Adm. 1920
E. A. Hottell	---
Billie Hall	Adm. 192?
Leroy Herider	Adm. 1914
Mrs. Roy Hycks	Adm. 1924
Katherine Hycks	Adm. 1924
Dorothy Hycks	Adm. 1924
Lilliam Hutchinson	Adm. 1924
W. I. Hall	Adm. 1924
Billie Hall	Adm. 1925
Mrs. Margaret Ish	Adm. 1866
E. J. Ish	Adm. 1891
Mrs. Lola Ish	Adm. 1889
Clarance	Adm. 1916
Mrs. Ann Igo	Adm. 1925
Lizzie Jarvis	Adm. 1910
G. W. Jarvis	Adm. 1889
Mrs. Mollie Jarvis	Adm. 1897, from the Methodist
W. M. Jarvis	Adm. 1898
Mrs. Nellie Jarvis	Adm. 1903, from the Methodist
Geo. Jaques	Adm. 1903
Mrs. Geo. Jaques	Adm. 1903
J. H. Julian	Adm. 1903
Jack Julian	Adm. 1913
F. O. Jenkins	Adm. 1909
Mrs. F. O. Jenkins	Adm. 1909
Bert Roe Jarvis	Adm. 1910
Mary Lynne Jarvis	Adm. 1911
Mrs. David Jones	Adm. 1913
Miss Hazel Jaques	Adm. 1911
Miss Mamie Jackson	Adm. 1913
F. L. Jenkins, Jr.	Adm. 1913
Clarance Julian	Adm. 1917
Vern Julian	Adm. 1917
Mrs. Cornelia Johnson	Adm. 1917
Mrs. A. L. Jones	Adm. 1907

Name	Comments
Louise Jarvis	Adm. 1918
Wm. Jarvis	Adm. 1910
P. D. Johnson	Adm. 1921
Mrs. P. D. Johnson	Adm. 1921
J. H. Julian	Adm. 1921
Stella Johnson	---
Eva Johnson	---
Myrtle Johnson	---
Elsie Johnson	---
Henry Johnson	---
Mary Johnson	---
Eulah Johnson	---
R. J. Johnson	---
Virginia Johnston	---
Miss Gertrude Kirby	Adm. 1907
Miss Jenice Keyton	Adm. 1911, Married Geo. Wright
Miss Esther Keyton	Adm. 1911, Married Oliver Johnson
Miss Nellie Keyton (Venable)	Adm. 1917
Bennie Keyton	Adm. 1917
Mrs. Eli Kidwell	---
Nadell Kidwell	---
Annabell Kirby	Adm. 1924
Mrs. Velma Keyton	Adm. 1927
Mrs. Hattie Kramer	Adm. 1924
Lillian Keith	Adm. 1928
Thelma Keith	Adm. 1928
Dorothy Keith	Adm. 1928
A. L. Liggett	Adm. 1888
Mrs. A. L. Liggett	Adm. 1916
Miss Pauline Liggett	Adm. 1888
Albert Liggett	Adm. 1913
Mrs. John Lane	---
W. C. Ligon	Adm. 1917
Mrs. W. C. Ligon	Adm. 1917
Willie Ligon	Adm. 1917
Elmer Ligon	Adm. 1917
Allen Ligon	Adm. 1917
Mary Ligon	Adm. 1917
Andrew Lane	Adm. 1917
Mrs. Kate Liggett	Adm. 1923, d. Jun., 1924
Mrs. Sam Lee	---
Cordie Long	Adm. 1921
Mrs. Cordie Long	Adm. 1921

Name	Comments
Mrs. Freda May Leinberry	---
Bess P. Liggett	---
Mr. & Mrs. Evan Lawler	---
A. G. Little	Adm. 1928
Dr. W. E. Lockwood	Adm. 1928
Mrs. Mary E. Moore	Adm. 1925
Thos. J. Moore	Adm. 1925
Mrs. Arimina Montgomery	Adm. 1880
Miss Montgomery	Adm. 1891
Hugh Montgomery	Adm. 1897
Mr. & Mrs. A. C. Minks	Adm. 1897
Wm. A. Meyers	---
Mrs. Lillie Meyers	Adm. 1897
Mrs. Emma McGee	Adm. 1897
Mrs. Allie Metcalf	---
Leonard McGee	Adm. 1911
Merle McGee	Adm. 1912
Frank Miller	Adm. 1913
Mrs. Frank Miller	Adm. 1911
Elvin Miller	Adm. 1913
Homer Miller	Adm. 1913
Miss Mary McIntosh	Adm. 1916, Married Sam Lee
Mr. McIntosh	Adm. 1917
Mrs. Ruby McAmis	Adm. 1916
Mrs. Bess Melligan	Adm. 1916
Mrs. Carl Martin	---
Mrs. Barney Mayfield	Adm. 1917
Ola May Morris	Adm. 1917
Claude Morris	Adm. 1917
Mrs. Annie Mendenhall	Adm. 1917
Frank Montgomery	Adm. 1917
Harry Montgomery	Adm. 1917
Mrs. Claude Morris	Adm. 1911
Willie McClain	Adm. 1913
Henry Means	Adm. 1917, d. Apr., 1925
Mrs. Henry Means	Adm. 1917, Married Thos. Woodward
Edna McDade	---
Mrs. J. H. May	Move to Mexico in 1927
J. N. Mendenhall	Adm. 1919
Annabell Mendenhall	Adm. 1924
Mary Means	Adm. 1924, Moved to Cal.

49

Name	Comments
	Sep., 1926
Mr. & Mrs. Walter Marksberry	Adm. 1924
Earline Myers	Adm. 1924
Mrs. Elvyn Miller	---
J. H. May	Adm. 1924, Moved to Mexico
Wilford Means	Adm. 1923, Moved to Cal.
	Sep., 1926
Martha A. Montgomery	Adm. 1923
Mary Helen Montgomery	Adm. 1923, Joined the Baptists
Mrs. J. H. May	Adm. 1922
Mrs. F. R. Miller	Adm. 1923
Oren Miller	Adm. 1923
Mrs. Oren Miller	Adm. 1923
Stephen McGee	Adm. 1923
Jas. Milligan	Adm. 1923
F. R. Miller	Adm. 1923
Mrs. Roy Marshall	---
Chas. Montgomery	Adm. 1923
J. W. Montgomery	---
Richard Martin	---
Henry Mattix	Adm. 1921
Mrs. Henry Mattix	---
C. O. Mallard	---
Mrs. C. O. Mallard	Adm. 1926
Lewis McAmis	Adm. 1926
Francis Metcalf	Adm. 1928
Mrs. Francis Metcalf	Adm. 1928
Mrs. Lou Netherton	---
Edward Neal	Adm. 1902
Mrs. Ed Neal	---
Florence Neal	Adm. 1914
R. M. Nugent	Adm. 1907
R. E. Nichols	Adm. 1910
R. M. Nichols	Adm. 1910
Ed. Neff	Adm. 1912
Mrs. Ed. Neff	---
Miss Grace Nunies	Adm. 1916, Married Jinks Barksdale
Lorine Thebold Newman	Adm. 1911
Mrs. Blanche Nutter	---
Mrs. Alice Neal	Adm. 1920, Married

Name	Comments
	Harry Christ
Fred Newman	Adm. 1923
Bonna Newman	Adm. 1923
Vance Nugent	Adm. 1922
Robt. Nugent	Adm. 1922
Mrs. Newman	Adm. 1923
Mrs. Eulah Nidefer	Adm. 1927, Letter from Bapt. Church Fairland, OK
Samuel J. Oots	---
Mrs. Samuel J. Oots	---
Walter Oots	Adm. 1881
Mrs. Mattie Oots	Adm. 1881
Claude Oots	Adm. 1895
Mrs. Claude Oots	Adm. 1908
Rule Oots	Adm. 1887
Mrs. Rule Oots	Adm. 1887
Mrs. Elizabeth Oots	Adm. 1897
Anna Marie Oots	Adm. 1920
Ray Henson	Adm. 1920
Wm. Officer	Adm. 1922
Mrs. Frank Officer	Adm. 1922
Marie Officer	Adm. 1922, Married Gene Brown
Frank Officer, Jr.	Adm. 1924
Wilma Phillips	Adm. 1917
Mrs. Ida Peel	Adm. 1917
Tehodore Parks	Adm. 1917
Jno. A. Page	Adm. 1894, Came from the Baptists
Mrs. Eva Page	Adm. 1894, d. 1926
Hubert Page	Adm. 1904
Allen Page	Adm. 1904
Mrs. Ella Pennock	---
Daniel Pope	---
Mrs. Mollie Pope	---
Ben Pilliam	Adm. 1913
Mrs. Ben Pilliam	---
Mrs. Allen Page	Adm. 1908
Sadie Page	Adm. 1908
Jessie Page	Adm. 1908
John Page, Jr.	Adm. 1911
Hazel Pulliam	Adm. 1913
Alta Pulliam	Adm. 1911

Name	Comments
Mamye Pulliam	Adm. 1911
Oma Pulliam	Adm. 1913
Mr. & Mrs. E. B. Parks	Adm. 1912
Richard Parks	---
Ralph Parks	---
Miss Lottie Pennock	---
Mrs. Harry Porter	Adm. 1907
Pearl Peel	Adm. 1916
Mrs. & Mrs. W. B. Phillips	Adm. 1917
Miss Frances Paull	Adm. 1918
Mrs. Lois Powell	Adm. 1911, Moved to K. C.
Linwood Page	Adm. 1924
Wilbur Phillips	---
Mrs. L. E. Phillips	Adm. 1924
Mrs. Hall Pledge	Adm. 1925
Robt. Porter	Adm. 1928
Glen Phillipps	Adm. 1928
Lucile Piper	Adm. 1928
Mrs. R. D. Quisenberry	Moved to Columbia in 1922
Geo. H. Reynolds	Adm. 1917
Mrs. Belle Ross	Adm. 1880
W. B. Robinson	Adm. 1900, From the Baptists
Miss Sally Robinson	Adm. 1897
Howard Robinson	Adm. 1913
Mrs. Ro	Adm. 1879
Bessey Rimby	Adm. 1905
Mae Robertson	Adm. 1907
Beulah Robertson	Adm. 1907
Wm. H. Robertson	Adm. 1907
Mrs. J. R. Robertson	Adm. 1913
Bess Robertson	Adm. 1907
Mrs. Alice Rice	---
Mrs. Alice Roberts	---
Mrs. Beryl Riley	Adm. 1919
Bernard Riley	Adm. 1923
Miss Alice Riley (Goodsn)	Adm. 1924
Mrs. J. J. Ralston	Adm. 1923
Mrs. H. Rudd	Adm. 1924
O. H. Ross	Adm. 1924
Mrs. O. H. Ross	Adm. 1924
Harry Ross	Adm. 1924
Virginia Riley	Adm. 1924
Mrs. Eva Riley	Adm. 1925
Janice Stafford	Adm. 1917
Dorothy Stafford	Adm. 1917

Name	Comments
Claud Stafford	Adm. 1917
Martie Smith	Adm. 1917
Wm. Summers	Adm. 1917
Mrs. L. S. Shanks	Adm. 1917
A. H. Snoddy	Adm. 1881
Mrs. Milley Snoddy	Adm. 1881, d. 1919
Ona Snoddy	Adm. 1895, Married ClarkMansfield, 1918.
August Smith	Adm. 1887
Mrs. August Smith	---
Jerome Smith	Adm. 1912
Margaret Smith	Adm. 1911
Mrs. Almeda Smith	---
Mark Shelton	---
Mrs. Mollie Short	---
Mrs. Ida Shoan	Adm. 1896
Mrs. Robert Scipes	---
Ruth Scipes	Adm. 1911
Martha Scipes	Adm. 1911
Chas. Spradley	Adm. 1907
Alberta Shannon	Adm. 1908
L. E. Shepard	Adm. 1913
Mrs. L. E. Shepard	Adm. 1913
Clyde Smith	Adm. 1913
Nadine Shatzer	Adm. 1913
Mrs. A. Shockley	Adm. 1913
Clay Surber	Adm. 1913
Mrs. Clay Surber	Adm. 1913
Louis Smith	Adm. 1913
Mr. & Mrs. Settle	Adm. 1914
Mrs. Della Smith	Adm. 1914
Mamie Short	Adm. 1914
Kathleen Short	Adm. 1911
Mrs. Claude Stafford	Adm. 1911
Mr. & Mrs. Frank Spencer	Adm. 1912
Era Sloan	Adm. 1914
Lucille Spencer	---
Russell Spencer	Moved to K. C.
Mrs. Russell Spencer	---
Mrs. Mevlin Stroud	Adm. 1907
Mrs. Earl Smith	---
Mrs. Inez Sharp	---
Mrs. Frank Skinner	Adm. 1919
Mabel Smith	Adm. 1921
Mr. G. W. Simco	Adm. 1921

Name	Comments
Joe Spencer	Adm. 1921
Sue Spencer	Adm. 1922
M. L. Stroud	Adm. 1921
Mrs. Chas. Spencer	Adm. 1923
Mr. & Mrs. E. W. Shockley	Adm. 1924
Verna Smith	Adm. 1925
Mrs. Joe Smith	---
Harold Smith	---
Mrs. Luella Smith	Adm. 1926
Joe Smith	---
Ralph Smith	Adm. 1928
Mrs. Clyde Smith	---
Elva Thebold	Adm. 1917
Floyd Turpin	Adm. 1917
Mrs. Martha Taylor	Adm. 1917
Fred Thebold	Adm. 1902
Mrs. Fred Thebold	Adm. 1902
Mrs. Ellen Tracey	Adm. 1906
Mrs. P. M. Thompson	---
Mrs. Gertie Thompson	Adm. 1897
Allyne Toohey	Adm. 1911
Frances Toohey	Adm. 1911
Mary Toohey	Adm. 1911
Hollis Toohey	Adm. 1914
Mrs. W. D. Toohey	Adm. 1911
Ruth Toohey	Adm. 1922
Claudine Toohey	---
Charles Townsend, Jr.	Adm. 1915
Murle Thebold	Adm. 1914
Cora Thompson	Adm. 1919
Creston Thebold	Adm. 1924
Lalla Thebold	---
Vernell Tillman	Adm. 1920, Married Claud Wood
Ophelia Tillman	Married Raymond Rudd
Mrs. C. Tillman	---
Mr. Taylor	Adm. 1927
Robert Thomas	Adm. 1928
Elene Thompson	Adm. 1928
C. R. Vaughan	---
Mrs. C. R. Vaughan	---
Nellie Keyton Venable	---
Joseph Wood	Adm. 1917
Anna Wood	Adm. 1917
Amos Wilhite	Adm. 1897
Mrs. May Wilhite	Adm. 1897

Name	Comments
A. W. Wilhite	Adm. 1870
Mrs. A. W. Wilhite	Adm. 1870
Mrs. Veta Whitten	Adm. 1908
Louise Woods	Adm. 1909
Mrs. Nellie Winn	Adm. 1911
Harry Way	Adm. 1911
Beth Wood	Adm. 1912
Ray Wood	Adm. 1912
A. C. Wood	Adm. 1912
Mrs. A. C. Wood	Adm. 1912
Nadine Wood	Adm. 1912
John Winn	Adm. 1912
Mrs. C. C. Waller	Adm. 1914
Russel Weir	From the Methodist
Mrs. Russel Weir	From the Methodist
Norene Winn	Adm. 1919
Mrs. Eva Weekley	Adm. 1920
Neola Worrell	Adm. 1921
Mary Bell Wilhite	Adm. 1921
Miss Beulah Way	Adm. 1921, Moved to Texas, Married a Mr. Roberts.
Mrs. A. L. Willis	Adm. 1921
Mrs. H. M. Watts	Gone to the Baptists
Mrs. Carter Williams	Adm. 1922, Gone to the Baptists
Mrs. Dan Williams	Adm. 1922
Geo. Walker	Adm. 1922
Leo Wilhite	Adm. 1922
Val Wasby	Adm. 1921
Iverson Weekley	Adm. 1924
Devere Weekley	Adm. 1924
Don Weekley	Adm. 1925
Mr. S. L. Yowell	Adm. 1917
Mrs. S. L. Yowell	Adm. 1917
Joe Yates	Adm. 1917
Gertrude Yates	Adm. 1917
Mr. S. J. Yowell	Adm. 1918
Mrs. S. J. Yowell	Adm. 1918
David Yates	Adm. 1921
J. P. Yates	Adm. 1923
Sherman Yowell	Adm. 1924
Mrs. Pat J. Yates	---

Name	Comments
Kenneth Yowell	Adm. 1928

Register of Elders

Name	Date
R. P. Gwinn	Feb. 23, 1919
Jno. A. Page	Feb. 23, 1919
G. W. Jarvis	Feb. 23, 1919
W. P. Dulaney	Feb. 23, 1919

Register of Deacons

Name	Date
T. R. Haynie	Feb. 23, 1919
W. G. Barksdale	Feb. 23, 1919
M. F. Allen	Feb. 23, 1919
P. L. Eubank	Feb. 23, 1919
W. H. Brown	Feb. 23, 1919
Allen Page	Feb. 23, 1919
A. H. Snoddy	Feb. 23, 1919
Roy Eubank	Feb. 23, 1919
Frank Featherstone	Jan. 9, 1921
Robt. T. Ham	Jan. 9, 1921
W. L. Decker	Jan. 9, 1921
Harry Christ	Jan., 1923
Earnest Ish	Jan., 1923
Walter Gwinn	Jan., 1928
J. G. Francis	Jan., 1928
M. L. Stroud	Feb., 1928
B. Riley	Feb., 1928
J. M. Mendenhall	Feb., 1928
F. E. Berry	Feb., 1928
S. T. Yowell	Feb., 1928
I. Weekley	Feb., 1928
Claud Oots	Feb., 1928
W. B. Phillips	Feb., 1928
David Byers	Feb., 1928

Record of Deaths

Name	Place of Death	Burial
Wm. Jarvis	Slater, MO	Slater
Dr. W. M. Jarvis	Fulton, MO	Slater
Mrs. A. Gorker	Slater, MO	Slater
Millie Fishbeck	Slater, MO	Slater
Vera Benedict	Kansas City, MO	K. C.
Guy Bradley	Slater, MO	Slater
Name	Place of Death	Burial
R. W. Compton	Slater, MO	Slater
P. H. Clifford	Slater, MO	Slater
Mrs. F. M. Day	Slater, MO	Slater
Mrs. W. S. Dillard	Slater, MO	Slater
Cleo Groce	County Home	Slater
W. I. Hockaday	Slater, MO	Slater

```
Mrs. Mike Short      Kansas City, MO      Slater
Mrs. Jno. Page       County Home          Slater
```

1883 State Census, Sedalia, Pettis County, Missouri.

```
A. J. Van Wagner            White     Male    36
Minister W. 6th St.
Fannnie                     White  Female 36
Anna Bell                   White  Female 36
```

Mount Hope Cumberland Presbyterian Church, Huntsville, Randolph County, Missouri

Register of Marriages

P. G. Turner and Fannie E. Jenkins, (MD) May 7, 1878, (MG) A. M. Buchanan.
Arthur (Bud) Jenkins and Mary J. Overby, (MD) September 8, 1876, (MG) T. G. Pool.

Register of Adult Baptisms

Name	Date	Reverend
Mary J. Welch	1876	Levi Haynes
Green Jenkins	Sep. 29, 1878	*S. D. Givens
		*(Holden, Mo)
Martha E. Jenkins	Sep. 29, 1878	S. D. Givens
Lucinda P. Hoover	Sep. 29, 1878	S. D. Givens
Malinda Hoover	Sep. 29, 1878	S. D. Givens
Jacob Hoover	Apr. 18, 1890	W. F. Manning
Alfred C. Smothers	Aug. 25, 1882	J. E. Sharp
Katie Cunningham	Aug. 25, 1892	J. E. Sharp
Wm. Arthur Frazier	Aug. 31, 1882	J. E. Sharp
Isola Jenkins	Aug. 31, 1882	J. E. Sharp
Nora Jenkins	Aug. 31, 1882	J. E. Sharp
Mollie Smothers	Aug. 31, 1882	J. E. Sharp
Lisie A. Cunningham	Aug. 31, 1882	J. E. Sharp
Flora B. Wilson	Aug. 31, 1882	J. E. Sharp
Adella E. Esra	Sep. 17, 1882	J. E. Sharp
Mary A. Esry	Sep. 4, 1883	A. M. Buchanan
Warren E. Esry	Sep. 4, 1883	A. M. Buchanan
Geo. F. Brock	Sep. 5, 1883	A. M. Buchanan
Edward E. Brock	Dec. 5, 1883	A. M. Buchanan
Tho. L. Pilkerton	Dec. 5, 1883	A. M. Buchanan
Amos Weeks	Dec. 5, 1883	*J. E. Sharpe

*(Reverend's name spelled two ways.)

```
E. Landon Heand      Dec.  5, 1883      J. E. Sharpe
```

Name	Date	Reverend
Jhon (sic) Kribs	Dec. 5, 1883	J. E. Sharpe
Eva L. Jenkins	Dec. 6, 1883	J. E. Sharpe
James H. Rout	Nov. 24, 1884	James Disert
Emit H. Hardister	Nov. 24, 1884	James Disert
Cora B. Adams	Dec. 25, 1884	G. W. Baker
Mary Pilkington	Dec. 25, 1884	G. W. Baker
Mattie A. Pilkington	Dec. 25, 1884	G. W. Baker
Eugene H. Pilkington	Dec. 25, 1884	G. W. Baker
Tomie J. Owen	Dec. 25, 1884	G. W. Baker
Amanda E. Esry	Dec. 25, 1884	G. W. Baker
Lizia Miller	Dec. 25, 1884	G. W. Baker
Sinie L. Miller	Dec. 25, 1884	G. W. Baker
Jno. Wm. McCollough	Oct. 18, 1885	A. M. Buchanan
Jas. G. Alverson	Oct. 18, 1885	A. M. Buchanan
Cyrus Frazier	Oct. 18, 1885	A. M. Buchanan
Charley A. Frazier	Oct. 18, 1885	A. M. Buchanan
Ollie Harris	May 2, 1886	A. M. Buchanan
Jas. L. McCullanah	May 2, 1886	A. M. Buchanan
Edwin J. Adams	Aug. --, 1886	A. M. Buchanan
Ida A. White	Aug. 8, 1886	A. M. Buchanan
Nowel Devore	Mar. 9, 1889	H. C. Yates
Warren B. Walker	Mar. 9, 1889	H. C. Yates
Geo. Vaugh	Mar. 9, 1889	H. C. Yates
Anna Vaugh	Mar. 9, 1889	H. C. Yates
Ernest D. Adams	Mar. 9, 1889	H. C. Yates
Magie E. Jackoby	Mar. 9, 1889	H. C. Yates
Martha A. Jacoby	Mar. 9, 1889	H. C. Yates
Minnie L. Wats	Mar. 9, 1889	H. C. Yates
James C. Jenkins	Jun. 2, 1889	A. M. Buchanan
Wm. T. Chapman	Jun. 2, 1889	A. M. Buchanan
Lura Reede	Jun. 2, 1889	A. M. Buchanan
Benjamin Deskins	Mar. 2, 1890	J. L. Routt
Mrs. S. A. Deskins	Mar. 2, 1890	---

Membership Register

Name	Admission	Dismissed
Mary J. Pilkington	Dec. 14, 1884	---
John W. Pilkington	Dec. 14, 1884	---
*Mattie A. Pilkington	Dec. 14, 1884	---

*(She claims an unregenerate hart (sic). Her name is dropped at her own request.)

Name	Admission	Dismissed
Eugene H. Pilkingtin	Dec. 14, 1884	Dis. Mar. 8, 1893
Josmie J. Owen	Dec. 14, 1884	---
Salie (sic) B. Owen	Dec. 14, 1884	---
Amanda E. Esry	Dec. 14, 1884	Dis. Sep. 18, 1888
Lizia Miller	Dec. 14, 1884	---
Jno. Wm. McCullough	Oct. 18, 1885	Dis. Dec. 6, 1902
Jas. G. Alverson	Oct. 18, 1885	d. Mar. 6, 1910
Wm. B. Walls	Oct. 18, 1885	Dis. Mar. 17, 1888
Sarah R. Watts	Oct. 18, 1885	Dis. Mar. 17, 1888
Emil Junker	Oct. 18, 1885	Dis. Nov. 20, 1886
Cyrus Frazier	Oct. 18, 1885	Dis. Mar. 26, 1902
Charity A. Frazier	Oct. 18, 1885	---
Charles H. Ramsey	Oct. 18, 1885	---
Sarah M. Ramsey	Oct. 18, 1885	---
Rachel A. McCullough	Oct. 18, 1885	Dis. Jan. 15, 1889
Eliza Shaw	Nov. 15, 1885	Dis. Aug. 7, 1903 Joinedthe Mormons
Samuel P. White	Dec. 6, 1885	---
Mary C. White	Dec. 6, 1885	---
Ida A. White	Dec. 6, 1885	Dis. Jun. 2, 1892
James L. McCullough	Dec. 6, 1885	---
Isaac Harris	Feb. 8, 1886	d. Apr. 2, 1888
Ollia Harris	Feb. 17, 1886	---
Wm. Henry Tuggle	Feb. 17, 1886	Dis. Aug. 8, 1889
Edwin J. Adams	Aug. 7, 1886	Dis. Aug. 6, 1892
Gerthie L. Jenkins	Aug. 7, 1886	---
Wm. T. Chapman	Nov. 21, 1888	---

Name	Admission	Dismissed
*James C. Jenkins	Nov. 21, 1888	Dis. Aug.
*(Went to Huntsville)		7, 1903
Norvel Devore	Mar. 9, 1889	---
Warren B. Walker	Mar. 9, 1889	---
Chas. E. Miller	Mar. 9, 1889	---
Geo. Vaughn	Mar. 9, 1889	---
Anna J. Vaughn	Mar. 9, 1889	---
Robbert (sic) W. Dutten	Mar. 9, 1889	Dis. Mar. 3, 1893
Ernest D. Adams	Mar. 9, 1889	Dis. Mar. 2, 1895
Magie E. Jackoby	Mar. 9, 1889	---
Martha A. Jackoby	Mar. 9, 1889	---
Minie L. Wats	Mar. 9, 1889	Dis. Mar. 3, 1893
Taura Reede	Jun. 2, 1889	Dis. Feb. 3, 1893
Alex. M. Frazer	Aug. 12, 1889	Dis. Jul. 6, 1901
Mrs. S. A. Deskin	Feb. 2, 1809	Dis. May 19, 1899
Benjamin Deskin	Mar. 2, 1890	Dis. May 19, 1899
Alice E. Frazier	May 4, 1890	Dis. Jul. 6, 1901
Clara Walker	Oct. 5, 1890	Married W. L. Gibson
Tomie E. Sheron	Oct. 5, 1890	---
Tomie J. Esry	Oct. 5, 1890	---
Joseph A. Calvert	Nov. 30, 1890	---
L. M. Calvert	Nov. 30, 1890	d. 1891
J. W. McCullough	Nov. 30, 1890	Dis. Nov. 3, 1894
Rachel A. McCullough	Nov. 30, 1890	Dis. Nov. 3, 1894
Wm. H. Robuck	Dec. 6, 1890	d. Feb. 19, 1924
Sarah E. Robuck	Dec. 6, 1890	---
Frank White	Oct. 30, 1892	---
Bertha Deskins	Oct. 30, 1892	Dis. May 19, 1899
Barbary Breusch	Dec. 4, 1892	---
Bula Rutte	Apr. 30, 1893	---
Jacob Brush	Aug. 16, 1893	---
John C. Cox	Aug. 16, 1893	---
Geo. Morris	Aug. 7, 1895	---

Name	Admission	Dismissed
Tura Morris	Aug. 7, 1895	---
Henrettie McCullough	Aug. 12, 1896	---
Laura Baker	Aug. 21, 1896	Joined the Baptists
Winnie Rais	Aug. 21, 1896	Married Robt. Harris
J. W. Baker	Aug. 21, 1896	---
Maggie Walker	Aug. 21, 1896	---
Aaron McCullough	Aug. 21, 1896	---
Edward Rais	Aug. 21, 1896	---
Thos. Gowings	Aug. 21, 1896	d. Mar. 16, 1897
Ida Gowings	Aug. 21, 1896	---
Thos. Shiflett	Aug. 21, 1896	---
Ella Shiflett	Aug. 21, 1896	---
Mrs. Bertha Shaw	Aug. 21, 1896	---
Milton F. Gooding	Aug. 21, 1896	---
Alise Shaw	Aug. 21, 1896	---
Burnard H. Shilfett	Aug. 21, 1896	---
Frank L. Baker	Aug. 21, 1896	---
Wm. W. Shaw	Aug. 21, 1896	Joined the Mormons
Willard E. Towles	Aug. 21, 1896	Dis. Mar. 14, 1902
James C. Towles	Aug. 21, 1896	---
Selmon Harris	Aug. 21, 1896	---
David Esry	Aug. 21, 1896	---
Emma Shiflett	Aug. 21, 1896	---
Geo. T. Shiflett	Aug. 21, 1896	---
Alfred Graves	Aug. 21, 1896	Dis. Mar. 14, 1902
Lizzie Graves	Aug. 21, 1896	Dis. Mar. 14, 1902
H. R. Walker	Aug. 21, 1896	Dis. Oct., 1904
Belle Walker	Aug. 21, 1896	Dis. Oct., 1904
Lula Routte	Aug. 21, 1896	---
Thos. H. Riley	Oct. 18, 1896	---
Lydia F. Polston	Apr. 24, 1898	Dis. 1902
R. S. Polston	Aug. 7, 1898	---
Walter Shiflett	Aug. 7, 1898	Joined at Moberley
Wm. J. Turner	Aug. 7, 1898	---
Josafine Hosa	Aug. 12, 1898	---
Mrs. Bill Ramsey	Aug. 12, 1898	---

Name	Admission	Dismissed
David G. Jones	Aug. 12, 1898	---
James Calvin Thomas	Aug. 12, 1898	---
Mrs. Nettie Thomas	Aug. 12, 1898	---
James Kidwell	Aug. 12, 1898	---

Watson Cumberland Presbyterian Church, Watson, Atchison Co- unty, Missouri

Register of Elders

Name	Ordained	Ceased to Act
Wm. L. Reeves	Feb., 1867	Feb., 1884
Jesse M. Cross	Feb., 1867	d. Jan. 1, 1871
Isaac B. Jones	---	---
David McNeal	---	Feb., 1884
W. M. R. Dean	Jun., 1876	---
Daniel B. Morgan	Feb., 1867	---
Thomas McAlravy	Feb., 1867	---
Whitley McNeal	Feb., 1867	---
Adam C. Good	Feb., 1867	---
Salrid Addington	Dec., 1877	---
A. S. Campbell	Mar. 22, 1878	---
M. M. Good	Mar. 14, 1886	---
Sylvester Hall	Mar. 14, 1886	---

Register of Deacons

Name	Ordained
David McNeal	Feb., 1867
Robert Furgeson	Feb., 1867
H. J. Good	Jan., 1871
Henry Barnhart	Jan., 1871
A. S. Campbell	Jan., 1871
John Garst	May, 1876
Manon Good	Mar. 22, 1878
Willie Good	Mar. 14, 1886
June Campbell	Mar. 14, 1886
John Garst, jr.	Dec. 14, 1888

Register of Adult Baptisms

Name	Date	Reverend
Jackson M. Brown	Feb., 1876	T. K. Roach
Martha Clodfelter	Feb., 1876	T. K. Roach
Sarah Hays	Feb., 1876	T. K. Roach
Elizabeth Good	Feb., 1876	T. K. Roach
Jammie C. McNeal	Feb., 1876	T. K. Roach
Mary E. McNeal	Feb., 1876	T. K. Roach
Permelia J. Turner	Feb., 1876	T. K. Roach
Lowley Martin	Feb., 1876	T. K. Roach
Laura M. Morgan	Feb., 1876	T. K. Roach
Landon W. Campbell	Feb., 1876	T. K. Roach
Eddie F. Reeves	Feb., 1876	T. K. Roach
David J. McNeal	Feb., 1876	T. K. Roach

Name	Date	Reverend
Abraham Bowman	Feb., 1876	T. K. Roach
John T. Clodfelter	Feb., 1876	T. K. Roach
Lafayette Morgan	Feb., 1876	T. K. Roach
Louisa J. Morgan	Feb., 1876	T. K. Roach
Anna Workman	Feb., 1876	T. K. Roach
Edmonia Barnhart	Feb., 1876	T. K. Roach
Thos. Wm. McIlravz	Feb., 1876	T. K. Roach
John L. McIlravz	Feb., 1876	T. K. Roach
Chas. R. Bushon	Feb., 1876	T. K. Roach
John H. Vanderslice	Feb., 1876	T. K. Roach
Daniel Vanderslice	Feb., 1876	T. K. Roach
Claib. J. Barnhart	Feb., 1876	T. K. Roach
John E. Davis	Feb., 1876	T. K. Roach
Mildred E. Rhodes	Feb., 1876	T. K. Roach
Catharine Harris	Feb., 1876	T. K. Roach
William H. Morgan	Feb., 1876	T. K. Roach
Alexander McLoed	Feb., 1876	T. K. Roach
Valentine Johnson	Feb., 1876	T. K. Roach
Henry R. Hales	Feb., 1876	T. K. Roach
Thomas Hays	Feb., 1876	T. K. Roach
W. L. Johnson	Feb., 1876	T. K. Roach
Wm. R. C. Clark	Nov. 15,1878	J. C. Moore
Chas. W. Goodwin	Nov. 15,1878	J. C. Moore
Burrell L. Goodwin	Dec. 10,1878	J. C. Moore
John E. Smith	Dec. 10,1878	J. C. Moore
John J. Hughes	Dec. 10,1878	J. C. Moore
Joseph B. Goodwin	Dec. 10,1878	J. C. Moore
Mary J. Reeves	Dec. 10,1878	J. C. Moore
Flora E. Winkle	Dec. 10,1878	J. C. Moore
Caroline King	Dec. 10,1878	J. C. Moore
Leora A. Clark	Nov. 15,1878	J. C. Moore
Mary M. Goodwin	Nov. 15,1878	J. C. Moore
Margaret Goodwin	Nov. 15,1878	J. C. Moore
Mary E. Brown	Nov. 15,1878	J. C. Moore
Hannah L. Reeves	Nov. 15,1878	J. C. Moore
Mary McFarland	Nov. 15,1878	J. C. Moore
Sarah Hannan	1870	O. D. Allen
Elisha R. Wood	Jan. 26,1879	J. C. Moore
Nettie E. Peacock	Jan. 26,1879	J. C. Moore
Sarah E. Goodwin	Jan. 26,1879	J. C. Moore
Wm. J. Goodwin	Jan. 26,1879	J. C. Moore
John J. Hughes	Dec. 10,1878	J. C. Moore
Joseph B. Goodwin	Dec. 10,1878	J. C. Moore
Mary J. Reeves	Dec. 10,1878	J. C. Moore
Flora E. Winkle	Dec. 10,1878	J. C. Moore
Caroline King	Dec. 10,1878	J. C. Moore
Leora A. Clark	Nov. 15,1878	J. C. Moore
Mary M. Goodwin	Nov. 15,1878	J. C. Moore

Name	Date	Reverend
Margaret Goodwin	Nov. 15, 1878	J. C. Moore
Mary E. Brown	Nov. 15, 1878	J. C. Moore
Hannah L. Reeves	Nov. 15, 1878	J. C. Moore
Mary McFarland	Nov. 15, 1878	J. C. Moore
Sarah Hannan	1870	O. D. Allen
Elisha R. Wood	Jan. 26, 1879	J. C. Moore
Nettie E. Peacock	Jan. 26, 1879	J. C. Moore
Sarah E. Goodwin	Jan. 26, 1879	J. C. Moore
Wm. J. Goodwin	Jan. 26, 1879	J. C. Moore
James M'Million	Jan. 26, 1879	J. C. Moore
Mary M'Million	Jan. 26, 1879	J. C. Moore
Salina C. Dunwoody	Feb., 1879	J. C. Moore
Mary E. Stifle	Feb., 1879	J. C. Moore
Dora Eastridge	Feb., 1879	J. C. Moore
Jacob Stephens	Feb., 1879	J. C. Moore
Nathan F. Hays	Feb., 1879	J. C. Moore
Andrew J. Ruble	Feb., 1879	J. C. Moore
James L. Craig	Jun., 1879	J. C. Moore
John E. Ruble	Jun., 1879	J. C. Moore
John H. Hays	Jun., 1879	J. C. Moore
Annie E. Hays	Jun., 1879	J. C. Moore
Carrie B. Warfield	Feb., 1880	J. C. Moore
Mary E. Campbell	Feb., 1880	J. C. Moore
Ada B. Peacock	Feb., 1880	J. C. Moore
Lorna J. Dunham	Feb., 1880	J. C. Moore
J. Russell McNeal	Jan., 1881	J. C. Moore
Jacob N. Campbell	Jan., 1881	J. C. Moore
Alice E. Sterritt	Jan., 1881	J. C. Moore
Adaline Browning	Jan., 1881	J. C. Moore
Dora Noble	Jan., 1881	J. C. Moore
Flora B. Rhodes	Jan., 1881	J. C. Moore
Ida F. Warfield	Jan., 1881	J. C. Moore
Emma B. Geele	Jan., 1881	J. C. Moore
Miriam Hannon	Apr., 1881	J. C. Moore
James H. Browning	May, 1881	J. C. Moore
M. A. Browning	May, 1881	J. C. Moore
Alice Thornhill	Jan., 1882	J. C. Moore
Sarah M. Addington	Jan., 1882	J. C. Moore
Henry A. Shandy	Dec., 1882	J. C. Moore
Dora A. Barnhart	Dec., 1882	J. C. Moore
Minnie D. Sliger	Dec., 1882	J. C. Moore
Elizabeth C. Hall	Dec., 1882	J. C. Moore
Mincie A. Hughs	Dec., 1882	J. C. Moore
Mary A. Hall	Dec., 1882	J. C. Moore
Elizabeth J. Brown	Dec., 1882	J. C. Moore
William E. Shandy	Dec., 1882	J. C. Moore
Wm. H. Eddington	Dec., 1882	J. C. Moore
Jacob C. Shandy	Dec., 1882	J. C. Moore

Name	Date	Reverend
Jasper M. Hughs	Dec., 1882	J. C. Moore
Alice J. Shandy	Dec., 1882	J. C. Moore
Wm. H. Eastridge	Jan., 1883	Rev. Hodges
Alonzo A. Watts	Jan., 1883	Rev. Hodges
Lee R. Horn	Jan., 1883	Rev. Hodges
Wm. H. Good	Jan., 1883	Rev. Hodges
John H. Hudson	Jan., 1883	Rev. Hodges
Charles M. Hale	Jan., 1883	Rev. Hodges
Geo. H. Morgan	Jan., 1883	Rev. Hodges
Ellenora Nix	Mar., 1883	J. C. Moore
Mary E. Hays	Jan., 1884	J. C. Moore
Chas. Pickett	Jan., 1884	J. C. Moore
Ada M. Noels	Feb., 1884	J. C. Moore
Ritha Hall	Jan., 1884	J. C. Moore
John B. Garst	Jul., 1884	J. C. Moore
William Garst	Jul., 1884	J. C. Moore
Nellie J. Goose	Feb., 1885	J. C. Moore
Mary E. Harrison	Dec., 1885	J. C. Moore
Seletha J. Morrow	Dec., 1885	J. C. Moore
Josephine Garst	Dec., 1885	J. C. Moore
Winford H. Morgan	Dec., 1885	J. C. Moore
Hannah E. Hay	Dec., 1885	J. C. Moore
Oscar York	Dec., 1885	J. C. Moore
Jesse O. Garst	Dec., 1885	J. C. Moore
Brookens Campbell	Dec., 1885	J. C. Moore
Oliver York	Dec., 1885	J. C. Moore
Minnie Good	Aug., 1887	J. H. Tharp
Nettie Hays	Aug., 1887	J. H. Tharp
Lillie Lane	Jan., 1888	Geo. W. Hawley
Susan Lane	Jan., 1888	Geo. W. Hawley
Mary C. Hays	Jan., 1888	Geo. W. Hawley
Alice Herron	Jan., 1888	Geo. W. Hawley
Chas. Buck	Jan., 1888	Geo. W. Hawley
Noah Lane	Jan., 1888	Geo. W. Hawley
Oran Garst	Dec., 1888	C. W. Powers
Effie Garst	Dec., 1888	C. W. Powers
Josie Dirnel	Dec., 1888	C. W. Powers
Charlotta Noble	Dec., 1888	C. B. Powers
Hugh L. Hays	Dec., 1888	C. B. Powers
Peter Newman	Dec., 1888	C. B. Powers
H. Newman	Dec., 1888	C. B. Powers
H. Fosket	Dec., 1888	C. B. Powers
May E. Matherly	Dec., 1888	C. B. Powers
Lillian Lutz	Dec., 1888	C. B. Powers
John Furgeson	Dec., 1888	C. B. Powers
Lulie B. Hay	Aug., 1890	C. B. Powers
Minnie Burns	Aug., 1890	C. B. Powers
Charles Unicore	Aug., 1890	C. B. Powers

Name	Date	Reverend
Cora Hall	Aug., 1890	C. B. Powers

Register of Communicants

Name	Comments
Mary Gains	Adm. Feb., 1867, d. in Il.
Mariah McNeal	Adm. Feb., 1867, Dis. in Holden, Missouri
Mary M. McNeal	Adm., Feb., 1867, d. Apr. 15, 1875
Cintha A. Reeves	Adm. Feb., 1867, Dis. Shiloh, Atch. Co.
Elizabeth McAdams	Adm. Feb., 1867, d. Apr. 6, 1877, Funeral by Baird Benington
Barbara A. Williams	Adm. Feb., 1867, Moved to south Missouri
Martha Marrs	Adm. Feb., 1867, Moved to south Missouri
Salina Marrs	Adm. Feb., 1867, Moved to south Missouri
Anna E. Lackard	Adm. Feb., 1867, Gone to Ill.
Elizabeth M. NcIlroy	Adm. Feb., 1867, Trans. to Mt. Carmel, Atch. Mo.
Sarah E. Ferguson	Adm. Feb., 1867
Ellen Lucas White	Adm. Feb., 1867, Joined the Baptists
Parilla M. Addington	(Barnhart), Adm. Feb., 1867
Mary Morrow	Adm. Feb., 1867
Mary L. McNeal	Adm. Feb., 1867
Margaret Jones	Adm. Feb., 1867
Martha E. Starns	(Trimble), Adm. Feb., 1867, Dis. Aug. 25, 1880
Saraphine Crockett	Adm. Feb., 1867
A. J. Rhodes	Adm. Feb., 1867
Juliett T. McNeal	Adm. Feb., 1867, Dis. Rockport
Nancy J. Odell	Adm. Feb., 1867, d. Mar. 17, 1871
Sarena Good (Bowers)	Adm. Feb., 1867
Salina Plasters	Adm. Feb., 1867
M. C. McAdams	Adm. Feb., 1867
Evaline Coorlane	Adm. Feb., 1867
Unice Rhodes	Adm. Feb., 1867, d. 1876
Malinda J. Garst	Adm. Feb., 1867, d. Sep. 15, 1870
Phebe A. Good	(Watts), *Adm. Feb., 1867, Moved to south Missouri

*(Note: There is a line drawn through the part

Name	Comments
about moving, with another word which might be Rutherford.)	
Susannah Good	Adm. Feb., 1867
Nancy A. Smith	Adm. Feb., 1867
Sarah Smith	(Barnhart), Adm. Feb., 1867
Sarah C. Morrow	(Taylor), Adm. Feb., 1867
Clara A. Morrow (Good)	Adm. Feb., 1867
Hannah A. Addington	Adm. Feb., 1867
Josephine Matthews	(Taylor), Adm. Feb., 1867
Laura Taylor (McNeal)	Adm. Feb., 1867, Removed to Tarkio
Grace A. Cross	(Warfield), Adm. Feb., 1867
Liddie A. Sliger	Adm. Feb., 1867
Francis Bowman	Adm. Feb., 1867
Martha Bowman	Adm. Feb., 1867
Mary C. Addington	Adm. Feb., 1867
Nancy W. Eastridge	Adm. Feb., 1867
Arminta J. Reeves	Adm. Feb., 1867
Nancy Morgan	Adm. Feb., 1867 Went to Ill.
Malissa A. Reevis	(Solomon), Adm. Feb., 1867
Mary J. Cross	Adm. Feb., 1867, died in south Misouri
Arena Moor	Adm. Feb., 1867
Nancy Eastridge	Adm. Feb., 1867
Earanda Barnhart	(Mann), Adm. Feb., 1867
Angeline Jones	(Lindsleg), Adm. Feb., 1867, Went to Ill.
Anna E. Starns	Adm. Feb., 1867, Went to Tennessee
Lucy A. Morgan	Adm. Feb., 1867
Mary E. Lawson	(Vanderpool), Adm. Feb., 1867, Died in Iowa in 1876
Nancy Campbell	Adm. Feb., 1867
Mary Brown	Adm. Feb., 1867
Martha A. Barnhart	(Good), Adm. Feb., 1867
Margaret Lindsley	Adm. Feb., 1867
Ann E. Lindsley	Adm. Feb., 1867
Jane Moorland	Adm. Feb., 1867
Elizabeth Mitchel	Adm. Feb., 1867
Laura M. Helman	Adm. Feb., 1867, Went to Pennslyvania
Alice C. Helman	Adm. Feb., 1867
Emma McAdams	Adm. Feb., 1867, Joined at Wish Grove

Name	Comments
Nancy Trimble	Adm. Feb., 1867, Dis. Rockport
Nancy Jones	Adm. Feb., 1867, Went to Tennessee
Katherine Neuminster	Adm. Feb., 1867, Moved to Milwauka (sic)
Allie B. Duncan	Adm. Feb., 1867, Went to Ill.
Lou A. Duncan	Adm. Feb., 1867, Joined the Methodists
Sarah Hannan	Adm. Feb., 1867
Martha Miller	Adm. Feb., 1867, Moved to Rockport
Nancy T. Lee	Adm. Feb., 1867
Harriett Ross	(Brozles), Adm. Feb., 1867, Went to Iowa
Louisa Horn (Morgan)	Adm. Feb., 1867
Mary A. Rummerfield	Adm. Feb., 1867
Emma Dean	Adm. Feb., 1867
Susan Campbell	Adm. Feb., 1867
Nancy Vanderslice	(Tanner), Adm. Feb., 1867
Ambrose Addington	Adm. Feb., 1867, d. 1883
Thos. McIlroy	Adm. Feb., 1867, Sus. Oct. 29, 1877
Wm. C. McNeal	Adm. Feb., 1867 Went to Tarkio
Wm. R. Branard	Adm. Feb., 1867
Jonas Odell	Adm. Feb., 1867
John Good	Adm. Feb., 1867, d. Apr. 23, 1878
Geo. W. Walker	Adm. Feb., 1867
James McNeal	Adm. Feb., 1867, Moved to Holden, Mo.
David McNeal	Adm. Feb., 1867, Trans. to Shiloh Cong. 1884
Samuel Odell	Adm. Feb., 1867
Jefferson Eastridge	Adm. Feb., 1867, d. May 8, 1872
Ralph Morgan	Adm. Feb., 1867, d. Feb. 13, 1869
Robert Good	Adm. Feb., 1867
Henry L. Moore	Adm. Feb., 1867, Went to Texas
Mattison Barnhart	Adm. Feb., 1867, d. Aug. 15, 1872
Luther G. Ferguson	Adm. Feb., 1867
Hezekiah Barnhart	Adm. Feb., 1867
Wm. R. Morgan	Adm. Feb., 1867

Name	Comments
James Stewart	Adm. Feb., 1867
Wm. P. Brown	Adm. Feb., 1867
Daniel P. Morgan	Adm. Feb., 1867
Norton Barnhart	Adm. Feb., 1867
Abraham Helman	Adm. Feb., 1867, Went to Pennsylvania
Arch. S. Campbell	---
A. O. Nieuimister	---
Harvey Duncan	Went to Illinois
John Solomon	Went to Nebraska
C. W. Harris	Went to St. Joe.
John Ross	---
Jeremiah A. York	---
Abigah Brown	Left the county
Alfred Lawson	Joined another church
Jack M. Brown	Adm. Feb., 1876, Sus. Oct. 27, 1878, Restored and trans. to Shiloh Feb., 1884.
John B. Eastridge	Adm. Feb., 1876, Sus. Jun. 20, 1877 for six months
Chas. M. Good	Adm. Feb., 1876
Robt. Bacon	Adm. Feb., 1876, Joined the Baptists
L. W. Campbell	Adm. Feb., 1876, Went to Rockport, Mo.
Ed. F. Reeves	Adm. Feb., 1876, Trans. to Shiloh, Feb., 1884
Abraham Bowman	Adm. Feb., 1876, Went to Kansas.
John T. Clodfelter	Adm. Feb., 1876, ranaway
Val. Johnson	Adm. Feb., 1876
Thos. Hains	Adm. Feb., 1876
Henry R. Hale	Adm. Feb., 1876, Went to Nebraska
W. L. Johnson	Adm. Feb., 1876, Left the County
Chas. R. Bushong	Adm. Feb., 1876, Sus. Dec. 22, 1878 until he repents
John H. Vanderslice	Adm. Feb., 1876
Claib J. Barnhart	Adm. Feb., 1876, trans. to Shiloh Feb., 1884
John E. Davis	Adm. Feb., 1876, trans. to Shiloh Feb., 1884
Jas. D. Vanderslice	Adm. Feb. 1876, Went to Ammajonia, Missouri
Wm. H. Morgan	Adm. Feb., 1876
Mary A. Hughs	Adm. Feb., 1876

Name	Comments
Laura C. Barnhart	Adm. Feb., 1876
Mary A. Sliga	Adm. Feb., 1876
Polly A. Barnhart	(Johnson), Adm. Feb., 1876, Dis. Oct. 15, 1877
Caroline Barnhart	(King), Adm. Feb., 1876, trans. to Shiloh, Atch. Co., Mo.
Martha R. Danforth	Adm. Feb., 1876
Lou M. Martin	Adm. Feb., 1876
Sarah E. Morton	Adm. Feb., 1876
Amanda L. Morgan	Adm. Feb., 1876, Went to Lincoln, Ill., Returned Jul. 22, 1883
Loniga J. Morgan	Adm. Feb., 1876
Anna Workman	Adm. Feb., 1876, Went to Linden
Edmonia Barnhart	Adm. Feb., 1876, Dis. Oct. 15, 1877
Sarah F. Garst	Adm. Feb., 1876
Phebe M. Brown	Adm. Feb., 1876, trans. Shiloh
Martha Clodfelter	Adm. Feb., 1876, d. 1881
Sarah Hays	Adm. Feb., 1876
Elizabeth Good	Adm. Feb., 1876
Qsleize (?) E. McNeal	Adm. Feb., 1876, trans. Shiloh
Mary E. McNeal	Adm. Feb., 1876
Permelia J. Turner	Adm. Feb., 1876
Sarah A. Barnhart	(Zork), Adm. Feb., 1876
Laura M. Morgan	Adm. Feb., 1876, Went to Lincoln, IL
Mildred Rhodes	Adm. Feb., 1876, Went to Nebraska
Catharine Harris	Adm. Feb., 1876
Elizabeth Dean	Adm. Feb., 1876
Lucilla Neil	Adm. Apr. 22, 1877
Nancy Robinson	Adm. Apr. 22, 1877, Dis. Nov. 11, 1880, married Wm. Anderson
Sarah J. Young	Adm. Apr. 22, 1877
Evelen Robinson	Adm. Apr. 22, 1877
Leora A. Clark	Adm. Nov. 15, 1878, Run Off
Mary M. Goodwin	Adm. Nov. 15, 1878
Margaret Goodwin	Adm. Nov. 15, 1878
Martha J. Goodwin	Adm. Nov. 15, 1878
Mary E. Brown	Adm. Nov. 15, 1878
Hannah L. Reeves	(Lawson), Adm. Nov. 15,

Name	Comments
	1878
Sarah E. Young	Adm. Nov. 15, 1878
Mary McFarland	Adm. Nov. 15, 1878
Mary J. Reeves	Adm. Dec. 10, 1878
Amis (sic) S. Smith	Adm. Dec. 10, 1878
Flora C. Winkle	Adm. Dec. 10, 1878
Nettie E. Peacock	Adm. Jan. 26, 1879, Went to Tarkio
Sarah E. Goodwin	Adm. Jan. 26, 1879
Mary M. Willon	Adm. Jan. 26, 1879
C. J. Warfield	Adm. Feb., 1879, Went to Nebraska
Hiram Hannon	Adm. Feb., 1879, Went to Nebraska
Salina C. Dunwoody	Adm. Feb., 1879
Mary E. Stifle	(Clevenger), Adm. Feb., 1879
Anna E. Hays	Adm. Feb., 1879
Casandra Hays	Adm. Feb., 1879
Minnie Good	Adm. Feb., 1879
Mary A. Stephens	Adm. Feb., 1879
Dora Eastridge	(Vanderslice), Adm. Feb., 1879
Emma Ruble	Adm. Feb., 1879
Mary Ruble	(wife of A. J.), Adm. Feb., 1879
Sarah E. Taylor	(widow), Adm. Feb., 1879
Lavina Rummerfield	Adm. Feb., 1879
Agnes Saines	Adm. Feb., 1880, Went to Ohio
Mary S. Moore	Adm. Feb., 1880
Carrie B. Warfield	(Hale), Adm. Feb., 1880, Went to Nebraska
Mary E. Campbell	Adm. Feb., 1880
Agnes E. Morgan	Adm. Feb., 1880, Went to Lincoln, Ill. Returned Jul. 22, 1883
Ada B. Peacock	Adm. Feb., 1880, Went to Tarkio
Laura J. Durham	Adm. Feb., 1880, Went to. St. Joe.
Alice E. Steritt	Adm. Jan. 1, 1881, Went to Nebraska
Adaline Browning	Adm. Jan. 1, 1881, Went to Nebraska
Dora Noble	Adm. Jan. 1, 1881
Flora B. Rhodes	Adm. Jan. 1, 1881, Went to Nebraska

Name	Comments
Ida F. Warfield (Applegate)	Adm. Jan. 1, 1881
Anna B. Keele	Adm. Jan. 1, 1881
Mary A. Browning	Adm. Mar., 1881
Alice Thornhill	Adm. Jan., 1882
Sarah M. Addington	Adm. Jan., 1882
Dora A. Barnhart	Adm. Dec., 1882
Minnie D. Sliger	Adm. Dec., 1882
Elizabeth C. Hall	Adm. Dec., 1882
Mincie A. Hughs	Adm. Dec., 1882 trans. to Shiloh
May A. Hull	Adm. Dec., 1882, trans to Shiloh
Elizabeth J. Brown	Adm. Dec., 1882
Alice J. Shandy	Adm. Dec., 1882
Alexander McLoed	---
Jessee Sliger	---
Marion M. Good	---
John C. York	---
W. H. R. Dean	Adm. Feb., 1876
Samuel L. Manns	Sus. Jun. 2, 1877 for six months
Lafayette Morgan	---
Andrew J. Edwards	Gone to Arkansas
John Garst	---
Thos. Wm. McIlravy	---
Joseph H. Young	Adm. Apr., 1877
John Robinson	Adm. Apr., 1877
James M. Sliger	Adm. Jan. 13, 1878, trans. to Shiloh, Feb. 1884.
David Addington	Adm. Dec., 1877
John A. Broyles	Adm. May, 1878, Went to Indiana
Wm. R. C. Clark	Adm. Nov. 15, 1878, runaway
Burrel H. Goodwin	Adm. Nov. 15, 1878, trans. to Shiloh, Feb., 1884
Chas. W. Goodwin	Adm. Nov. 15, 1878, suspended
Samuel W. Dunlap	Adm. Dec. 10, 1878
Burrel Log. Goodwin	Adm. Dec. 10, 1878, d. 1883
Harvey O. Sitken	Adm. Dec. 10, 1878
John E. Smith	Adm. Dec. 10, 1878
John J. Hughs	Adm. Dec. 10, 1878
Joseph B. Goodwin	Adm. Dec. 10, 1878
Samuel O. Howlett	Adm. Jan. 26, 1879,

Name	Comments
	left the county.
Elisha R. Woods	Adm. Jan. 26, 1879, Went to Tarkio, Missouri
William J. Goodwin	Adm. Jan. 26, 1879
Mary E. Eastridge	Adm. Jan., 1883
Mollie Billick (Crane)	Adm. Mar., 1883
Ellenora Nox	Adm. Mar., 1883, Went to Kansas
Mary E. Hays	Adm. Dec., 1883
Laura C. Martin	Adm. Dec., 1883
May Vanderslice	Adm. Dec., 1883
Belle Vanderslice	Adm. Dec., 1883
Anna Lutz	Adm. Dec., 1883
Rosa J. Prather	Adm. Dec., 1883
Mary E. Hays	Adm. Dec., 1883
Sleta A. Brown	Adm. Dec., 1883, trans. to Shiloh
Sarah D. West	Adm. Dec., 1883, trans to Shiloh
Delia A. Carter	Adm. Jan., 1884
Josephene Taylor (Vannala)	Adm. Jan., 1884
Jayne E. Hays	Adm. Jan., 1884
Sarah Raleigh	Adm. Jan., 1884
Mary C. Vanderslice	Adm. Jan., 1884
Anna Pickett	Adm. Jan., 1884
Rutha Hall	Adm. Jan., 1884
Ada M. Noels	Adm. Jan., 1884
Nellie J. Good	Adm. Feb. 8, 1885
May Morgan	Adm. Feb. 8, 1885
Rutha Good	Adm. Feb. 8, 1885

Surprise Cumberland Presbyterian Church, Clinton, Lafayette County, Missouri, (Note: This church was once located in Gaines, Missouri.)

Register of Elders

Name	Ordained	Ceased to Act
Jas. Miller	Mar. 23, 1859	Jul. 7, 1872
Hugh B. Witherspoon	Mar. 23, 1859	---
Jas. E. Hutton	---	---
Joseph Simmons	Oct. 26, 1867	---
Jas. Smith	Sep. 27, 1868	d. Nov. 7, 1871
Albert Hornbeck	Sep. 27, 1868	---
John H. Parks	Jul. 27, 1870	Aug. 23, 1897
Joseph Smith	Jul. 27, 1870	---
James W. Miller	Feb. 13, 1879	---
Alex Gaines	Sep., 1896	---

Wilson Parks   Sep., 1896   ---

Register of Deacons

Name	Ordained	Ceased to Act
George Nichols	Feb. 13, 1879	---
M. Read	Apr. 23, 1881	---
R. E. Trenay	---	---
Alx. Gaines	May 27, 1895	Sep., 1896
Jas. Wilson	Sep., 1896	Jun., 1899
A. L. McCoun	Sep., 1896	Jul., 1897

Register of Communicants

Name	Comments
Lucinda Gillam	Adm. Mar. 23, 1859, Dis. Mar. 7, 1871
Elizabeth Parks	Adm. 1859, Dis. Sep. 20, 1870
James Smith	Dis. Apr., 1873, d. Nov. 7, 1871 (?)
Mary Smith	Dis. Apr., 1873
Hugh B. Witherspoon	Dis. Dec. 21, 1908
Sarah A. Quick	d. 1896
James M. Miller	Adm. Aug. 24, 1859, Dis. Jul. 7, 1872, d. Apr. 5, 1896
Hetty Miller	Adm. Aug. 24, 1859, Dis. Mar., 1887
Margaret M. Miller	Adm. Apr. 27, 1859, Dis. Dec. 28, 1885
Elisa Miller	Adm. 1859, Dis. Mar. 18, 1887
Elisabeth McCown	Adm. Dec. 12, 1859, Dis. Oct. 12, 1877
Rebeca Havens	Adm. Feb. 12, 1860, d. Dec., 1897
M. Mathes	Adm. Aug. 28, 1860
Thomas C. Miller	Adm. May 25, 1867, Dis. May 28, 1876
William Gillam	Adm. Jul. 27, (?), Dis. Aug. 7, 1871
James W. Miller	Dis. Aug. 28, 1871
Jacob Gilliam	Dis. Aug. 7, 1871
F. B. Davidson	Dis. Aug. 7, 1871
Mary A. Mercer	Dis. Aug. 7, 1871
Elisa J. Dempsey	Dis. Sep. 20, 1870
Julia A. Finks	Dis. Sep. 20, 1870
Lewella M. Witherspoon	---
Susan Nichols	---
Salina Davidson	Dis. May 7, 1871
Hugh Galbraith	---
W. H. McCown	---

Name	Comments
A. E. Witherspoon	Dis. Dec. 21, 1908
Manson B. Simmons	Adm. Jul. 27, 1867, Dis. May 27, 1870
Sarah A. Simmons	Dis. May 27, 1870
Joseph Simmons	Exp. Nov. 15, 1871
An. E. Anderson	---
Tinis P. Witherspoon	---
E. B. Dempsey	d. Feb., 1879
Anna Eliston	Dis. Nov. 15, 1871
Corneluis Williams	d. Jan., 1876
Joseph H. Smith	---
James Hutton	Adm. Jul. 29, 1867, Dis. Sep. 27, 1868
Fannie Hutton	Dis. Sep. 27, 1868
Marthy Irwin	---
Mary E. Irwin	---
Amandy E. Reed	---
Weston Dempsey	Dis. Jul. 23, 1870
Ruthy Dempsey	Dis. Apr., 1873
Albert Hornbeck	Adm. Nov. 23, 1867, Dis. Aug. 28, 1870
Mary Hornbeck	Dis. Aug. 28, 1870
Melvin McCown	Dis. Jul. 23, 1870
Catherine Nichols	---
Joseph Dempsey	Adm. Feb. 28, 1869, Dis. Sep. 20, 1870
Sarah Duckworth	Adm. Feb. 28, 1869, Dis. May 17, 1879
Mary Reed	1878
John Parks	Adm. Aug. 1, 1869, Dis. Aug. 3, 1897
Zillah Parks	---
James Parks	Dis. Apr., 1875
F. A. Dory	Adm. Jan. 30, 1870
S. A. Dory	---
John E. Smith	---
Mary E. Smtih	---
Susana M. Trenary	---
Nancy J. Trenary	---
Magy E. Melton	Dis. Sep., 1874
Mary A. Trenary	Adm. Jan. 31, 1870, Dis. Jun. 22, 1884
Mary C. Slavens	---
Francis E. Smith	---
Nannie J. Mills	Dis. Aug., 1875
Norwood Parks	Dis. 1876
Louisa Mills	Adm. Feb. 4, 1870, Dis. Aug., 1873

Name	Comments
Louis Stricklan	d. Aug., 1873
Luther McCown	d. Apr., 1888
Jas. G. Fike	Adm. Mar. 27, 1870, Dis. Sep., 1873
Margret M. Fike	Adm. Mar. 27, 1870, Dis. Sep., 1873
Docena Fike	Adm. Mar. 27, 1870, Dis. Sep., 1873
George Smith	Adm. Mar. 27, 1870, Dis. Sep., 1873
Alice M. Witherspoon	Adm. Mar. 27, 1870
Alfred M. Chiles	Adm. Aug. 28, 1870, d. 1876
Amandy E. Chiles	Adm. Aug. 28, 1870, Dis. Jan. 14, 1889
Matty Chiles	Dis. Nov., 1876
Agness McKinsey	---
Cary Micklson	---
William Snider	Dis. Sep. 28, 1879
Western Trenary	Adm. Dec. 8, 1871, d. Mar., 1888
John Miller	Adm. Dec. 8, 1871, Dis. Aug., 1881
Bell Parks	Adm. Dec. 12, 1871, Dis. Feb. 12, 1881
Nana J. Parks	Adm. Dec. 12, 1871, d. Aug. 22, 1874
Elisa Supeona	Adm. Dec. 12, 1871, Dis. Sep., 1874
Lelana Write	Adm. Dec. 12, 1871, Dis. 1876
Ewel H. Smith	Adm. May 7, 1871, Dis. 1887
Ethia Smith	Adm. May 7, 1871, Dis. Jan. 14, 1889
Amanda Tremary	Adm. May 7, 1871
Margaret J. Renfro	Adm. Jul. 7, 1872
Maggie Quick	Adm. Sep. 1, 1872
Mary Quick	Adm. Sep. 1, 1872
Jose Jemison	Adm. Sep. 1, 1879
George Burch	Adm. Oct. 26, 1873
Wilson Parks	Adm. Oct. 26, 1873, Dis. Aug. 3, 1897
Darius Lee	Adm. Jan. 25, 1874, d. Feb., 1878
Frederick Hammond	Adm. Jul. 25, 1874, Dis., 1897
Catharine Moore	Adm. Aug. 27, 1874

Name	Comments
Emma Miller	Adm. Aug. 30, 1874, d. Apr., 1896
Elvina Snyder	Adm. Dec. 28, 1874, Dis. Sep. 28, 1879
Ida Smith	Adm. 1874
George Nickols	Adm. 1874
Norah S. Witherpsoon	Adm. 1874
Roseabell Johnson	Adm. Aug., 1875
Mariah ---ller	Dis. Aug., 1881
Wm. White	Adm. Jan., 1876, d. 1886
Sarah E. Bogard	Adm. Aug. 14, 1878, d. 1880
Amanda A. Trenary	Adm. Aug. 14, 1878, Dis. Sep. 8, 1878
Martin R. Snider	Adm. Aug. 14, 1878, Dis. Jun. 21, 1881
George W. Parks	Adm. Aug. 14, 1878
Rachel Bogard	Adm. Jun. 5, 1879, d. Sep., 1880
Hatty Trenary	Adm. Sep. 7, 1879
Marsh Reed	Adm. Nov., 1880
Benjamin Trenary	Adm. Aug. 27, 1881
Armilda Trenary	Adm. Aug. 27, 1881
Cynthia Riddle	Adm. Aug. 27, 1881
Laura Quick	Adm. Aug. 27, 1881
Susie Quick	Adm. Aug. 27, 1881
Catherine Hammon	Adm. Aug. 27, 1881
Elen Witherspoon	Adm. Aug. 27, 1881
William Smith	Adm. Nov. 28, 1883
P. W. Kimbrough	Adm. Jun. 22, 1884
Mrs. Sarah E. Wright	Adm. Mar. 26, 1885
Miny Hoover	Adm. Mar. 26, 1885
Beney Trenary	Adm. 1890
Ben J. Gaines	---
Alexander Painis	Adm. Nov., 1892
William L. Hornback	Adm. Nov., 1892
Noah Read	Adm. Nov., 1892
Addam Eberting	Adm. Nov., 1892
Nancy Ebberting	Adm. Nov., 1892
Sarah Trenary	Adm. Nov., 1892
John W. Fisher	Adm. Jun., 1893
Mr. C. Fisher	Adm. Jun., 1893
James W. Fisher	Adm. Jun., 1893
William Parks	Joined the Baptists
Emmuel Smith	---
Pinkney Smith	---
Albert Roberts	Adm. Nov. 4, 1896
Jas. Wilson	Adm. Nov. 4, 1896

Name	Comments
Netty Willson	Adm. Nov. 4, 1896
Timothy Hoover	Adm. Nov. 4, 1896
Elmer J. Smith	Adm. Nov. 4, 1896
Mrs. C. Hagen	Adm. Nov. 4, 1896
P. R. Wi-----	Adm. Nov. 4, 1896
A. L. McCowen	Adm. Dec. 28, 1895, Dis. Aug. 3, 1879
Susie McCowen	---
Ida Smith	---
Albert Roberts	---

Revised Register of Communicants, Nov. 5, 1905

Name	Comments
Zillah J. Parks	Adm. Aug. 1, 1869
Elisebeth Tirrell	Adm. Mar. 10, 1860
Hattie Gaskell	Adm. Sep. 9, 1879
Sarah E. Parks	Adm. Mar. 26, 1885
George W. Parks	Adm. Aug. 14, 1878, d. Mar. 15, 1912
Bennie Trenary	Adm. 4th Sunday, Aug., 1890, d. Mar. 21, 1916
J. R. Witherspoon	Adm. Nov. 4, 1896
Wilson W. Parks	d. Mar. 11, 1912

Crooked Creek Cumberland Presbyterian Church, Keysville, Crawford County, Missouri.
Statistical Church Record

Name	Comments
Washington Carter	d. Nov. 13, 1870, married
Catherine Carter	Married
E. H. Carter (male)	d. Sep. 17, 1871, single
Alfred Y. Carter	Single
G. W. Bullock (male)	Dis. Aug. 5, 1878
Eliza L. Bullock	Dis. Aug. 5, 1878, married
E. J. Dunlap (male)	Married, moved to SW MO
O. E. Dunlap (male)	Married, moved to SW MO
Lucinda Dunlap	Married
E. C. Dunlap (male)	Married
Polly Dunlap	Married, d. Dec. 23, 1881
Elijah Key	Married
Matilda Key	Married
James N. Key	Married
Jesse B. Key	Married

Name	Comments
Obadiah Key	Single, Sus. Jan. 9, 1876
Wm. O. Wilkerson	Married
Sarah A. Wilkerson	Married
Catharine Wilkerson	Single
George W. Browne	Age 36Y, Prof. Hopewell, Bellefountaine, Wash. Co., MO, 1847, married
Mary J. Browne	Age 31Y, Prof. Union Church, Crawford Co.
L. A. Dunlap (male)	Married, Dis. Dec. 14, 1879
Nancy Dunlap	Married, Dis. Dec. 14, 1879
A. J. Bullock (male)	Married
Wm. M. Bennett	Married, joined M. E. Church
F. J. Vaughan (male)	Married
E. J. Key (male)	Married, Restored Dec. 19, 1883
L. L. Culp (male)	Married, Dis. Nov. 14, 1879
J. E. Key	Single, Dis. Aug., 1867
Wm. E. Speer	Married, Dis. Nov., 1865
Henry Trotter	Married, d. Crawford Co.
John Dunlap	Married, d. Jan. 1, 1867, Crawford Co., MO
O. W. Carter (male)	Married, Dis. Dec. 9, 1865
Noah Angle	Married, Dis. Nov. 12, 1879
Jeremiah Key	Married
Lewis Key	Married
John Kelley	Married
H. N. Key (male)	Single, d. Aug., 1867
Wm. Baker	Married
R. A. Carter (male)	Married, Dis. Aug. 13, 1871
H. C. Vaughan (male)	Married
Jacob Humble	Married

Name	Comments
Rebecca Bullock	Married, d. Apr. 4, 1877, Crawford Co.
Maris Dunlap	Married, d. Jan. 2, 1877, Crawford Co.
Elizabeth J. Dunlap	Married
Mary E. Key	Married, moved southwest
S. C. Dunlap (female)	Single, d. Aug. 26, 1878
Harriett E. Dunlap	Single, d. Mar. 16, 1877, Crawford Co.
Mirah D. Vaughan	Married
Margaret H. Dunlap	Single, Dis. Oct., 1865
Matilda A. Key	Married
Mary H. Carter	Married, Dis. Feb., 1866
Sarah J. Baker	Married
Charlotte Burton	Single, Dis. Dec., 1865
Nancy Kelly	Married
Ann A. Wilkerson	Single, Dis. Jan. 23, 1880
Martha E. Carter	Single
Martha E. Harman	Married, Dis. Jan. 20, 1872
Susan Culp	Married
Susan Eaton	Married
Lewis Key	Restored Sep. 20, 1874
William Key	Married
Elvira Key	Married
Sarah E. Russell	Married, Dis. Mar. 12, 1881
Isaac E. Key	Single, Bapt. by A. O. Melvin
Welshy Ann Keller	---
Jennie Key	Single, Bapt. by E. M. Johnson
Rosa Key	Married
Obadiah Key	Single
Samuel A. Key (male)	---
Lutie Dunlap	Single, Never Bapt.
L. P. Key (male)	Married, Bapt.

Name	Comments
Louisa J. Key	Dec. 19, 1883, by Rev. J. Campbell Married, Bapt.
Mary E. Key	Dec. 19, 1883, by Rev. J. Campbell Single, Bapt. Dec. 19, 18833, by Rev. J. Campbell
Nora Key	Single, Bapt. Dec. 19, 1883, by Rev. J. Campbell
Laura Key	Single, Bapt. Dec. 19, 1883 by Rev. J. Campbell
Mantra Butt	Single, Bapt. Dec. 19, 1883 by Rev. J. Campbell
Lulie Butt	Single, Bapt. Dec. 19, 1883, by Rev. J. Campbell
Jas. Davis	Married, from Canaan, Prf. Faith at Cook Station, Bapt. Dec. 19, 1883.
Matilda Davis	Married, from Canaan, Prf. Faith at Cook Station, Bapt. Dec. 19, 1883
Mark L. Butt	Married, former Member Methodist, Baptised Dec. 19, 1883
Matilda A. Butt	Married, Bapt. Dec. 19, 1883
Samuel Duncan	Single, Bapt. Dec. 19, 1883
John Powell	Married, Bapt. Dec. 19, 1883, by Rev. J. Campbell
Malissa R. Key	Single, Bapt. Dec. 19, 1883

Rochester Cumberland Presbyterian Church, Helena,
Andrew County, Missouri.

Register of Elders

Name	Ceased to Act	Ordained
Henry Blanket	---	Jun. 11, 1871
Wm. Hayter	1875	---
S. A. Irvin	---	---
George Loues	1875	Jun. 17, 1871
M. V. Piper	1874	Jun. 17, 1871
W. P. Slade	---	---
John J. Signist	---	1875
M. R. Mickles	---	Feb., 1892
J. F. Martin	---	Jun., 1892
Henry Maddock	---	Jun. 24, 1896
George Tethro	---	Jun. 24, 1896
Jas. D. Elder	---	Jun. 24, 1896

Register of Deacons

Name	Ordained	Ceased to Act
W. M. Shanks	Jun. 17, 1876	d. 1878
D. G. Caldwell	Feb., 1892	d. 1898
Lura Wiloughby	Mar., 1894	d. 1907
Mrs. M.F. Nuckols	Mar., 1894	d. Jan. 8, 1932

Register of Marriages

L. Buler and Sophia Slade, (MD) October 2, 1870,
(MG) A. Guthery.

James S. Blount and Flora Simmons, (MD) October,
1874, (MG) C. B. Powers.

Register of Deaths

Name	Death Date
Sarah McLathlue	April 19, 1878

Register of Adult Baptism

Name	Date	Reverend
Mrs. C. Frame	Mar. 20, 1871	Layette Munkers
Edward B. Willoby	Mar. 20, 1871	Layette Munkers
Susan A. Shanks	Mar. 20, 1871	Layette Munker
Susannah Shreve	Mar. 20, 1871	Layette Munker
Elizabeth E. Peper	Mar. 20, 1871	Layette Munker
Price Summers	Mar. 20, 1871	Layette Munker
Wm. Hector	Mar. 20, 1871	Layette Munker
Laura Mitchel	Mar. 20, 1871	Layette Munker
William Piper	Mar. 20, 1871	Layette Munker
Mary Slade	Mar. 20, 1871	Layette Munker
Rhoda Piper	Mar. 20, 1871	Layette Munker
Mrs. Sallie Brown	Mar. 20, 1871	Layette Munker
Charles McGlothlin	Mar. 20, 1871	Layette Munker
Martin V. Piper	Jun., 1871	Layette Munker

Name	Date	Reverend
Louisa Piper	Jun., 1871	Layette Munker
Louisa Hayter	Feb., 1870	A. W. Guthery
Psafine (?) Fales	Mar. 20, 1871	Layette Munker
James Blount	Nov., 1872	Layette Munker
Alice Metcalf	Nov., 1872	Layette Munker
Mrs. Belton	Jul., 1872	Layette Munker
Susan Osburn	May, 1872	Layette Munker
Wm. Cook	Jan., 1874	T. M. Miller
Hannah E. Cook	Jan., 1874	T. M. Miller
Maud Jayne	Jan. 29, 1893	J. S. Wayman
Claud Caldwell	Jan. 30, 1893	J. S. Wayman
Earl Bloomer	Oct. 29, 1899	H. W. Fisher
Thos. N. Jaynes	Oct. 29, 1899	H. W. Fisher
Ruby Bloomer	Oct. 29, 1899	H. W. Fisher

Register of Communicants

Name	Comments
H. H. Blount	Adm. Sep. 5, 1870
Mrs. H. Blount	Adm. Aug. 7, 1870
James S. Blount	Adm. Sep., 1871
Geoganna Baker	Adm. Jan. 24, 1872, Dis. 1874
Mrs. Sarah Brown	Adm. Jan. 17, 1871
Mary Baker	Adm. Mar. 22, 1871, Dis. 1874
Miss Psaphene File	Adm. Aug. 7, 1870, Dis. 1872
Wm. Frame	Adm. Mar. 20, 1871, d. 1884
Elizabeth Belton	Adm. Apr., 1872
Mrs. Joannah Grey	Adm. Sep. 18, 1870, d. 1871
Mrs. Sarah Page	Adm. Mar. 20, (?)
Mrs. Elvira P. Hicklen	Dis. 1882
Wm. Hayter	Adm. Aug., 1867, Dis. 1879
Louisa Hayter	Adm. May, 1868
James H. Hill	Adm. Nov., 1867, d. 1874
Margaret Hill	Adm. Nov., 1867, d. 1874
Wm. Hector	Adm. Mar. 20, 1870
Jane Hector	1872
Henry Boltzer	Adm. Jan. 23, 1874, d. 1874
S. A. Irwin	---
Isabel J. E. Irwin	Adm. Aug., 1868
Joseph Irwin	Adm. Aug., 1868
R. A. Irwin	Adm. Apr. 21, 1872

Name	Comments
Sarah I. Irwin	Adm. Aug., 1868
Wm. Cook	Adm. Mar., 1871, d. 1873
Hannah Cook	Adm. Mar., 1871, d. 1873
Malinda Cook	Adm. Mar., 1871, d. 1873
George W. Louis	Adm. Aug. 7, 1870, Dis. 1878
Susannah Louis	Adm. Aug. 7, 1870
Lena Louis	Adm. Aug. 7, 1870, Dis. 1878
Elizabeth Millaken	Adm. May, 1868
Elizabeth McGlothlen	Adm. Mar., 1871, d. 1870
Charles McGlothlen	Adm. Mar., 1871, d. 1879
Sarah McGlothlen	Adm. Feb., 1871, d. Apr., 1878
Laura Mitchell	Adm. Mar., 1871, Dis. Jan. 20, 1873
Alice Medcalf	Adm. Sep., 1871, Dis. 1872
Henry Mattox	Adm. Jan. 24, 1872
Mrs. Jenny Mattox	Adm. Jan. 24, 1872
Francis Patton	Adm. Feb., 1868
Clarissa Patton	Adm. Aug., 1868, Dis. 1879
Margaret Patton	Adm. Aug., 1868
Marten U. Piper	Adm. Mar., 1871, Dis. 1878
Elizabeth C. Piper	Adm. Mar., 1871, Dis. 1878
Wm. Piper	Adm. Mar., 1871, Dis. 1882
Rhoda Piper	Adm. Mar., 1871, Dis. 1882
Cyntha Ann Piper	Adm. Mar., 1871, Dis. 1882
Mrs. Louisa Piper	Adm. Jun. 17, 1871, Dis. 1882
Eliza Patton	Adm. Apr. 21, 1872, Dis. 1876
W. W. P. Slade	Adm. Sep., 1854
Isabel Slade	Adm. Aug., 1840
Elizabeth Slade	Adm. Mar., 1871
Achcy (?) Shrete	Dis. 1881
Lucy Simmons	Adm. Aug., 1868, Dis.

Name	Comments
	1878
Sophiah SLade	Adm. Aug., 1868
F. A. Simmons	Adm. Aug. 7, 1870, Dis.
	1878
Lucinda Simmons	Adm. Mar. 20, 1871
Anna Catharine Sharp	Adm. Aug. 7, 1870, Dis.
	1873
Mrs. Mary Signist	Adm. Aug. 7, 1870
J. S. Sharp	Adm. Sep. 6, 1870, Dis.
	1873
Frances E. Shrieves	Adm. Sep. 6, 1870
Catharine Signist	Adm. Sep. 6, 1870
Mary A. Shrieves	Adm. Sep. 6, 1870
Emma Sharp	Adm. Sep. 6, 1870, Dis.
	1873
Rachel Scott	Adm. Sep. 6, 1870, Dis.
	1874
Mary Slade	Adm. Mar., 1871
M. M. Shanks	Adm. Feb., 1871
Susan A. Shanks	Adm. Feb., 1871
Price Summers	Adm. Feb. 20, 1871,
	Dis. 1871
Rebecca Sale	Adm. Feb. 20, 1871
Marshel Shint (?)	Adm. Feb., 1871
John P. Sigrist	Adm. Mar. 20, 1871,
	Dis. 1873
Armina Shrite	Adm. Sep., 1872
Lucinda Shreve	Adm. Apr., 1872
Jonathan Snowden	Adm. 1874
Henry B. Turner	Adm. Sep. 6, 1870, Dis.
	1873
Amanthe J. Turner	Adm. Sep. 6, 1870, Dis.
	1873
Sarah Tumbleson	Adm. Sep. 6, 1870, Dis.
	1873
Mrs. Tethro	Adm. Sep. 6, 1870
Edward B. Willoughby	Adm. Mar. 20, 1871,
	Dis. 1879, d. 1881
Armenta Woodard	Adm. Aug. 7, 1870
Ferneler (?) Woodward	Adm. Sep. 6, 1870
J. R. Williams	Adm. Mar., 1872

Jacksonville Union Chapel, Jacksonville, Randolph County, Missouri.

Register of Pasters

Name	Ordained
F. Z. Shearon	April 3, 1898
R. S. Maupin	May 7, 1899

Register of Elders

Name	Ordained
Martin C. Adams	February 27, 1898
John A. Adams	February 27, 1898

Register of Communicants, February 27, 1898

C. H. Johnston, Lutharia F. Johnston, John M.
Johnston, Allen J. Hines, Susan J. Hines, David G.
Hines, George A. Hines, Henry M. Hines, Susie
Hines, John A. Hines, Joseph S. Adams, Martin C.
Adams, Ann Mary Adams, Mattie T. Adams, Ida M.
Adams, John A. Adams, Sallie Adams, Guite B.
Hudson, Fannie Henderson, Sallie Johnson, Vina D.
Garner, Daisy Garner, Amelia C. McCully, Henry M.
Poers, A. B. Burton, Tula Gray, Margarite E. Terry,
Elijah M. Terry, Mary F. Travis, Francis P. Brown,
George F. Powers

Jackson County, Missouri, United Blue River Association, Twenty-Third Annual Session Minutes, October 4, 1856.

Attendee's Name	County	Congregation
J. W. Ward	Lafayette	Lexington
E. D. Dulin	Lafayette	Lexington
Jas. Waddell	Lafayette	Lexington
M. F. Price	Lafayette	Lexington
L. Franklin	Jackson	Six Mile
J. Highlower	Jackson	Six Mile
J. Petty	Jackson	Six Mile
J. R. Franklin	Jackson	Six Mile
E. Wood	Jackson	Blue Springs
N. Crisman	Jackson	Blue Springs
J. R. Wood	Jackson	Blue Springs
J. M. Burruss	Jackson	Blue Springs
W. Duvall	Cass	Liberty
J. Herryman	Cass	Liberty
H. Y. Proctor	Cass	Liberty
W. L. Hornbuck	Cass	Liberty
J. Farmer	Cass	Harrisonville
S. G. Allen	Cass	Harrisonville
M. Griffin	Cass	Harrisonville
William Jones	Cass	Harrisonville
H. Farmer	Cass	Union
William Farmer	Cass	Union
H. Gurgess	Cass	Union
W. Hodges	Cass	Union
James Holloway	Jackson	Westport
A. B. Earle	Jackson	Westport
B. Hornbuckle	Jackson	Westport
J. B. Wornal	Jackson	Westport

Attendee's Name	County	Congregation
C. G.T. Gibbon	Johnson	Post Oak
E. Eppright	Johnson	Post Oak
R. J. Jacob	Johnson	Post Oak
C. M. Kavanuagh	Johnson	Post Oak
B. M. Adams	Cass	New Hope
J. B. Meadow	Cass	New Hope
J. Devenport	Cass	New Hope
J. W. Adams	Cass	New Hope
J. C. Martin	Jackson	Lone Jack
M. W. Easley	Jackson	Lone Jack
Martin Rice	Jackson	Lone Jack
Noah Hunt	Jackson	Lone Jack
J. J. Robinson	Jackson	West Fork
H. Chisim	Jackson	West Fork
William A. Durfey	Jackson	West Fork
A. Brooking	Jackson	West Fork
P. C. Pool	Lafayette	Mound Prairie
E. A. Eddy	Lafayette	Mound Prairie
William Lankford	Lafayette	Mound Prairie
B. F. Vickers	Lafayette	Mound Praire
John Brady	Cass	Grand River
John Franse	Cass	Grand River
William Jackson	Cass	Grand River
William Brady	Cass	Grand River
Stephen Adams	Jackson	New Salem
J. M. Morris	Jackson	New Salem
L. Dickerson	Jackson	New Salem
William Rice	Jackson	New Salem
W. P. C. Caldwell	Johnson	Providence
D. More	Johnson	Providence
C. T. Woolfork	Johnson	Providence
S. Evans	Johnson	Providence
C. S. White	Lafayette	Concord
G. Kesterson	Lafayette	Concord
H. Fickle	Lafayette	Concord
J. Williamson	Lafayette	Concord
E. Roth	Lafayette	Dover
S. B. New	Lafayette	Dover
William Kirtley	Lafayette	Dover
William Fristoe	Lafayette	Dover
J. H. Kemper	Jackson	Blue Ridge
T. G. Colgin	Jackson	Blue Ridge
A. M. Adams	Jackson	Blue Ridge
J. P. Smith	Jackson	Blue Ridge
J. Kelly	Johnson	Bethel
M. C. Blades	Johnson	Bethel
G. C. Devenport	Johnson	Bethel
W. R. Taylor	Johnson	Bethel

Attendee's Name	County	Congregation
A. P. William	Johnson	Warrensburg
G. W. Johnson	Johnson	Warrensburg
W. Adams	Johnson	Warrensburg
R. Smith	Johnson	Warrensburg
Thomas Campbell	Jackson	Pleasant Val.
C. C. Rive	Jackson	Independence
Samuel Rufner	Jackson	Independence
J. D. Meadow	Jackson	Independence
James Rufner	Jackson	Independence
James Warren	Cass	Mount Pisgah
William A. Temple	Cass	Mount Pisgah
H. Sheets	Cass	Mount Pisgah
J. Oldham	Cass	Mount Pisgah
A. G. Newgent	Cass	Austin
D. Hartsell	Cass	Austin
James Holloway	Cass	Austin
William Thompson	Cass	Austin
Ed. Price	Lafayette	Harmony
J. D. Horn	Lafayette	Harmony
Bevill Whitworth	Lafayette	Harmony
J. Kemper	Bates	Red Dirt
L. Dillon	Bates	Red Dirt
H. M. Marly	Bates	Red Dirt
S. Hill	Jackson	Oak Hill
W. C. Harding	Jackson	Oak Hill
J. W. Ray	Jackson	Oak Hill
J. Patterson	Jackson	Oak Hill
R. S. Thomas	Jackson	Kansas
R. Holmes	Jackson	Kansas
T. M. James	Jackson	Kansas
A. J. Martin	Jackson	Kansas
J. C. Teas	Cass	Mount Nebo
J. S. Wheeler	Cass	Mount Nebo
C. T. Preston	Cass	Mount Nebo
W. M. Bruscie	Cass	Mount Nebo
Joseph WHite	Johnson	Black Water
W. W. Murry	Johnson	Black Water
M. Hammond	Johnson	Black Water
F. German	Jackson	Bone Hill
J. Gray	Jackson	Bone Hill

Clay County, Missouri, Baptist References
Abstracted from the Liberty Tribune.
Mrs. Sophia Rollins, age 90, died May 16th at
the home of her daughter-in-law, Mrs. Susan Rollins
near Smithville, Clay County. The deceased was
born in eastern Maryland on June 6, 1777. Her
father was John Kennedy, Revolutionary War soldier.

John Kennedy was captured by the British at Guilford Court House, North Carolina and perished in the infamous Jersey prison ship. At the age of two her parents moved to Bedford County, Virginia. At age 15 years she emigrated to Bourbon County, Kentucky with her Mother and her siblings. At age 20 she married Joshua Rollins, a native of Maryland, who died in 1801. Sophia and Joshua had two daughters and one son. She never remarried. In 1830 she moved to Missouri with her son, Lee and his family. She joined the Old Baptist Church at Stoney Point, Bourbon County, Kentucky. She outlived her brothers and sisters and her own children. (I) June 12, 1868.

John C. Hawkins, age 65, died on April 5th of heart disease. He was born in Woodford County, Kentucky and had been a Clay County resident for forty years. He was a member of the Baptist Church. (I) June 19, 1868.

Henry H. Estes died in the 8th inst. He was born in Vir- ginia on May 11, 1788. He moved with his father to Madison County, Kentucky in 1792. In 1816 he moved to Howard County, Missouri, then in 1817 moved to Saline County and finally moved to Clay County in 1819. In 1811 he joined the Old Baptist Church and later married in 1814. (I) September 18, 1868.

Mrs. Mary A. Garret, age 42, died at Liberty on December 15, 1868. She was a member of the Baptist Church. (I) February 19, 1869.

John T. Pollard, a mason, died on the 28th ult. He had been ill about two months. He was born in Owen County, Kentucky and moved to Missouri with his father. He attended William Jewell College and was admitted to the bar in 1859. He married Mrs. E. E. Snyder on June, 1861, at Harrisonville. After the Civil War he moved to Independence in February, 1867. He was a member of the Baptist Church. (I) April 9, 1869.

Elder William M. Jenkins, age 60, died a few days ago. He was a teacher and leader of the Old Baptist Church. (I) October 15, 1869.

Dr. Herman S. Major, age 40, died on the 23rd ult. He had lived in the county about twenty years. He was a member of the Baptist Church. (I) January 7, 1870.

Mrs. Martha Shaver, age 21, died on December 26, 1869. She was the daughter of John E. and Sarah M. Whitsett. She married Archibald Shaver and was the

mother two children. She was baptised in 1865 by
Rev. A. N. Bird at Crooked Creek Baptist Church.
She leaves her husband, two children, her mother
and brother to mourn her passing. (I) February 4,
1870.

At the Baptist Church on the 4th inst. Edward E.
Tooner, of Mobile, Alabama, married Miss Anna
Rambaut. She is the daugh- ter of Dr. Thomas
Rambaut, President of William Jewell Col- lege.
The ceromony was perfomred by Rev. Thomas Raubuat.
(I) October 6, 1871.

Mrs. Nancy Rice, daughter of John and ELizabeth
Arnold, age 59, passed away. She was the wife of
Rev. William Rice. She was born January 22, 1797
in Woodford County, Kentucky. She moved with her
family to Liberty in 1835. For the last four years
she has been residing with her son in Kansas City.
She was a member of the Baptist Church and was
buried on October 10th. (I) October 27, 1871.

Rev. James E. Welsh, of Troy, Lincoln County,
Missouri, was 84 years old on the 28th ult. He
celebrated his 60th anniversary of his ministry
with a sermon at the Troy Baptist Church on the 3rd
inst. (I) March 22, 1872.

Elder Thomas Fristo, age 81, died at his home in
Howard County. He had been a preacher of the
Baptist Church for many years. (I) March 22, 1872.

Mrs. Anna McCarty, mother of Capt. Thos.
McCarty, age 89, died Monday night. She had been a
member of the Baptist Church for over forty years.
(I) July 26, 1872.

John S. Major, age 84, died at his home near
Kearney on the 16th. He was born in Culpepper
County, Virginia on March 26, 1788. He moved with
his family in 1799 to Franklin County, Kentucky
where he lived for fifty-one years. He came to
Clay County in 1850. He served under Gen. Harrison
in the War of 1812 and participated in the
Northwest Campaign. After the war he became a
Baptist minister. (I) September 27, 1872.

Mrs. Elizabeth E. Hubbell, of Columbia,
Missouri, age 68 years died on January 26, 1874.
She was the daughter of John and Susan Gano Price.
She was born on November 24, 1806 in Franklin
County, Kentucky. She married Capt. W.D. Hubbell
on September 17, 1822. Elizabeth and her husband
joined the Buckrun Baptist Church in 1824 in Howard
County. Two years later they moved to Liberty and
raised eight children. Her childred are John P.

and C. G. Hubbell, Columbia, Missouri; P. and R. M. Hubbel, Richmond, Missouri; Mrs. Gano, Chicago; and Mrs. Darneale, San Francisco. Her third son, F. L. Hubbell, member of the Third Missouri Confederate Infantry, died at Vicksburg. (I) February 13, 1874.

Margaret Elizabeth Roberts, widow of Jos. Roberts, dec., died at her home on March 20th near Edgerton, Platte County, Missouri. She was the daughter of John and Nancy Howard and was born on September 24, 1835 in Howard County. She was married in Platte County on April 15, 1852. Rev. J. Clay baptized her in 1871 and she became a member of the Zion Baptist Church in Platte County. She later became a member of the Olive Branch Baptist Church. She was 39 years old and leaves four children to mourn her passing. (I) April 20, 1874.

Rebuen Searcy was born June 30, 1799 in Union District, South Carolina. He moved to Kentucky in 1814 and to Missouri in 1850. He joined the Baptist Church in 1819 and became a minister in 1840. (I) September 23, 1870.

Ebenezer Titus was born April 11, 1782 in Augusta County, Virginia. His father moved to Madison County, Kentucky in 1782. He joined the Separate Baptists in 1800. His father died on April 23, 1838 in Howard County. Ebenezer joined the United Baptists in 1818 and moved to Howard in 1824 where he lived for eighteen years. In 1849 Ebenezer moved to Ray County where he lived until 1869. He nows lives with his daughter, Elizabeth, and her husband John McCorkle. (I) September 23, 1870.

Married at the Columbia Baptist Church on June 25th, Irwin Switzler to Miss Ellen Runyan. The service was performed by Rev. E. S. Dulin and Rev. R. S. Campbell. (I) July 3, 1874.

On September 17th by Elder W. T. Fleenor. Thos. B. Stone married Miss Martha A. Wadley, daughter of Rev. F. M. Wadley at Utica Baptist Church, Utica, Missouri. (I) September 25, 1874.

Elder James Barnes died at the home of his son, James Barnes, jr., on February 6, 1875 in Moberly, Missouri. He moved to central Missouri in 1811 and was the first sheriff of Boone County. Most of his life, he was a minister of the old Baptist Church. (I) February 19, 1875.

The Haynesville Lodge AF & AM, July 25, 1875,

wish to pay a tribute of respect to E. E. Lindsey who died on July 24, 1875. He was 57 years old and was buried at Mr. Zion Baptist Church. (I) July 30, 1875.

Died on the 23rd ult. in Boone County, Mrs. Patsey Step- hens, mother of J. L. Stephens of Columbia. She was 85 years old at the time of her death and moved to the farm where she lived her life in 1819. She was a member of the Old Baptist Church for over 50 years. (I) September 10, 1875.

Rev. James E. Welch, age 87, of Warrensburg, called on us today. He came to Missouri in 1814 and has been an active minister of the Baptist church for sixty-four years. He was ordained in 1812. (I) March 24, 1876.

Rev. Wm. C. Ligon, age 81, Baptist minister, died at his home in Dover, Lafayette County, on April 13th. (I) April 27, 1877.

Miss Mary D. Dudsworth died on October 6th in Gallatin Twonship. She was baptised in the Olive Brnch Baptist Church in 1876 and was born on October 29, 1859. She leaves a mother, stepfather and stepbrother to mourn her passing. (I) October 12, 1877.

Cass County, Missouri, New Hope Baptist Church, West Union.

Register of Members

Name	Name
Thomas Jackson	Able Massy
Hiram Harris	Eli G. Harris
Harris C. Jackson, deceased	Robt. H. Thompson
Hunphrey P. Thompson	Thomas J. Harris
Elijah Thompson, d. 1851	Mary Jackson, deceased
Judeth Massey, dead	Elizabeth Harris, dead
Sarah A. Harris	Mary Bayley, dead
Martha J. Bayley	Anna Preston
Margaret Alderidge, dead	Mary Bean
Isiah Lynch	Oliver W. Harris
Nathan Aldridge	Edmon Bean
J. Blackston Dailey,Dis. 1866	Francis L. Harris
Louisa Ann Harris, dead	Andrew Power
George W. Wolf	James L. Harris
Jessy Lynch	Sary Lynch
Malinda Noel	Moses Sparks
Elizabeth Sparks	Matilda Sparks, dead

Name	Name
Mary A. Thompson	Rebecca Jackson
James Hood	Isabel Hood
Malinda Sparks	Permelia Sparks
Jane Roddy	Jessy Roddy
Mary Adkins	Elizabeth Adkins
Moses Bailey	Elinor Newkird
Mary Sparks	Benjamin Sparks
Sarah Sparks	Martha, woman of color
Calvin Powell, dead	Milton Jackson, dead
Elizabeth J. Lightner	Mary Malone
Absalom Hicks	Crissy Hicks
Catharine Johnson	Diadama Sparks
Emeline Harris, dead	William Thompson
Lieauann Magers	David Magers
Martha Harris	Rachiel Harris
John Haselip, died 1850	Doshoann Hood
Malinda Aldridge	Richard Sparks
John Aldridge	Elizabeth McNutts
Eliza. A. Spears, exc. Jan.,1850	Lucinda Throop
Jane Preston	Henry Sugs
Sarah Freeman	Felise Muligan
Rachel Muligan	John Caloway,dead
Sarah Caloway, dead	Mary M. Caloway
Wilson Davenport	Hugh L.T. Caloway
Julia A. Mossell (Caloway)	Sarah A. Webb
Nancy C. Webb	Tinkney, man of color
Rosin, man of color	Clowey, woman of color
Elender Jones	Martha Shipley
James Davenport	Frances Janes Davenport
Mary Taul	Susanna Davenport
Mary Rogers	Sarah J. Mockbee
Lydia Edmason	Mary J. Shipley
Nancy E. Shipley	Wm. P. Shipley
Elizabeth Haskins	John Holloway
Mary Holloway, dead	Genianah White
Ann E. Bailey, dead	Mary Ann Thompson

Eliz. Preston, dis. Aug.,1860 Melvin Lynch
Charlotte Andrews (Preston), dis. Aug., 1860
Jas. Davenport, d. Mar., 1860 Caroline Jones
Frances Jane Warner (Davenport), dis. 1867
Clementine E. Bailey Powell Malinda Haslip
Elizabeth Williams   Betsy Ann Harris

Name	Name
Nancy Mitchell	Hannah Majors
Matilda Savage	Louis A. Todd, dead
Nancy A. Suttles (Majors)	Thos. Prettyman
Ruth Ann Harris (Thiswater)	Sarah Kinamon
Nancy Mitchell	Chas. Jackson, dead
Martha J. Jackson, d. Jun.,1860	
Wm C. Hicks	Anne Hicks
Jane Cummins (Adams)	Riley Adams
William Hagans	Nat E. Thompson
Mary Lynch, No Baptist	Wm. Bailey, jr.
Mary Ann Prettyman (Majors),	dis. 1857
Martha J. Thompson, ex. 1851	Winepee Savage
Ruth E. Spears (Massey), ex.	Jan., 1858
James T. Harris	Robert Wood
Susanah Kincaid (Davenport)	Mary Paul
Susan Glass	Nancy Harris, dis. 1857
Jessie V. Meadow	Prescilla Yanall
James Adams, dis. 1857	Sidney Adams, dis. 1857
Eleanor E. Edwards, d. 1851	Abram Koots
Annah Powell, d. May, 1860	Rosey A. Laffoon
James Dolan, dis. 1867	Sarah O. Paul, dis. 1867
Juli Ann Paul, dis. Feb.,1867	Sarah Ann Voil
Nancy Ann Voil	Polly Ann Pitman
George Voilman, dead	Elexander Jackson
Elizer White, No Baptist	James M. Magers
Mary Kath. Eledge, dis. 1861	Mary Jane McGill, dead
Mary Meek, No Baptist	Elenor Jones
B. M. Adams	Caroline M. Adams
Martha Price, dis. Dec., 1857	Abel Massey, d. 1857
Eda Massey, ex. Jan., 1858	James Methers
Susan Glass	Mary Glass
William Meadow	Elizabeth McGill
John B. Laffoon	Joseph Eledge, d. 1863
Alvis Powel, dead	Reason Pitman
Margaret Daily, d. 1865	Mary Beets
John B. Keton, ex. May 2,1857	Martha Jane Beets
M. A. Keton, ex. Feb. 15,1858	Allena Meadow
J. W. Adams, dis. 1866	M. S. Adams, dis. 1866
J. B. Porter, dis. 1859	Mary Powell

Name	Name
Catharine Porter, dis. 1859	Hannah Porter, dis. 1859
Louisa Wamlton (Porter), d. Jun., 1860	
Mary J. Simmons, dead	Mary J. Adams
Susan E. Allen Dis. June, 1859	Martha C. Adams, dead
Preston Bowen, ex. Jun., 1860	Henry Chapel
Robert W. Adams	A. B. Allen, dis. 1859
Josiah Porter, ex. Nov., 1860	S. W. Hoover, Dis. 1868
J. Wallen Adams, dis. 1866	Ann Judson Adams
Silvanus Echolds, dis. 1858	T. N. Abslin
Lucinda Echolds, dis. 1858	Elizabeth Ann Thompson
Ann Powell	William Hoover
William Thompson, dis. 1866	Martha Magill
J. B. Peterson, dis. 1867	Drewry Laffoon
Elizabeth Duvall, dis. 1867	Maninne Laffoon
Sarah Abslin, d. Aug., 1860	Nancy York (Laffoon)
John Carneal	T. G. Carneal
Levi J. Butts	E. N. Butts
Sallie N. Adams, dis. 1866	James Marpin
Ed, prop. of J. R. Williams	Celia Jones
Geo. W. Burgess, dis. 1868	Fanny E. Phillips
Susannah Rice, dead	Nancy Jane Bailey
Sary Bailey	Mary H. Hough
James York	W. A. Iles
A. W. C. York, d. Apr., 1868	Joseph Hought
George Elis	Ann E. Powell
Nichlas Hedington, dis. 1867	Mathew Isle
Wm. Dwly	Mary E. Dewly
C. R. Collins, dead	Almeda Hoage
Margaret Davis	E. B. Collins
Rebecca Hedington, dis. 1867	Sary Ligget
Nancy Kendel, dis. 1867	Thomas Powell
Elizabeth Laffoon	Dallas Williams
Coldwell Jones	Syntha Young
Mary York (Jones)	Elen Isle
Margaret Lowes	Richard Meador, dead
Sary Twitty, dis. Apr., 1868	W. T. Bailey
L. W. Bailey	Matilda Rice
Isaac T. Rice	Eliz. A. Jones
Elizabeth Short, d. 1868	Susan Gillenwater
James Zimerman	Ellen Burgess
Ambros M. Twitty, dis. 1868	Jane Steward

Name	Name
John Gillenwater	Francis C. Powel
Steven Laffoon	Lou Ann Jones
Nancy Sears	Luticra Sutton
Elizabeth Iles	Lucinda Smith
George Sutton	Andrew Philips
William Powell	B. F. Hurley
Christofer Treakel	Isaac Powel
Alvin Addams	Katie Addams
Eliza Bailey	E. M. Bailey
Ann Sheppard	Sarah Walls
Mary Laffoon, dis. Sep., 1868	William Davis
Marion York, dis. Sep., 1868	Elizabeth Price
Elizabeth Medder	James Davis

Saline County, Missouri, First Baptist Church, Miami.

Register of Members

Name	Admission Date and Comments
W. C. Batchelor	Nov. 20, 1849, Dis. Apr. 4, 1850
Winson Rice	Nov. 20, 1849
C. W. Pendleton	Nov. 20, 1849
W. H. Cunningham	Nov. 20, 1849
Ann P. Rice	Nov. 20, 1849
Catherine Strother	Nov. 20, 1849
Judith Haynie	Nov. 20, 1849, d. Mar. 13, 1850
Elizabeth Graham	Nov. 20, 1849, d. May 13, 1852
Eliza Campbell	Nov. 20, 1849, Dis. Oct. 10, 1850
Nancy Batchelor	Nov. 20, 1849, Dis. Apr. 6, 1850
E. W. Lewis	Sep. 8, 1850, d. Apr. 29, 1855
Rebecca Lewis	Sep. 8, 1850
Catherine Randolph	Sep. 8, 1850
Loize Graham	Sep. 8, 1850
Hannah Surbaugh	Sep. 8, 1850
Loucy Daniels	Sep. 8, 1850
Sarah Parson	Oct. 2, 1850
Elizabeth Vanmeter	Oct. 2, 1850
Sousan Wallis	Oct. 2, 1850
Louinda Miner	Oct. 2, 1850
Lolman Wellen	Oct. 2, 1850
George Runnels	Oct. 9, 1850, Moved to Calif.
Lewis E. Scott	Oct. 12, 1850

Name	Admission Date and Comments
Jemina Scott	Oct. 12, 1850
Thornton Strother	Oct. 12, 1850
Herman Strother	Oct. 12, 1850, d. Jun., 1852
Pollyanna Strother	Oct. 12, 1850, Joined the Cumberland Presbyterian
Elvira Scott	Nov. 20, 1850
Mary M. Smith	Feb. 8, 1851
Jane B. Harwood	May 10, 1851
Serena Wheeler	May 10, 1851
Martha Hufman	May 10, 1851
Elizabeth F. Johnson	Jul. 11, 1851
French S. Johnson	Jul. 13, 1851
Mary, a colored	Jul. 13, 1851
Alfred Wheeler	Jul. 13, 1851
Eliza Jane Haynie	Jul. 13, 1851
Mary Perry	Jul. 13, 1851
John, a colored man	Jul. 13, 1851, Property of N. Wolkskill
Elizah Martin	Jul. 14, 1851
Elizabeth Ferrell	Jul. 13, 1851
William E. Harl	Jul. 14, 1851
Hemetter F. Harl	Jul. 14, 1851
Hannah Kile	Jul. 14, 1851
Barton McMahon	Jul. 14, 1851
George W. Denham	Jul. 15, 1851
Emily B. Denham	Jul. 15, 1851
Retter Casebolt	Jul. 15, 1851
Adam, a colored man	Jul. 15, 1851
Wm. P. Hicklin	Jul. 16, 1851
Mary Ann Pendleton	Jul. 16, 1851
Jacob Milsaps	Jul. 16, 1851
B. Coats	---
Simon, a colored man	Jul. 16, 1851, Property of W. S. Robertson
Mary Cunningham	Jul. 17, 1851
William Surbaugh	Jul. 17, 1851
Eliza Perry	Jul. 18, 1851
Joseph Milsaps	Jul. 18, 1851
Martha Ann Mullens	Jul. 18, 1851
Fredrick Haynie	Jul. 18, 1851
John P. Campbell	Jul. 18, 1851
Frderick Smith	Jul. 18, 1851
Clark M. Smith	Jul. 18, 1851
Emiline Haynie	Jul. 20, 1851
Patten, colored woman	Jul. 21, 1851
T. N. Minor	Jul. 21, 1851
Elizabeth Minor	Jul. 21, 1851

Name	Admission Date and Comments
Emelony A. Lent	Jul. 21, 1851
Lydia Sidenstricker	Jul. 21, 1851
Willis Houts	Jul. 21, 1851
Benjamin Simmons	Jul. 21, 1851
Emily M. Simmons	Jul. 21, 1851
John Martin	Jul. 22, 1851
Oliver Howe	Jul. 22, 1851
Barsheba Mullens	Nov. 8, 1851
Lougan Mullens	Nov. 8, 1851
P. S. Reynolds	Jan. 13, 1852
Peter Huff	Mar. 13, 1852
Miss Swann	Apr. 10, 1852
Miss Martha Hicklin	Apr. 10, 1852
Reuben Seay	May 8, 1852
Susan Carthee	May 8, 1852
M. Hicklin	Jul. 11, 1852, Formerly a Presbyterian
Miss Williams	Jul. 12, 1852
M. A. McMahan	Aug. 7, 1852
Dianah Haynie	Aug. 7, 1852
John Davis	Aug. 12, 1852
Mary Ann Denham	Aug. 12, 1852, Bapt. at the Bethel Church
Jno. Graham	Aug. 31, 1852
A. B. Lewis	Nov. 13, 1852
Martha J. Lewis	Nov. 13, 1852, d. Jan. 11, 1855
Sarah J. Colvin	Nov. 13, 1852
Mary M. Desavom	Nov. 14, 1852
Agniss, colored	Nov. 14, 1852
Saml. H. Colman	Dec. 11, 1852
Sent Mullins	May 8, 1853
Susan Mullins	May 8, 1853
Jane Akers	Jul. 9, 1853
Susan Walden	Jul. 9, 1853
Elivan Cardwell	Jul. 9, 1853
John Hornbeck	Jul. 9, 1853
--- Guiner	Jul. 9, 1853
Milton Clemons	Aug. -, 1853
Alexander Martin	Sep. 10, 1853
Charles Alexander	Sep. 11, 1853
Sarah Wilson	Sep. 11, 1853
Leander Rickman	Oct. 9, 1853
Jane E. Rickman	Oct. 9, 1853
S. B. Lewis	Nov. 12, 1853
Maiah Lewis	Nov. 12, 1853
Ellen A. Martin	Mar. --, 1854
Janes P. Tocoles	Apr. 8, 1854

Name	Admission Date and Comments
Sarah Rickman	May 13, 1854
James Rickman	May 13, 1854
Josephine Mullins	Jul. 8, 1854
William Mullins	Jul. 8, 1854
N. Varnell	Jul. 8, 1854
Miss E. Lewis	Jul. 8, 1854
Catharine Varnell	Jul. 8, 1854
Angelia Miller	Jul. 13, 1854
Margaret Tishlock	Jul. 15, 1854
Catharine A.M. Lewis	Jul. 15, 1854
Nancy E. Wheeler	Jul. 15, 1854
Wm. B. Cox	Jul. 15, 1854
L. M. Haynie	Jul. 15, 1854
Jno. W. Steels	Jul. 15, 1854
Elizabeth Wheeler	Jul. 15, 1854
Minerva Steels	Jul. 15, 1854
Sarah O. Hicklin	Jul. 15, 1854
Mary Ann Parsons	Jul. 15, 1854
Judith Marg. Haynie	Jul. 15, 1854
May Eliza Cox	Jul. 15, 1854
Mary Columbia Lewis	Jul. 15, 1854
Ann Eliza Surbaugh	Jul. 15, 1854
Wm. Hicklin	Jul. 18, 1854
Jno. G. Latimer	Jul. 18, 1854
Emma L. Latimer	Jul. 18, 1854
Mary, colored	Nov. 1, 1854, Property of W. Surbaugh
Sophia, colored	Jan. 13, 1855, Property of N. Betts
Lestha, colored	Jan. 13, 1855, Property of N. Betts
A. T. Jones	May 24, 1855
--- Jones	May 24, 1855
B. F. Reynolds	Jun. 28, 1855
Virginia Reynolds	Jun. 28, 1855

Jackson County, Missouri, West Fork Baptist Church, Raytown.

Membership Register

Name	Admission	Dismissed
John Davis	Dec., 1842	---
Lewis Jones	Dec., 1842	---
Alvin Brookings	Dec., 1842	---
C. S. Stribling	Dec., 1842	---
Joseph C. Davis	Dec., 1842	---
Jas. Beckham	Dec., 1842	---
Edwin Allen	Dec., 1842	---
Thomas Stayton	Dec., 1842	d. Sep., 1843

Name	Admission	Dismissed
John J. Fox	Mar., 1843	Mar., 1845
Wm. W. Jones	Mar., 1843	Jul., 1850
John Shelton	Apr., 1843	Jul., 1848
Presley Muir	Jul., 1843	Nov., 1846
Wm. Cornet	Jul., 1843	Dec., 1846
Peter Courtney	Jul., 1843	Sep., 1844, dis. Mar., 1845
Jacob Fox	Aug., 1843	Mar., 1845
Shelby West	Aug., 1843	---
Eli House	Aug., 1843	---
John George	Aug., 1843	Restored Jan., 1846, d. 1857.
Simeon Stayton	Aug., 1843	Sep., 1857
Richard Fristoe	Aug., 1843	d. Nov., 1845
Alexander Harris	Aug., 1843	---
Henry Cox	Aug., 1843	1849
Wesley Cornet	Aug., 1843	Mar., 1845
George Smith	Aug., 1843	Feb., 1857
Robert Brooking	Aug., 1843	Mar., 1845
Alvin Adams	Aug., 1843	Jul., 1848
Asa Campbell	Dec., 1843	---
Robert Word	Jan., 1844	Aug., 1844
Hukman SMith	May, 1844	---
Milton Quisenberry	Jul., 1844	d. Sep. 18, 1845
John Flanery	Aug., 1844	---
Thos. D. Chism	Sep., 1844	Aug., 1847
Christopher Star	Sep., 1844	1853
William Ross	Sep., 1844	May, 1847
Foster F. Henderick	Sep., 1844	Sep., 1844
Charles Story	Sep., 1844	Mar., 1845
Zion Flanery	Oct., 1844	---
John Chrisman	Oct., 1844	---
Jeremiah Farmer	Dec., 1844	Dec., 1846
Noah Halhan	Apr., 1845	---
Daniel Meade	Mar., 1846	1850
Thomas Colgin	Apr., 1846	---
James Robinson	Apr., 1846	---
James Commins	May, 1846	Nov., 1856
Thomas P. Fristoe	Aug., 1846	1848
Benjamin F. Fisher	Sep., 1846	1855
Valentine Hamton	Sep., 1846	1847

Buchanan County, Missouri, "St. Joseph Gazette," October 24, 1845, Delegates to the Platte River Baptist Association.

Name	Church
John M. Evans	Union
Strother Ball	Union

Name	Church
Littleton S. Roberts	Union
Nelson Witt	Union
Thornton Gwinn	Pleasant Grove
Lance Woodard	Pleasant Grove
Isaac Lynch	El-Bethel
Isaac Agee	Bethlehem
William Thornton	Bethlehem
Abram Brown	Mill Creek
Greenberry Thorp	Mill Creek
John Evans	Flag Spring
James C. C. Patton	Flag Spring
Jared Tribble	Flag Spring
Samuel King	Flag Spring
Joshua Anderson	Bee Creek
Hiram Hurst	Bee Creek
Zebediah Baker	Bee Creek
Henry W. Baker	Bee Creek
Eli P. Harden	Lebanon
William Shurer	Sugar Creek
H. Cook	Sugar Creek
Zachariah Garton	Sugar Creek
John Butler	Providence
Sampson Langston	Providence
William H. Miller	Mount Gilead
William Miller (sic)	Mount Gilead
Isaac Farns	Mount Gilead
William C. Garrett	Concord
John Barnett	Concord

Benton County, Missouri, Big Buffalo United Baptist
Church.
Membership Register
As follows: Margaret Taylor, Mary R. Taylor,
Rebecca Brown, Susan Bradshaw, Sintha Ann Wallis,
Angeline Wilcoxson, Eliza Gehart, Margaret
Christian, Melissa Bradin, Elzada Franklin, Georgia
E. Taylor, Martha Crenshaw, Lib Brown, Martha Brim,
Sarah E. Silvey, Rosie Hunter, Mollie Willis, Annie
Williams, John R. Taylor, Isaac E. Brown, Wm.
Bradden, Nathan Wilcoxsen (adm. Nov. 2, 1872),
Joseph Franklin, James Bradin, Robert S. Brown,
Robert Hunter, W. A. Taylor, Walter Brown, Emaline
Campbell, S. A. Williams, Elin Smith, Catharine
Wallis, Rhoda Bradin, Ann C. Hunter, Lorence
Coontz, Mary Ann Bradin, Mary Wallis, Helin Brown,
Mary Foster, Minerva Gary, Sarah E. Taylor, Julia
Johnson, Sarah William, Margaret M. Chewning, Mary
Williams, Minnie Hunter, Mollie Taylor, Sard (sic)

Taylor, Jacob Wallis, James Wallis, Andrew Braden, John Braden, Andy Huff (Bapt. Nov. 2, 1873), Peter Silvey, Charley Gary, Luther Taylor, B. Sanburn, Jacob Weaver, T. Gary, W. T. Weaver.

Minutes

Albert and Margaret Braden, (BAPT) September, 1869, (P) 2.

Mary Brown, (BAPT) May 7, 1870, (P) 6.

J. E. Brown, John Braden, W. S. Barnett, Jacob Wallis, J. R., Building Site Committe, (P) 24.

W. S. and Mary V. Barnett, (Dis) April 5, 1873, (P) 43.

Elzada Taylor, Restored, (P) 46.

Peter and Sarah E. Silvey, Admitted, (P) 59.

D. S. and Martha Brim, (Adm) December, 1879, (P) 66.

James Wallis, Received preaching license, December, 1880, (P) 69.

Dan Bowers opened the church meeting. James Wallis was ordained. B. R. Sanburn received his preaching license. (P) 82.

Robert S. Brown, J. R. Taylor, (Adm) December, 1885, (Dis) James Wallis, Mary Wallis, Molly Wallis, (P) 86.

Jacob Weaver, (Adm) September 21, 1887, (P) 92.

W. A. Taylor, Joined church, (P) 93.

Effie Taylor, Baptised; Fannie Weaver, Afternoon funeral, (P) 94.

R. S. Brown, Ordained, (P) 96.

Luther Taylor, (Adm) January 30, 1891, (P) 99.

S. V. Williams and Luther Taylor, (BAPT) May 24, 1891, (P) 100.

St. Francois County, Missouri, "St. Louis Free Press," October 17, 1833, Bethel United Baptist Association, Meeting September, 1833.

Name	Church Congregation
Wingate Jackson	Hepzibah
Noe Hunt	Hepzibah
Joel Hammar	Hepzibah
Jesse Bound	New Hope
John Blanton	New Hope
John Carter	New Hope
James Halbert	New Hope
James Ritter	New Hope
Joshua Kinworthy	New Hope
Elijah O'Banion	Providence
John Strickland	Bethany
Samuel Vance	Wolf Creek

Name	Church Congregation
Richard Cobb	Wolf Creek
Stephen Colyer	Wolf Creek
William Polk	----

Pike County, Missouri, Salt River Baptist Association, September 9-11, 1842, Meeting at Mt. Pleasant Church, "Bowling Green Radical," October 22, 1842.

Name	Church
A. D. Landrum	Ramsey's Creek
Newton McDonald	Ramsey's Creek
J. C. Duvall	Ramsey's Creek
Terisha Turner	Ramsey's Creek
William Biggs	Peno Creek
E. Ferrell	Peno Creek
W. H. Doyle	Peno Creek
William Shannon	Peno Creek
Levi Moore	Siloam Church
Bazel Riggs	Siloam Church
John D. Biggs	Salem Church
Joseph McGrew	Thomas Ellis
Francis Conner	Salem Church
G. Mock	Mount Pleasant
Timothy Rodgers	Mount Pleasant
William Brown	Mount Pleasant
R. Vermillion	Mount Pleasant
John T. Hedges	Noix Creek
G. W. Peay	Noix Creek
T. H. Hedges	Noix Creek
S. B. Clark	Noix Creek
T. T. Johnson	Mt. Pisgah
W. G. Hawkins	Mt. Pisgah
B. T. Hawkins	Mt. Pisgah
Thomas Dunbar	Mt. Pisgah
David Hubbard	Six Miles
William Mitchell	Six Miles
Robert Gilmore	Sulphur Lick
Ira Bailey	Sulpher Lick
John M. Rieds	Sulpher Lick
J. M. Johnson	Bethel Church
J. Culbertson	Bethel Church
Mark Shults	Bethel Church
W. H. Vardeman	Bethel Church
Jeremiah Vardeman	Death Mentioned
Peter Moss	Adiel Church
Robert Sloss	Adiel Church
John Woods	Adiel Church
Moses Hawkins	Adiel Church

Saline County, Missouri, "Marshall Democrat," Vol. 1, No. 33, September 2, 1859, Marshall, List of Baptist Ministers.

Name	Post Office	County
S. G. Allen	Harrisonville	Cass
T. S. Allen	St. Catherine	Linn
B. Anderson	Huntsville	Randolph
G. Anderson	St. Louis	St. Louis
J. M. Ashburn	Kansas City	Jackson
N. Ayres	Palmyra	Marion
--- Babb	Centralia	Boone
B. Baker	Columbia	Boone
T. Barbee	Linneus	Linn
W. Barnhurst	St. Louis	St. Louis
T. W. Barrett	Hainsville	Clinton
A. T. Batteron	Bloomington	Macon
S. A. Beauchamp	Chilicothe	Livingston
W. M. Bell	Miami	Saline
M. T. Bibb	Williamsburg	Callaway
J. D. Black	Victoria	Daviess
J. D. Blakely	Middleburg	Mercer
B. F. Bowles	Pisgah	Cooper
T. Bradley	Trenton	Grundy
J. P. Bridewell	Charleston	Miss. Co.
M. Brown	Tipton	Moniteau
P. Brown	Hogle's Creek	St. Clair
X. X. Buckner	Columbia	Boone
W. C. Busby	Hannibal	Marion
B. T. F. Cake	New Franklin	Howard
W.P. C. Caldwell	Walls Store	Johnson
G. Carey	Rocheport	Boone
J. M. Chaney	Versailles	Morgan
H. Chism	Independence	Jackson
J. A. Clark	Cape Girardeau	Cape Gir.
S. Clevinger	Fredericksburg	Ray
R. N. Coffey	Camden Point	Platte
S. W. Coker	Greene	Bollinger
Wm. Cromell	St. Louis	St. Louis
J. J. Daniel	New Market	Platte
J. G. Davenport	Louisiana	Pike
D. Doyle	Ashland	Boone
E. S. Dulin	Kansas City	Jackson
L. Duncan	Louisville	Lincoln
M. W. Duncan	California	Moniteau
R. S. Duncan	Lost Branch	Lincoln
W. A. Durfey	Independence	Jackson
W. H. Duvall	Blue Springs	Jackson
A. Estes	Versailles	Morgan
H. Farmer	Pleasant Hill	Cass

Name	Post Office	County
W. Ferguson	Georgetown	Pettis
J. Farmer	Harrisonville	Cass
N. Flood	Huntsville	Randolph
L. Franklin	Independence	Jackson
T. Fristoe	Glasgow	Howard
J. B. Fuqua	Bridgeton	St. Louis
C. Gentry	Salem	Ralls
C. Gentry	Shelbyville	Shelby
J. J. Gipson	Louisiana	Pike
J. Goen	Linneus	Linn
A. C. Goodrich	Paris	Monroe
B. F. Goodwin	Walls Store	Johnson
J. M. Goodson	Carrollton	Carroll
J. Gott	Fayetteville	Johnson
W. D. Grant	Hawk Point	---
F. Graves	Hainesville	Clinton
H. B. Graves	Farmington	St. Francois
R. C. Graves	Kingston	Caldwell
W. A. Gray	Calhoun	Henry
J. S. Green	Palmyra	Marion
J. D. Gregory	Portland	Callaway
T. V. Grier	Tipton	Moniteau
J. N. Griffin	Hickory Creek	Audrain
R. H. Harris	Pisgah	Cooper
N. Hawley	Middleburg	Macon
P. N. Haycraft	New Market	Platte
A. Heaussler	St. Louis	St. Louis
J. Hickman	St. Louis	St. Louis
A. T. Hite	Glasgow	Howard
A. B. Hogard	Perryville	Perry
J. A. Hollis	Lexington	Lafayette
J. M. Holt	Williamstown	Lewis
A. Horne	Fayetteville	Johnson
J. E. Hughes	Stewartsville	DeKalb
D. V. Inlow	Florida	Monroe
W. Jennings	Louisiana	Pike
G. W. Johnson	Warrensburg	Johnson
J. M. Johnson	Frankford	Pike
J. T. M. Johnson	Columbia	Boone
T. T. Johnson	High Hill	Mont. Co.
R. Kayler	Newark	Knox
J. H. Keach	New London	Ralls
B. F. Kenney	Victoria	Daviess
H. King	Shelbyville	Shelby
G. S. Kinnard	Carrollton	Carroll
J. W. Lacey	Camden	Ray
T. F. Lockett	Jefferson City	Cole

Name	Post Office	County
A. I. Landrum	Windsor	Henry
B. Leach	Owensville	Gasconade
J. Leake	Richmond	Ray
W. C. Ligon	Carrollton	Carroll
J. M. Lillard	Monticello	Lewis
J. B. Link	Liberty	Clay
W. Luck	Troy	Lincoln
J. Lurme	Trenton	Grundy
J. H. Luther	Kansas City	Jackson
J. Lykens	Kansas City	Jackson
J. P. McAdam	Keytesville	Chariton
W. H. McClelland	Millville	Ray
W. McQuie	Middletown	Mont. Co.
J. Major	Liberty	Clay
W. H. Mansfield	Roanoke	Randolph
J. C. Maple	Cape Girardeau	Cape Gir.
A. F. Martin	Linneus	Linn
W. A. May	Bloomington	Macon
W. J. Mimms	Kansas City	Jackson
A. G. Mitchell	New Hope	Lincoln
G. Mitchell	St. Louis	St. Louis
M. M. Modisett	Lagrange	Lewis
W. H. Morris	Roanoke	Randolph
J. D. Murphy	Owensville	Gasconade
L. C. Musick	Hickory Creek	Audrain
J. Nichols	Warrenton	Warren
M. D. Noland	Jefferson City	Cole
D. W. Nowlin	Tivoit	Mont. Co.
T. N. O'Bryan	Liberty	Clay
J. Oliver	Ten Mile	Macon
S. H. Olmstead	Fayette	Howard
E. J. Owen	Platte City	Platte
Dr. Paramour	Bloomfield	Stoddard
M. Powers	Florida	Monroe
M. Powers	Paris	Monroe
N. S. Prentice	Lagrange	Lewis
W. Price	St. Joseph	Buchanan
R. M. Rhoades	Palmyra	Marion
A. H. Right	Liberty	Clay
W. P. Right	Hogle's Creek	St. Clair
J. Roan	Huntsville	Randolph
John Roan	Middlefork	---
N. Roberts	Ridgely	Platte
W. M. Robertson	California	Montieau
G. W. Robey	Philadelphia	Marion
J. M. Robinson	Columbia	Boone
G. W. Rodgers	Liberty	Clay
A. P. Rogers	Bowling Green	Pike

Name	Post Office	County
E. Roth	Dover	Lafayette
T. Rucker	Ridge Prairie	Saline
Scott Kemp	Carrollton	Carroll
J. F. Smith	Glasgow	Howard
J. G. Smith	Fulton	Callaway
P. H. Steen-bergen	Columbia	Boone
P. H. Steenstra	St. Louis	St. Louis
B. C. Stephens	Hannibal	Marion
C. W. Stewart	Rushville	Buchanan
J. Swinney	Carbon	Macon
C. J. Teas	Clinton	Henry
B. Terrill	Huntsville	Randolph
J. Terrill	Roanoke	Randolph
J. W. Terrill	Roanoke	Randolph
B. T. Thomas	Lexington	Lafayette
H. Thomas	Shelbina	Shelby
W. H. Thomas	Camden Point	Platte
W. Thompson	Liberty	Clay
H. H. Tilford	Shelbyville	Shelby
G. D. Tolle	New Bloomfield	Callaway
P. Turner	Athens	Clarke
J. H. Tuttle	Hibernia	Callaway
W. H. Vardiman	Wellsburg	St. Charles
W. W. Walden	Chillicothe	Livingston
J. Walkup	Linneus	Linn
W. B. Walthal	Jefferson City	Cole
J. W. Warder	Lexington	Lafayette
J. E. Welch	Hickory Grove	Warren
B. Wheeler	Gentryville	Gentry
J. T. Wheeler	Cornersville	Hickory
W. R. Wiginton	Centralia	Boone
A. P. Williams	Cambridge	Saline
J. T. Williams	Ridgely	Platte
M. F. Williams	Sparta	Buchanan
J. M. Willis	Columbia	Boone
E. Wood	Independence	Jackson
B. Woods	Sturgeon	Boone
--- Woolridge	---	Chariton
J. Wyatt	Charleston	Mississippi

Carroll County, Missouri, Big Creek Baptist Church, Near Big Creek, 1844 - 1872, Membership Rooster.

Name	Received Date	Dismissed Date
William David Allee	Jul., 1856	Mar., 1857
Gilbert Allen	Feb., 1869	---
Emma Agard	Nov., 1870	---

Name	Received Date	Dismissed Date
Jabez Calvert, Sr.	Jul., 1845	Apr., 1855
Malinda Calvert	Jul., 1845	---
Elizabeth Colley	Sep., 1846	Oct., 1854
*John B. Calvert	Oct., 1848	Dec., 1855

*(Dismissed by letter Aug., 1858)

John F. Calvert	Dec., 1846	May, 1851
*John F. Calvert	Jul., 1853	May, 1868

*(Elected deacon Aug., 1847; Ordained Sep., 1847; Received as deacon Jul., 1853; Appointed assistant clerk Apr., 1858.)

Elizabeth Calvert	Jul., 1847	May, 1851
Mrs. Calvert	Jul., 1853	May, 1868
Wm. Calvert, Sr.	May, 1848	---
Martha Ann Calvert	May, 1848	Nov., 1864
*James Calvert	Oct., 1848	---

*(Elected trustee Jul., 1859 and in Feb., 1870.)

William N. Calvert	Oct., 1848	Apr., 1854
David A. Calvert	Oct., 1848	Feb., 1858
M. E. Calvert	Jul., 1852	---
*Johnathan Calvert	Oct., 1848	Mar., 1851

*(Dismissed by letter Dec., 1853.)

Jabez Calvert, Jr.	Oct., 1848	---
Eri M. Calvert	Oct., 1848	Dec., 1855
William H. Calvert	Oct., 1848	Nov., 1854
Noding Calvert	Aug., 1853	Dec., 1854
Gabriella Calvert	Aug., 1853	Dec., 1854
*Ambrose Calvert	Mar., 1855	Oct., 1858

*(Appointed trustee Apr., 1855)

Nancy A. Calvert	Jul., 1852	---
Mary Jane Calvert	Oct., 1848	---
---- Crocker	Jul., 1853	Apr., 1855
*William N. Calvert	Aug., 185?	---

*(Elected clerk Feb., 1858.)

Wm. R. Creel	Jul., 1866	---
Elizabeth Creel	Jul., 1866	---
Thomas A. Calvert	Jul., 1866	---
Nancy E. Calvert	Jul., 1866	May, 1868
Melinda J. Calvert	---	---
Samuel M. Calvert	Dec., 1865	---
Margret J. Calvert	Dec., 1865	May, 1871
Benjamin F. Calvert	Dec., 1865	Nov., 1870
*Woods S. Creel	Jul., 1866	Mar., 1871

*(Joined the Reformer Chruch.)

Harriett Colston	Feb., 1869	---
John W. Colston	Feb., 1869	---
Paulina Calvert	Feb., 1869	---
Margaret J. Creel	Nov., 1867	---

Name	Received Date	Dismissed Date
Wm. R. Creel, Jr.	Nov., 1867	---
*Jane Calvert	May, 1870	---
*(Letter from Bethlehem Church)		
John F. Calvert	---	May, 1868
Elizabeth Calvert	---	May, 1868
Louelza Creel	Nov., 1870	---
Josephine K. Creel	Nov., 1867	---
*Henry S. Doty	Dec., 1847	Nov., 1853
*(Appointed treasurer Jul., 1853)		
Francis Doty	Dec., 1847	Nov., 1853
Isaac Doty	Feb., 1849	Nov., 1853
Aloina L. Dean	Aug., 1848	1856
John J. Dean	Jul., 1852	Dec., 1855
Cyntha Durnil	Jul., 1854	1856
Sarah Dean	Jun., 1866	d.Mar., 1870
Alexander J. Dean	Feb., 1869	---
Francis M. Dean	Feb., 1869	---
Mary A. Dean	Feb., 1869	Apr., 1869
Elizabeth Dean	Feb., 1869	---
*Lavina Dean	May, 1870	---
*(Letter from Bethlehem Church)		
*Martha Dean	May, 1870	---
*(Letter from Bethlehem Church)		
Jane Dean	Nov., 1870	---
*Emily (Servant)	Sep., 1844	Nov., 1850
*(Slave of Ambrose Callaway)		
John J. Fristoe	Jul., 1852	Jul., 1855
*Elbridge Finch	May, 1854	1856
*(Appointed assistant clerk Mar., 1856)		
Sinah Finch	May, 1854	1856
Malinda Finch	May, 1854	1854
Mary E. France	Jul., 1852	---
George France	May, 1855	---
Priclla Finch	May, 1855	1856
*John Finch	Jun., 1856	---
*(Appointed church clerk, Mar., 1857)		
Elizabeth Finch	Jun., 1856	---
Lydia French	Feb., 1869	---
Nancy A. France	Nov., 1870	---
Allen J. Gabriel	Jun., 1852	Apr., 1854
Nancy Gabriel	Jun., 1852	Feb., 1854
*Marry (sic) E. Gabriel	Dec., 1865	Jul., 1869
*(Joined a church of a different order.)		
Frances M. Grim	Jun., 1866	---
A. J. Grim	Feb., 1869	d.Jan. 13, 1872
Jerome Gillespie	Feb., 1869	---
Margaret Gillispie	Feb., 1869	Mar., 1872

Name	Received Date	Dismissed Date
Burley Godsey	Sep., 1870	Mar., 1872
Nancy Godsey	Sep., 1870	Mar., 1872
Martha Ann Godsey	Sep., 1870	Mar., 1872
Thomas G. Godsey	Sep., 1870	Mar., 1872
Jane Hudson (Joined a separate Baptist Church)		
Rhoda A. Hill	Oct., 1848	---
Benjamin S. Hawkins	Jun. 22, 1844	Oct., 1848
Nancy Hawkins	Jun. 22, 1844	Oct., 1848
William Hill	Jun. 22, 1844	Jun. 20, 1849
*Pleasant M. Hill	Jun. 22, 1844	Feb., 1849

*(Elected church clerk Jul. 6, 1844; Elected trustee May 2, 1846; Elected church treasurer Sep., 1847.)

Name	Received Date	Dismissed Date
Gideon Hill	Jun. 22, 1844	Mar., 1853
James Hill	Aug., 1844	Jul., 1855
Nancy Hill	Aug., 1844	Jul., 1855
*Newton J. Halsy	Mar., 1849	Mar., 1854

*(Licensed to preach Aug., 1853)

Name	Received Date	Dismissed Date
Nancy Hill	Jun., 1847	Mar., 1853
*Daniel Hill	Nov., 1850	Nov., 1853

*(Appointed church clerk Feb., 1851)

Name	Received Date	Dismissed Date
Sarah Hill	Oct., 1849	Nov., 1853
George Harman	May, 1852	Mar., 1854
Abriham Horton	Jan., 1854	---
Matilda Horton	Mar., 1855	Aug., 1869
Elender Howard	May, 1851	Aug., 1861
Mary Ellen Horton	Jul., 1852	Jan., 1862
? W. Horton	May, 1855	---
Richard Hewitt	Dec., 1865	d.Jul., 1870
Huldah A. Hewitt	Dec., 1865	Mar., 1870
Eri Hawkins	Dec., 1865	Jan., 1866
Sarah J. Hudson	Jan., 1866	---
Marry A. Hubbard	Jun., 1866	Apr., 1870
John W. Hudson	Feb., 1869	---
John R. Hewitt	Feb., 1869	---
John R. Hewitt	Feb., 1869	Nov., 1869
Mary Hewitt	Feb., 1869	---
Virginia Hill	Nov., 1870	---
Phebe Johnson	Sep., 1847	Oct., 1850
Samuel H. Johnson	Jun., 1866	---
*H. J. Kelley	Jan., 1866	---

*(APpointed church clerk Jul., 1867)

Name	Received Date	Dismissed Date
Marry (sic) B. Kelley	Jan., 1866	---
*Frances Kelley	Jun., 1870	May, 1871

*(Letter from Bethlehem Church)

Name	Received Date	Dismissed Date
Mary Little	Feb., 1847	---
James C. Linvill	Jun., 1854	---
*Johnas (sic) Little	Feb., 1847	---

Name	Recevied Date	Dismissed Date

*(Appointed trustee Jan., 1850; Appointed
assistant church clerk Nov., 1853, Died
Jun., 1855.)

Name	Recevied Date	Dismissed Date
Sena Leeton	Mar. 11, 1851	Apr., 1854
Sarah Little	Jun., 1855	---
Nancy Linvill (sic)	Dec., 1865	---
Jerem. S. Linville	Nov., 1870	---
James C. Linville	Dec., 1871	---
David T. McWilliams	Oct., 1848	Jan., 1854
Eliz. McWilliams	Oct., 1848	---
Mary Mitchel	Mar., 1851	---
Wm. K. Medlin	Jul., 1852	1856
Winaford Medlin	Aug., 1854	1856
Sarah Ann Medlin	Jul., 1852	1856
M. E. McWilliams	Jul., 1852	---
Robert Mitchel	Oct., 1848	Mar., 1849
Lidea McWilliams	May, 1855	---
James Medlin	May, 1855	1856
*Eliz. McWilliams	Jan., 1858	Aug., 1860

*(Joined the Reformed Church.)

Name	Recevied Date	Dismissed Date
Angaline McClain	Jan., 1866	Feb., 1869
*Wm. H. Miller	Jan., 1866	Jun., 1869

*(Joined the Methodist Church)

Name	Recevied Date	Dismissed Date
Mary E. McLain	Feb., 1869	---
Robert McLain	Feb., 1869	---
James McLain	Feb., 1869	---
Asa McLain	Feb., 1869	---
John McLain	Feb., 1869	---
Sarah Mizner	1859	May, 1868
*Wm. Morney	Mar., 1870	---

*(Letter from Carrollton sexton Jan., 1870)

Name	Recevied Date	Dismissed Date
Norflet Newsom	Jun. 22, 1844	Apr., 1854
Nancy Newsom	Oct., 1846	Apr., 1854
James Newsom	Mar. 10, 1851	Mar., 1857
Sarah Newsom	Mar. 10, 1851	---
Sefus Newsom	Mar. 11, 1851	Apr., 1854
Bunion Newsom	Sep., 1853	Apr., 1854
Sarah Newsom	Mar. 11, 1851	1852
Larry Newsom	Mar. 10, 1851	Apr., 1854
Polly Newsom	Mar. 10, 1851	---
Sarah Philips	Oct., 1848	---
Louisa Philips	Oct., 1848	---
Elizabeth Philips	Oct., 1848	---
James Rippetoe	Jun. 22, 1844	Apr., 1854
Eliz. Rippetoe	Jul. 21, 1844	Apr., 1854
A. S. Reynolds	Feb., 1869	---
Mrs. Martha Ruark	May, 1873	---
Mary J. Scott	Oct., 1848	---

Name	Received Date	Dismissed Date
*Daniel Sharp	Jul. 21, 1844	Aug., 1847
*(Excluded for communing with the Presbyterians)		
Zilpah Sharp	Jul. 21, 1844	---
Lewis E. Scott	Feb., 1847	Jun., 1850
Lewis E. Scott	Aug., 1853	---
Jemina Scott	Oct., 1848	Jun., 1850
Mrs. Lewis Scott	Aug., 1853	---
Kemp Scott	Feb., 1847	1856
Ann Scott	Feb., 1847	1856
Ann Scott	Apr., 1847	Sep., 1851
Francis Sercy	Jul., 1848	Feb., 1852
Nancy Sercy	Jul., 1848	Feb., 1851
David K. Scott	Oct., 1848	Apr., 1852
David K. Scott	Mar., 1854	1856
Elizabeth Scott	Mar., 1854	1856
Thomas A. Scott	Oct., 1848	1856
Eliza Ann Scott	Apr., 1855	1856
*Ralph P. Scott	Jan., 1850	1856
*(Appointed deacon Jan., 1850; Appointed church treasurer Nov., 1853; Licensed to preach Jun., 1856.)		
Martha W. Scott	Jan., 1850	1856
Beuford Scott	Mar., 1852	1854
Peter W. Scott	Jul., 1852	1856
Loucinda Scott	Jul., 1852	1856
Elizabeth Scott	May, 1852	1856
Charrity Scott	May, 1852	1856
Mosis (sic) Smith	Jul., 1853	Jul. 1, 1854
Rebecer (sic) Smith	Jul., 1853	Dec., 1854
William Smart	Jun. 7, 1845	Apr., 1852
Hannah Sharp	Mar. 9, 1851	Apr., 1854
Wm. H. Smart	Jan., 1866	Mar., 1866
C. E. Shinn	Jan., 1866	---
*George M. Smith	Aug., 1870	---
*(Letter from the Dewitt Church)		
*Mary A. Smith	Aug., 1870	---
*(Letter from the Dewitt Church)		
Hamilton Shinn	Nov., 1870	---
Margaret Shurley	---	May, 1871
Henry Temple	Nov., 1870	---
*John Teter	Nov., 1870	Mar., 1871
*(Joined the Reformed Church.)		
Robert Parker Williams	Mar., 1851	---
Lewis Waldon	Sep., 1852	Mar., 1853
Joseph P. Whorton	May, 1855	---
Mary Waggamon	Jul., 1856	---

Name	Received Date	Dismissed Date
John Woolverton	Nov., 1870	Mar., 1872
Angeline Woolverton	Nov., 1870	---
Mr. Waughtal	Nov., 1870	---
George Whorton	---	Aug., 1869
A. W. Whorton	Feb., 1854	---
Matilda Whorton	Feb., 1854	---
*Mary E. Whorton	---	Aug., 1860

*(Joined the Reformed Church.)

Name	Received Date	Dismissed Date
J. R. Yates	Dec., 1872	---
Ellen Yates	Dec., 1872	---

Abstracts from Church Minutes

On the first Sat., July, 1844, Bro. Ely wrote a letter to the Grand River Association at Mt. Nebo, Lynn Co. (Linn), Mo. (P) 6.

On the first Sat., March, 1845, the church met at the home of James M. Waldens. (P) 7.

May, 1850, Bro. J. M. Goodson preached. Bro. T. Blakely preached Nov., 1850. (P) 23.

Abraham Rife mentioned in the minutes June, 185. (P) 30.

John Mathew mentioned in the minutes July, 1853. (P) 35.

On April, 1854, the follwowing members were dismissed to form a church on the Hurricane: Norfleet Newsom, Bunion Newsom, James Rippetoe, Cephes Newsom, Laury Newsom, Allen Ball, Sr., Allen Ball, Jr., Nancy Newsom, Mazany Newsom, Elizabeth A. Rippetoe, Seeny Leeton, Avy J. Hudson, Sarah H. Bush, Martha Ball. (P) 44.

Death of Bro. Kinnard mentioned Oct., 1866. (P) No Numbers.

Oct., 1867, Br. Wm. Keen, Tennessee, preached. (P) No Numbers.

St. Louis County, Missouri, Manchester Methodist Church, Manchester, MO, Hwy-141.

Register of Baptism

Harold Thurman Gregg, (PRTS) George H. and Delia Gregg, (BAPT) Apr., 1893.

Myrtle Gregg, (PRTS) George H. and Delia Gregg, (BAPT) Apr., 1893.

Freddie Wm. Andrae, (PRTS) B.F. and Lavina Andrae, (BAPT) Sep. 3, 1893.

Esther Julia Andrae, (PRTS) B. F. and Lavina Andrae, (BAPT) Sep. 3, 1893.

Leslie Storck, (PRTS) Albert and Josie Storck, (BAPT) May, 1901.

Ralph Buford, (PRTS) John and Fannie Buford,

(BAPT) Apr. 20, 1902.

Elizabeth B. Buford, (PRTS) John and Fannie Buford, (BAPT) Apr. 20, 1902.

Mollie Buford, (PRTS) John and Fannie Buford, (BAPT) Apr. 20, 1902.

Emma Corina Buford, (PRTS) Walter and Emma C. Buford, (BAPT) Apr. 20, 1902.

John William Brooks, (PRTS) Hays M. and Ellen Brooks, (BAPT) Dec. 23, 1903.

John William Scheffing, (PRTS) Wm. H. and Mattie N. (nee Schafer) Scheffing, (BAPT) Apr. 14, 1904.

Raymon Buford, (PRTS) Marshall M. and Mattie N. (nee Preiss) Buford, (BAPT) Jun. 10, 1904.

Marguerite Johnson, (PRTS) Clarence and D'Olive (nee Ebricht) Johnson, (B) Sep. 11, 1904, (BAPT) Oct. 11, 1904.

Frederick Jos. Vancher, (PRTS) Gustave and Carrie Vancher, (B) Oct. 5, 1904, (BAPT) May 18, 1905.

Charles William Herzig, (PRTS) Joseph and Neva Herzig, (BAPT) May 18, 1905.

Ellen Maude Brooks, (PRTS) Hays M. and Ellen M. Brooks, (B) Mar. 3, 1905, (BAPT) Aug. 20, 1905.

Eliza Doris Jones, (PRTS) Gleen L. and Lila (nee Brooks) Jones, (B) May 19, 1905, (BAPT) Aug. 20, 1905.

Major Storck, (PRTS) Albert and Josie Storck, (B) Feb. 24, 1905, (BAPT) Oct. 29, 1905.

Alvin Defoe Gregg, (PRTS) George H. and Delia Gregg, (B) Jul. 12, 1899, (BAPT) Jan. 14, 1906.

Jessie Holmes Buford, (PRTS) Mashiel and Mattie (nee Price) Buford, (B) Sep. 8, 1906, (BAPT) Oct. 25, 1906.

Melvina Grothpeter, (PRTS) Julius and Melvina Grothpeter, (B) Mar. 22, 1895, (BAPT) Jan. 24, 1906.

Cora Edna Grothpeter, (PRTS) Julius and Melvina Grothpeter, (B) Jan. 23, 1897, (BAPT) Jan. 24, 1906.

Oliver Grothpeter, (PRTS) Julius and Melvina Grothpeter, (B) Jan. 4, 1901, (BAPT) Jan. 24, 1906.

Ollie Grothpeter, (PRTS) Julius and Melvina Grothpeter, (B) Jan. 4, 1901, (BAPT) Jan. 24, 1906.

Melvin Grothpeter, (PRTS) Julius and Melvina Grothpeter, (B) Sep. 6, 1903, (BAPT) Jan. 24, 1906.

John Haskel Buford, (PRTS) John H. and Fannie B. (nee Hayes) Buford, (B) Apr. 8, 1906, (BAPT) May 18, 1906.

Alice Dorothy Stoge, (PRTS) John E. and Louisa Catherine Stoger, (B) Jan. 26, 1905, (BAPT) Aug. -- , 1905.

Oliver Powell, (PRTS) T. Cole and Emma (nee Huntley) Powell, (B) Oct. 10, 1898, (BAPT) Sep. 24, 1905.

Marie Powell, (PRTS) T. Cole and Emma (nee Huntley), Powell, (B) Mar. 31, 1903, (BAPT) Sep. 24, 1905.

Willie Dell Westbrook, (PRTS) Paul and May (nee Scry) Westbrook, (B) May 28, 1903, (BAPT) Sep. 24, 1905.

Ruth Catherine Longgrear, (PRTS) Del and Clara (nee Huntley) Longgrear, (B) Jan. 28, 1904, (BAPT) Sep. 24, 1905.

John Del Conrad Longgrear, (PRTS) Del and Clara (nee Huntley) Longgrear, (B) Aug. 23, 1905, (BAPT) Sep. 24, 1905.

Clara Mary Longgrear, (PRTS) Del and Clara (nee Huntley) Longgrear, (B) Jan. 16, 1902, (BAPT) Sep. 24, 1905.

Edgar Gregg Ferguson, (PRTS) Benj. F. and Anna S. E. (nee Gregg) Ferguson, (B) May 20, 1904, (BAPT) Sep. 16, 1906.

George Edna Miller,(orphan), (PRTS) Adopted by Mrs. Cora L. Defore, (B) Jul. 25, 1899, (BAPT) Jul. 22, 1906.

Louisa Christina Terry, (PRTS) Robert and Dora Terry, (B) Aug. 24, 1898, (BAPT) Aug. 21, 1904.

George Edward Walker, (PRTS) Joseph and Clara Walker, (B) Oct. 12, 1904, (BAPT) Dec. 25, 1904.

Jeanette Powell, (PRTS) T. Cole and Emma (nee Huntley) Powell, (B) Nov. 4, 1893, (BAPT) Sep. 24, 1905.

Bessie Powell, (PRTS) T. Cole and Emma (nee Huntley) Powell, (B) Nov. 10, 1900, (BAPT) Sep. 24, 1905.

Hellen (sic) Powell, (PRTS) T. Cole and Emma (nee Huntley) Powell, (B) Feb. 11, 1905, (BAPT) Sep. 24, 1905.

Charles Henry Hoeh, (PRTS) Henry John and Lily Louisa (nee Weber) Hoeh, (B) Sep. 25, 1906, (BAPT) Nov. 25, 1906.

Elsie Mabel Starck, (PRTS) Wm. amd Annie (nee Albright) Starck, (B) Feb. 24, 1902, (BAPT) Dec. 5, 1906.

Dellie May Wycoff, (PRTS) Andrew and Mathilda Kathryn (nee Key) Wycoff, (B) Jun. 30, 1894, (BAPT) Dec. 24, 1906.

Ervin Nathaniel Wycoff, (PRTS) Andrew and Mathilda Kathryn (nee Key) Wycoff, (B) May 16, 1896, (BAPT) Dec. 24, 1906.

Millard Elmer Wycoff, (PRTS) Andrew and Mathilda Kathyrn (nee Key) Wycoff, (B) Jan. 26, 1899, (BAPT) Dec. 24, 1906.

Ruth Armenia Wycoff, (PRTS) Andrew and Matilda Kathyrn (nee Key) Wycoff, (B) Mar. 17, 1901, (BAPT) Dec. 24, 1901.

Dorothy Frances Wycoff, (PRTS) Andrew and Matilda Kathyrn (nee Key) Wycoff, (B) Apr. 21, 1903, (BAPT) Dec. 24, 1901.

Clifford Wycoff, (PRTS) Andrew and Matilda Kathyrn (nee Key) Wycoff, (B) Jan. 28, 1905, (BAPT) Dec. 24, 1906.

Chester Emil Kessler, (PRTS) John F. amd Christina (nee Fitzinger) Kessler, Jr., (B) Dec. 20, 1906, (BAPT) Jan. 13, 1907.

Mary Eliza Schroeder, (PRTS) A. J. J. and Ruth (nee Brooks) Schroeder, (B) Jan. 13, 1907, (BAPT) Sep. 8, 1907.

Fred Christian Schroeder, (PRTS) A. J. J. and Ruth (nee Brooks) Schroeder, (B) Feb. 24, 1908, (BAPT) Aug. 1, 1909.

Dorothy Engler, orphan, (PRTS) Adopted by Mrs. Cora Defore, (BAPT) Feb. 26, 1911.

Joseph James August Walka, (PRTS) Joseph and Mrs. Joseph Walka, (BAPT) Mar. 17, 1912.

Marriage Register

Groom	Bride	Date
George Young	Sally Lash	1884
David Cooters	Luella Eatherton	Jan. 17, 1886
Walter Orr	Lorena Eatherton	Jan. 21, 1886
Dr. Chas. Zuppann	Kate Gregg	Jun. 23, 1866
George W. Gieger	Delia Defore	Dec. 25, 1889
William Finlay	Grace Gillham	Oct. 9, 1890
J. H. Buford	Fannie Hays	Dec. 31, 1890
James W. McElvoy	Katherine Appel	Apr. 23, 1893
Andrew T. Bennett	Daisy Reinhard	Jun. 5, 1893
Jas. W. Eatherton	Rosa Johnson	Nov. 23, 1898
Henry J. Hicke	Clara M. Hildebrand	Dec. 28, 1898
Edward B. Lambeth	Mary E. Hill	Apr. 19, 1899
Theodore T. Bayer	Mary H. Sutton	Jun. 7, 1899
Fred Jesse Hewitt	Eliz. N. Bopp	Jun. 14, 1906
Samuel C. Wilson	June Woody	Jun. 20, 1904
George Bopp	Mattie Linss	May 11, 1904
Julius Eberwein	Olive Nichols	Jul. 4, 1906
Hays M. Brooks	Mrs. Emma Buford	Mar. 17, 1906

Groom	Bride	Date
August J. J. Scrader	Ruth Brooks	Apr. 8, 1906
Nicholas P. Meyer	Beulah Nichl. Nivin	Aug. 8, 1906
Emil L. Ruwwe	Lydia Hubbrand	Oct. 6, 1906
E. Eberwin	Magie Kroning	Feb. 8, 1910
Thomas Wright	Amelia Eberwein	Jan. 18, 1911
Lester Turley	Ethel L. Burks	Oct. 2, 1911

Church Minutes
Conference, 1852
Members: Wesley Browning, W. D. Shumate, J. M. Hardy, W. Wharton, Joseph Sappington, W. T. Willis, S. A. Hall, William Smith, William W. Robertson.

Conference, September 9, 1854
Members: Wesley Browning, Eldras Smith, William Bacon, Geo. White, Bro. Locker, Joseph Sappington, William Brook, James Sappington, William P. Smith, Enoch Berry.

Conference, July 2, 1858
Members: Wesley Browning, Robert Orr, Philipp Tippitt, Enoch Berry, William D. Bacon, Larkin Williams, Langston Bacon, Robert Orr.

September 10, 1859
John Ball died on the last day of August last. He was buried beside his wife, Mary. The church was originally a carding-machine house owned by James Neal.

September 10, 1859
J. H. Jones forged the signature of J. R. Bennett stating that he, Jones, was a preacher.

September 22, 1860
Samuel Rudder, member of the church for forty years, passed away. Levi Ashley was elected as his replacement.

Conference, September 6, 1862
Members: Rev. T. M. Finney, Rev. J. Boyle, Rev. J. N. Springer, Rev. W. D. Shumate, Enich Berry, P. S. Bunberry, Jacob Lash.

Conference, September 17, 1864
Members: Rev. William Alexander, Rev. W. D. Shumate, P. S. Lanham, K. Shotwell, William Smizer, Larkin Williams, W. D. Bacon, A. B. Barbee, Jesse Underwood.

August 5, 1865
John Finney, L. H. Baker abd Nathaniel Colman were elected trustee. B. F. Lacy passed away.

February 17, 1866
Alexander Kincaid was elected to fill the

vacancy created by Kenneth Shotwell.

Iron County, Missouri, "Iron County Register," Participating Church Members of St. Pauls Episcopal Church.
November 18, 1897
Lunch Committee: Mrs. Myers, Mrs. Shelby, Mrs. T. Newman, Mrs. Gross, Mrs. Watkins.

Baby Picture Gallery: Miss Leah O'Brien, Miss Belle Whitworth, Mrs. Geo. Gay.

Auction of Souvenirs: Mrs. O'Brien, Mr. Melhado, Mr. Talbott.

Fish Pond: Mrs. Roehry, Miss Mamie Byers, Irene Goulding, Meda Baldwin, Clara Hill, Maude Welch.

Confectionery: Mrs. Kendall, Miss Fairchild, Miss Andrews, Miss Myers.

Doll Booth: Mrs. Wemp, Miss Bradley, Mrs. Davis, Miss Haller.

Knitting/Crochet Booth: Mrs. T. Beard, Miss Ada Byers.

Embroidery: Mrs. K. Delano, Miss Hattie Davis.

Sewing: Mrs. Ringo, Miss May Bradley.
December 16, 18897
Prize Winners/Food: Mrs. Thomas Beard, Mrs. Wm. A. Fletcher, Mrs. Helen O'Bien, Mrs. Jas. Hatton, Miss Marie Gratiot.

Prize Winners/Baby Picture: Miss Georgia Muffley, Miss Lucille Moore.

Prize Winners/Dolls: Miss Marie Gratiot, Mrs. Lottie Talbott.

Prize Winners/Sewing: Mrs. Kate E. Delano, Miss Mari Gratiot, Miss Nettie Beard.

Prize Winner/Lunch Tickets: Francis G. Delano.

Lafayette County, Missouri, Christ Episcopal Church, Baptism Register,
Edith Elisa Clagett, (PRTS) Milton M. and S. E. Clagett (B) Jul. 23, 1855, (BD) Jan. 6, 1860, (MG) Rev. G. K. Dunlop.

Samuel Zachariah Clagett, (PRTS) Milton and S. E. Claggett, (B) Apr. 15, 1857, (BD) Jan. 6, 1860, (MG) Rev. G. K. Dunlop.

Henry Mortimer Claggett, (PRTS) Milton and S. E. Claggett, (B) Sep. 24, 1858, (MG) Rev G. K. Dunlop.

Margaret Cobb Dunlop, (PRTS) G. K. and Mary W. Dunlop, (B) Oct. 20, 1859, (BD) Jan. 22, 1860, (SP) Mrs. Anna Shields, (MG) Rev. G. K. Dunlop.

Sue Trigg Shilds, (PRTS) T. W. and Elizabeth

Shields, (B) Sep. 18, 1859, (BD) Jan. 22, 1860, (SP) R. N. Smith, Mrs. A. Shields, Mrs. S. H. Trigg, (MG) Rev. G. K. Dunlop.

Edward Anderson Martin, (PRTS) Charles C. and Virginia C. Martin, (B) Dec. 7, 1859, (BD) Mar. 18, 1860, (SP) Mrs. Arnold, (MG) Rev. G. K. Dunlop.

Adeline Hackett, (PRTS) T. M. and M. A. Hackett, (B) Jan. 21, 1860, (BD) Mar. 18, 1860, (MG) Rev. G. K. Dunlop.

James Alexander Bond, (PRTS) Benson and Sallie Bond, (B) Aug. 4, 1857, (BD) Apr. 8, 1860, (MG) Rev. G. K. Dunlop.

William Gray Early, (PRTS) R. H. and H. A. Early, (B) Jan. 10, 1858, (BD) Jul. 11, 1860, (SP) G. K. Dunlop, Miss Maria A. Sinton, (R) Mrs. Early, (MG) Rev. G. K. Dunlop.

Lewis Eugene Francis Walmsley, (PRTS) John and Emma H. Walmsley, (B) Aug. 24, 1848, (BD) Aug. 9, 1860, (MG) Rev. G. K. Dunlop.

Prentiss Heathman, (PRTS) John N. and Nancy E. Heathman, (B) Oct., 29, 1857, (BD) Aug. 13, 1860, (SP) Zachariah Thomason, (MG) Rev. G. K. Dunlop.

Haywood Heathman, (PRTS) John N. and Nancy Heatham, (B) Jul. 23, 1859, (BD) Aug. 13, 1860, (SP) Zachariah Thomason, (MG) Rev. G. K. Dunlop.

Mary Virginia Cunningham, (PRTS) C. E. and Elis. Cunningham, (B) May 22, 1856, (BD) Aug. 18, 1860, (R) Willian Hill, (MG) Rev. G. K. Dunlop.

James Cunningham, (PRTS) C. E. and Elis. Cunningham, (B) Mar. 1, 1859, (BD) Aug. 18, 1860, (R) William Hill, (MG) Rev. G. K. Dunlop.

Lillian Thornton Bedinger, (PRTS) H. C. and S. W. Bedinger, (B) Dec. 25, 1859, (BD) Aug. 18, 1860, (MG) Rev. G. K. Dunlop.

Henry Clay Bedinger, (PRTS) S. S. and M. B. Bedinger, (B) Sep. 13, 1859, (BD) Aug. 18, 1860, (R) William Hill, (MG) Rev. G. K. Dunlop.

Ch. Horace Asbury, (PRTS) Squire and Mary E. Asbury, (B) Jan. 27, 1860, (BD) Aug. 18, 1860, (SP) Father C. E. Cummingham, Aug. Little, (R) William Hill, (MG) Rev. G. K. Dunlop.

Eliza Mansfield Smith, (PRTS) J. W. and Georgianna Smith, (B) Feb. 1, 1859, (BD) Aug. 18, 1860, (SP) Mrs. S. Bedinger, (R) William Hill, (MG) Rev. G. K. Dunlop.

Mary May Hill, (PRTS) William and Helen Hill, (B) Aug. 31, 1858, (BD) Aug. 18, 1860, (SP) Fanny Hill, (R) William Rose, (MG) Rev. G. K. Dunlop.

Margaret Susan Hill, (PRTS) William and Helen

Hill, (B) Apr. 10, 1853, (BD) Aug. 18, 1860, (R)
William Rose, (NG) Rev. G. K. Dunlop.
    Ernest A. W. Walmsley, (PRTS) John and Emma H.
Walmsley, (B) Apr. 10, 1853, (BD) Sep. 9, 1860,
(MG) Rev. G. K. Dunlop.
    Albert C. E. Walmsey, (PRTS) John and Emma H.
Walmsley, (B) Dec. 18, 1854, (BD) Sep. 9, 1860, (S)
John Ivey, Emilia Fabing, (MG) Rev. G. K. Dunlop.
    Annie Moreland, (PRTS) Jos. P. and Bettie E.
Moreland, (MG) Rev. G. K. Dunlop.
    James Richard Clark, (PRTS) Richard B. and
Louisa Clark, (B) Jun. 20, 1859, (BD) Oct. 7, 1860,
(R) Mr. Oliphant, (MG) Rev. G. K. Dunlop.
    James Black, (PRTS) James W. and Joanna H. N.
Black, (B) Apr. 6, 1860, (BD) Oct. 7, 1860, (S)
Alex and Martha Oliphant, (MG) Rev. G. K. Dunlop.
    Kate Elisa Arnold, (PRTS) W. E. and S. M.
Arnold, (B) Sep. 2, 1858, (BD) Sep. 9, 1860, (MG)
Rev. G. K. Dunlop.
    Julia Gloyn Smith, (PRTS) R. B. and Sallie Ann
SMith, (B) Nov. 8, 1860, (BD) Jul. 28, 1861, (S)
Col. Smith, Mrs. M. E. (?), Mrs. E. S. Smith, (NG)
Rev. G. K. Dunlop.
    Sophia Lewis Dunlop, (PRTS) G. K. and Mary
Dunlop, (B) Jun. 11, 1861, (BD) Jul. 28, 1861, (S)
Mrs. Juliet Beck.
    Ellen Lee Smith, adult, (BD) Jul. 28, 1861, (MG)
G. K. Dunlop.
    Roberta Terry, (PRTS) Joseph B. and Mary W.
Terry, (B) Dec. 5, 1851, (BD) May 9, 1862, (R) Col.
Terry, (MG) Rev. G. K. Dunlop.
    Minnie Boothman, (PRTS) Wm. and Mary Boothman,
(B) Aug. 26, 1861, (BD) May 18, 1862, (S) Elizabeth
Boothman, John Ivey, (R) M. Farrar.
    Marion Chase Little, (PRTS) Geo. W. and Mary I.
Little, (B) Sep. 3, 1860, (BD) Jun. 17, 1862, (S)
Clara E. and Carris S. Little, (R) Mr. Little's,
Jackson Co., MO.
    Charlotte, adult servant, of John Reid, (R) Mr.
Reid, (BD) Dec. 7, 1862, (MG) Rev. G. K. Dunlop.
    Liburn McIntyre Shields, (PRTS) T. W. and S. H.
Shields, (B) Aug. 12, 1862, (BD) Feb. 1, 1863, (S)
R. N. Smith, Raul Reinhard, (R) Gen. Shields, (MG)
G. K. Dunlop.
    William Shields Grigg, (PRTS) Daniel and A. McI.
Grigg, (B) Apr. 7, 1857, (BD) Feb. 1, 1863, (S) R.
N. Smith and Paul Reinhard, (MG) G. K. Dunlop.
    Nannie Hickman, (PRTS) Daniel and A. McI. Grigg,
(B) Nov. 10, 1859, (BD) Feb. 1, 1863, (S) R. N.

Smith and Paul Reinhard, (MG) Rev. G. K. Dunlop.
Charles Dennison Dunlop, (PRTS) G. K. and M. C.
Dunlop, (B) Jan. 18, 1863, (BD) Feb. 1, 1863, (S)
R. N. Smith, (MG) Rev. Thomas L. Smith.

Isabel Hackett, (PRTS) T. M. and M. A. Hackett,
(B) Nov. 10, 1862, (BD) Feb. 1, 1863, (R) Mr.
Hackett, (MG) Rev. Thomas L. Smith.

Finetta Wilson, (PRTS) R. C. and M. H. Ewing,
(B) Oct. 17, 1859, (BD) Feb. 1, 1863, (R) Col.
Ewing, (MG) Rev. Thomas L. Smith.

Robert Finis Ewing, (PRTS) R. C. and M. H.
Ewing, (B) Oct. 17, 1859, (BD) Feb. 1, 1863, (R)
Col. Ewing, (MG) Rev. Thomas L. Smith.

Susan Martin, (PRTS) ?, (BD) Mar. 4, 1866, (S)
Mr. and Mrs. McCausland, (MG) Rev. Thomas L. Smith.

Elias Spruce, (BD) Mar. 4, 1866, (MG) Rev.
Thomas L. Smith.

William Samuel Boothman, (PRTS) William and Mary
Boothman, (BD) May 6, 1866, (S) Mrs. Farrar, (MG)
Rev. Thomas L. Smith.

Herbert Essex Stell, (PRTS) Michael A. and
Fannie B. Steel, (B) May 12, 1862, (BD) Dec. 6,
1866, (MG) Rev. Thomas L. Smith.

Mary Effie Steel, (PRTS) Michael A. and Fannie
B. Steel, (B) Aug. 25, 1863, (BD) Dec. 6, 1866,
(MG) Rev. Thomas L. Smith.

Cora Bell Steel, (PRTS) Michael A. and Fannie B.
Steel, (B) Jul. 16, 1863, (BD) Dec. 6, 1866, (S)
Miss Fannie Wentworth, (MG) Rev. Thomas L. Smith.

Edward Arnold Wilson, (PRTS) Hugh T. and Mary
Wilson, (B) Jun. 16, 1866, (BD) Dec. 30, 1866, (MG)
Rev. Thomas L. Smith, (S) Susan McCausland.

Elizabeth Martin, (PRTS) Charles and Jennie
Martin, (B) Oct. 16, 1866, (BD) Dec. 30, 1866, (MG)
Rev. Thomas L. Smith, (S) Susan McCausland.

Elizabeth Marion Smallwood, (PRTS) Mr. & Mrs.
Smallwood, (B) Oct. 25, 1866, (BD) Dec. 30, 1866,
(S) Paul Reinhard, (MG) Rev. Thomas L. Smith.

Stewart Higgins, (PRTS) Dr. amd Mrs. Mary
Higgins, (BD) Apr., 1867, (S) Rev. T. L. Smith, Mr.
I. Gooden, Miss M. Stewart, (MG) Rev. Thomas L.
Smith.

Irving Higgins, (PRTS) Dr. and Mrs. Mary Higgns,
(BD) Apr., 1867, (S) Rev. T. L. Smith, Mr. I.
Gooden, Miss M. Stewart, (MG) Rev. Thomas L. Smith.

Miss Virginia Austin, adult, (BD) Mar. 3, 1867,
(MG) Rev. Thomas L. Smith.

Mr. W. M. Carpenter, adult, (S) Mrs. McCasuland,
(BD) Mar. 3, 1867, (MG) Rev. Thomas L. Smith.

Thomas Walter Hackett, (PRTS) Thomas M. and Mary A. Hackett, (B) Apr. 5, 1867, (BD) Jun. 20, 1867, (MG) Rev. Thomas L. Smith.

William Russell Huston, (PRTS) Joseph and Susannah Huston, (B) Jun. 1, 1866, (BD) Jun. 20, 1867, (S) Thomas Hackett, (MG) Thomas L. Smith.

Alice Page Smith, (PRTS) R. B. and Sallie R. Smith, (B) Apr. 29, 1866, (BD) Aug. 13, 1867, (MG) Rev. John W. Dunn.

William Webb, (PRTS) Wm. Webb and Ada Lamborn, (B) Jul. 24, 1862, (BD) Aug. 15, 1867, (S) Frances Weaver, (MG) Rev. John W. Dunn.

Francis Morris Webb, (PRTS) Wm. Webb and Ada Lamborn, (B) Dec. 8, 1864, (BD) Aug. 15, 1867, (S) Francis Weaver, (MG) John W. Dunn.

John Henry Webb, (PRTS) Wm. Webb and Ada Lamborn, (B) Jul. 5, 1867, (BD) Aug. 15, 1867, (MG) John W. Dunn.

Joseph Lyle Thomas, adult, (BD) Aug. 15, 1867.

Edward Byron Stoughton, (PRTS) Seth and Annie N. Stoughton, (B) Apr. 17, 1867, (BD) May 17, 1868, (S) R. N. Smith, Joseph L. Thomas, (MG) Rev. John W. Dunn.

Edward Lee Dunn, (PRTS) Rev. John W. and Ann M. Dunn, (B) Jul. 8, 1868, (BD) Aug. 23, 1868, (S) Paul Reinhard, Mrs. Susan McCaus- land, (MG) John W. Dunn.

Hattie May Hixon, (PRTS) Wm. and Phebe Hixon, (B) Dec. 15, 1861, (BD) Mar. 28, 1869, (S) Jas. Gooden, Mrs. Caroline Buckingham, (MG) John W. Dunn.

Miss Ella Limrick, (BD) Dec. 6, 1869, (W) J. L. Thomas, (MG) Rev. John W. Dunn.

Miss Birdie Mahaffey, (BD) Mar. 21, 1869, (W) Mrs. Susan McCausland, (MG) John W. Dunn.

Margaret Jane Berge, (PRTS) Jacob and Elizabeth Berge, (B) May 10, 186?, (BD) May 22, 1869, (S) Mrs. Caroline Buckingham, Miss Lelia Arnold, (MG) John W. Dunn.

George Thomas, (PRTS) Jacob and Elizabeth Berge, (B) Feb. 11, 1863, (BD) May 22, 1869, (S) Mrs. Caroline Buckingham, Miss Lelia Arnold, (MG) John W. Dunn.

William Augustus Howard, (PRTS) Alex I. and Nellie B. Howard, (B) Nov. 24, 1868, (BD) Jul. 25, 1869, (S) Mrs. A. M. Dunn, (NG) Rev. John W. Dunn.

Conn Ready Evans Shaw, (PRTS) Thomas Shaw and Mary Eliza Belt, (B) May 25, 1868, (BD) Dec. 17, 1869, (S) Miss M. P. Howard, (MG) Rev. John W.

Dunn.

William Talbot Shaw, (PRTS) Thomas Shaw and Mary Eliza Belt, (B) Sep. 23, 1869, (BD) Dec. 17, 1869, (S) Miss M. P. Howard, (MG) Rev. John W. Dunn.

Mary Octavia Lesueur, (PRTS) Alex A. and Florence Lesueur, (B) Aug. 29, 1869, (BD) Dec. 24, 1869, (S) Elizabeth M. and Annie B. Beck, Frank S. Trigg, (MG) Rev. John W. Trigg.

David Otey Heathman, (PRTS) John N. and Nancy E. Heathman, (B) May 20, 1869, (BD) Apr. 15, 1870, (MG) J. W. Dunn.

Austin Gustavus Standish, (PRTS) Thomas and Adelia Standish, (B) Oct. 13, 1869, (BD) Apr. 15, 1870, (S) Mr. Limrick, Wm. G. Pigot, (MG) Rev. J. W. Dunn.

Mary Clarkson Wilson, (PRTS) Hugh T. and Mary G. Wilson, (B) Dec. 2, 1869, (BD) Jul. 3, 1870, (S) John E. Arnold, Mrs. Virginia K. Wright, (MG) Rev. J. W. Dunn.

Kate Ewing Smith, (PRTS) Rev. T. L. and Mrs. Smith, (B) Apr. 1, 1870, (BD) Aug. 4, 1870, (MG) Rev. T. L. Smith, Baptized in sickness.

Lizzie Hoyt Purnell, (PRTS) Isaac B. and Mary A. Purnell, (B) Jan. 8, 1870, (BD) Aug. 17, 1870, (MG) Rev. J. W. Dunn.

Florence Lesuer Dunn, (PRTS) J. W. and A. M. Dunn, (B) Aug. 30, 1870, (BD) Nov. 24, 1870, (S) W. R. Boggs, Mrs. Boggs, Mrs. Mary C. Wilson, (MG) Rev. J. W. Dunn.

Joseph Bent Terry, adult, (BD) May 2, 871, (MG) Rev. J. W. Dunn.

Alexander Oliphant, (PRTS) Ralph and Catherine Oliphant, (B) Dec. 7, 1869, (BD) May 3, 1871, (S) Alexander and Martha Oliphant, Grandparents, living near Richmond, Ray Co., MO., (MG) Rev. J. W. Dunn.

Elizabeth Boothman, (PRTS) Wm. and Mary Boothman, (B) Oct. 17, 1869, (BD) May 7, 1871, (S) Miss Elizabeth Boothman, (MG) Rev. J. W. Dunn.

John Walton Talbot, (PRTS) Levi and Mary E. Talbot, (B) Dec. 9, 1861, (BD) May 15, 1871, (S) J. W. and A. M. Dunn, Dover, MO., (MG) Rev. J. W. Dunn.

Nannie Stonewall, (B) Aug. 28, 1865, (BD) May 15, 1871, (MG) Rev. J. W. Dunn.

John Thomas Spruce, (PRTS) Samuel and Emma Spruce, (B) Aug. 20, 1871, (BD) Sep. 24, 1871, (S) Thomas Walton and Elizabeth Walton, (MG) Rev. J. W. Dunn.

Glin Limerick Standish, (PRTS) Thomas and Adelia

Standish, (B) May 15, 1871, (BD) Oct. 8, 1871, (S) Alexander A. Lesueur, Jos. O. Lesueur, Miss Aurelia A. Miller, (MG) Rev. J. W. Dunn.

Eliza Brown Reams, (PRTS) Bartlett and Rebecca Reams, (B) Sep. 20, 1871, (BD) Oct. 8, 1871, (MG) Rev. J. W. Dunn, Baptized in sickness,

Ann Preston Towers Mills, (PRTS) Nathaniel P. and Ann T. Mills, (B) Dec. 26, 1870, (BD) Oct. 24, 1871, (S) Henry Pillkington, Mrs. Emily Mills, Miss Jennie Pillkington, (MG) Rev. J. W. Dunn.

William Reed Trotter, (PRTS) Richard and Sarah Trotter, (B) Sep. 19, 1867, (BD) Apr. 11, 1873, (S) Wilson and Mrs. A. M. Dunn, (MG) Rev. John W. Dunn.

Miss Lutie Fleurnoy Moreland, (W) Mrs. Kate Reed, (BD) Apr. 13, 1873, (MG) Rev. J. W. Dunn.

Joseph Shewalter, (BD) Apr. 27, 1873, (MG) Rev. J. W. Dunn.

Miss Lillian Wiley, (S) Jos. L. and Elizabeth Thomas, (BD) May 4, 1873, (MG) Rev. J. W. Dunn.

---- (?), (PRTS) Wm. and Phoebe Hixon, (BD) Oct. 13, 1872, (MG) Rev. J. W. Dunn.

Ellen Elizabeth Standish, (PRTS) Thomas and Adelia Standish, (B) Mar. 8, 1873, (BD) Sep. 21, 1873, (S) Mrs. Juliet Beck, Mrs. Mary Terry, (MG) Rev. J. W. Dunn.

Emma Tillard Hays, (PRTS) Richard E. and Elizabeth B. Hays, (B) Apr. 4, 1871, (BD) Nov. 3, 1871, (S) Abraham Hays, Miss Mary Elizabeth Hays, Miss Sarah Smith, (MG) Rev. J. W. Dunn.

Florence Amelia Boothman, (PRTS) Wm. and Mary Boothman, (B) Aug. 19, 1871, (BD) Dec. 10, 1871, (S) Chas. R. and Mary W. Kriehn, (MG) Rev. J. W. Dunn.

Juliet Preston Thomas, (PRTS) Joseph L. and Elizabeth H. Thomas, (B) Aug. 19, 1871, (BD) Dec. 28, 1871, (MG) Rev. J. W. Dunn.

Miss Alice Larrick, (W) Miss Ball, (BD) Feb. 16, 1872, (MG) Rev. J. W. Dunn.

Charles William Taubman, (PRTS) Henry and Mary Elizabeth Taubman, (B) Jul. 15, 1861, (BD) Mar. 29, 1872, (S) Thomas Taubman, (MG) Rev. Olcutt Bulkly, Saline Co., MO.

Annie May Taubman, (PRTS) Henry and Mary Elizabeth Taubman, (B) Mar. 27, 1863, (BD) Mar. 29, 1872, (S) Thomas Taubman, (MG) Rev. Olcutt Bulkly, Saline Co., MO.

Charlotte Jane Taubman, (PRTS) Henry and Mary Elizabeth Taubman, (B) Dec. 26, 1864, (BD) Mar. 29, 1872, (S) Thomas Taubman, (MG) Rev. Olcutt Bulkly,

Saline Co., MO.

John Franklin Taubman, (PRTS) Henry and Mary Elizabeth Taubman, (B) Nov. 19, 1866, (BD) Mar. 29, 1872, (S) Thomas Taubman, (MG) Rev. Olcutt Bulkly, Saline Co., MO.

Albert Edwin Taubman, (PRTS) Henry and Mary Elizabeth Taubman, (B) Feb. 18, 1869, (BD) Mar. 29, 1872, (S) Thomas Taubman, (MG) Rev. Olcutt Bulkly, Saline Co., MO.

Tessa Mildred Taubman, (PRTS) Henry and Mary Elizabeth Taubman, (B) Nov. 3, 1859, (BD) Mar. 29, 1872, (S) Thomas Taubman, (MG) Rev. Olcutt Bulkly, Saline Co., MO.

Lulu Becount Kerdolff, (PRTS) Wm. F. and Martha E. Kerdolff, (BD) Aug. 14, 1872, (S) Sarah Smith, (MG) Rev. J. W. Dunn.

Edward Collins Kerdolff, (PRTS) Wm. F. and Martha E. Kerdolff, (B) Sep. 20, 1859, (BD) Aug. 14, 1872, (S) Sarah Smith, (MG) Rev. J. W. Dunn.

Mattie Louise Kerdolff, (PRTS) Wm. F. and Martha E. Kerdolff, (B) Mar. 17, 1862, (BD) Aug. 14, 1872, (S) Sarah Smith, (MG) Rev. J. W. Dunn.

John Thompson Heathman, (PRTS) John and Nancy E. Heathman, (B) Jul. 15, 1871, (BD) Apr. 16, 1872, (MG) Rev. J. W. Dunn.

Mrs. Adelia Francis Flint, (W) Mrs. Buckingham, (BD) Apr. 28, 1872, (MG) Rev. J. W. Dunn.

Mrs. Ella Frances Wood, (W) Miss Elizabeth Arnold, (BD) Apr. 30, 1872, (MG) Rev. J. W. Dunn.

Annie Lilburn Lesueur, (PRTS) Alexander A. and Florence E. Lesueur, (B) Dec. 2, 1871, (S) Jos. O. and Annie Lesueur, Miss Mary P. Howard, (BD) May 5, 1872, (MG) Rev. J. W. Dunn.

George Alexander, (PRTS) Gustavus and Lucy Alexander, (B) Mar. 12, 1872, (S) Geo. and Mary S. Wilson, (R) Geo. Wilson, (BD) Aug. 4, 1872, (MG) Rev. J. W. Dunn.

Susan Oliphant, (PRTS) Ralph and Catherine Oliphant, (B) Nov. 4, 1871, (S) Alexander and Mary Oliphant, granparents, (BD) Jul. 18, 1872, (MG) Rev. J. W. Dunn.

Helen Maitland, (PRTS) Alexander and Mary Maitland, (B) ??? 23, 1871, (S) Alexander and Martha Oliphant, (MG) Rev. J. W. Dunn.

Mary Bell Lane, (PRTS) Levin A. and Sophia H. Lane, (B) Oct. 14, 1871, (BD) Aug. 10, 1872, (MG) Rev. J. W. Dunn.

Charles Alden Morris, (PRTS) Henry V. and Emma J. Morris, (B) Oct. 14, 1871, (BD) Aug. 10, 1872,

(S) Mr. and Mrs. Kerdolff, George Wilson, (MG) Rev. J. W. Dunn.

Joseph Samuel Walton, (PRTS) Thomas and Elizabeth Walton, (B) Jul. 24, 1872, (BD) Sep. 4, 1872, (MG) Rev. J. W. Dunn.

John Webster Dunn, (PRTS) Rev. John W. and A. M. Dunn, (B) Dec. 5, 1872, (BD) Apr. 11, 1873, (S) Geo. Wilson, A. A. Lesueur, Mrs. Mary Wilson.

Sue Estill Lesueur, (PRTS) Jos. O. and Annie Lesueur, (B) Jan. 27, 1873, (BD) Sep. 21, 1873, (S) A. A. and Florence Lesueur, Mrs. Jennie Martin, (MG) Rev. J. W. Dunn.

Mrs. Elizabeth Scott, (BD) Dec. 29, 1873, (MG) Rev. J. W. Dunn.

Henry Carter, (PRTS) Andrew and Mrs. Carter, (B) Nov. 22, 1867, (BD) Mar. 15, 1874, (MG) Rev. J. W. Dunn.

John Carter, (PRTS) Andrew and Mrs. Carter, (B) Nov. 29, 1869, (BD) Mar. 15, 1874, (MG) Rev. J. W. Dunn.

Robert Carter, (PRTS) Andrew and Mrs. Carter, (B) Jan. 6, 1872, (BD) Mar. 15, 1874, (MG) Rev. J. W. Dunn.

James McClelland, (PRTS) M. V. L. and Sarah McClelland, (B) Jul. 15, 1872, (BD) Mar. 31, 1874, (MG) Rev. J. W. Dunn.

Charles Oscar Kidweel, (PRTS) Chas. and Carrie Kidwell, (B) Jan. 10, 1874, (BD) Apr. 5, 1874, (S) Mary Kreihn, Albert Kidwell, (MG) Rev. J. W. Dunn.

Margaret Hill Lane, (PRTS) Levin A. and Sophia H. Lane, (B) Jul. 25, 1873, (B) Jul. 25, 1873, (BD) Apr. 5, 1874, (S) A. M. and J. W. Dunn, Mrs. Buckingham, (MG) Rev. J. W. Dunn.

Armand Alexander Lesueur, (PRTS) A. A. and Florence E. Lesueur, (B) Jan. 31, 1874, (BD) May 24, 1874, (S) Wm. Trigg, Sr., J. V. and Mrs. Annie Lesueur, (MG) Rev. J. W. Dunn.

Hannah Augusta Trotter, (PRTS) Richard and Sarah Trotter, (B) Aug. 9, 1874, (BD) Aug. 28, 1874, (MG) Rev. J. W. Dunn.

Edward Kemper Drane, (PRT) Kemper and Mary Drane, (B) May 24, 1874, (BD) Sep. 5, 1874, (S) C. F. Smith, Miss Annie D. Beck, (MG) Rev. J. W. Dunn.

Lavina Rodney Thomas, (PRTS) Jos. L. and Elizabeth M. Thomas, (B) Feb. 16, 1874, (BD) Sep. 29, 1874, (S) Wm. and Miss Annie D. Beck, Miss Lavina Rodney, (NG) Rev. J. W. Dunn.

Fannie Rebecca Herndon, (PRTS) Thomas J. and Mary McGrew Herndon, (B) Apr. 8, 1874, (BD) Nov. 5,

1874, (S) Jos. O. and Mrs. Annie Lesueur, Mrs. Mary E. Wilson.

Lucien Dumaine Lesueur, (PRTS) Jos. O. and Annie Lesueur, (B) Sep. 28, 1874, (BD) Mar. 28, 1875, (S) A. A. and Mrs. Florence Lesueur, (MG) Rev. J. W. Dunn.

Nina Blanch McLean, (PRTS) Dr. George and Nancy McLean, (B) Apr. 1, 1875, (BD) May 16, 1875, (MG) Rev. J. W. Dunn.

Fanny May Earl, (PRTS) Samuel S. and Anna Earl, (B) Feb., 1868, (BD) May 16, 1875, (S) Mrs. Caroline Buckingham, (MG) Rev. J. W. Dunn.

Jacob Edward Earl, (PRTS) Samuel S. and Anna Earl, (B) Nov. 20, 1870, (BD) May 16, 1875, (S) Mrs. Caroline Buckingham, (MG) Rev. J. W. Dunn.

Henry Turner Earl, (PRTS) Samuel S. and Anna Earl, (B) Feb. 11, 1872, (BD) May 16, 1875, (S) Mrs. Carolibe Buckingham, (MG) Rev. J. W. Dunn.

Maggie Alice Kerdolff, (PRTS) Wm. F. and Martha E. Kerdolff, (B) Aug. 26, 1874, (BD) Jun. 9, 1875, (S) Mrs. Mary Alldtadt, Mrs. Kate Davis, (MG) Rev. J. W. Dunn.

Miss Martha Ann Phelps, adult, (BD) Jun. 22, 1875, (MG) Rev. J. W. Dunn.

George Ing Smith, (PRTS) George K. Smith, (B) Apr. 18, 1861, (BD) Nov. 6, 1875, (MG) Rev. J. W. Dunn.

Reginald Heber Dunn, (PRTS) Rev. J. W. and A. M. Dunn, (B) Sep. 11, 1875, (BD) Dec. 28, 1875, (S) C. T. Wood, Miss Ella Wood, Thos. Standish, (MG) Rev. J. W. Dunn.

Virginia Wilson, (PRTS) Hugh T. and Mary C. Wilson, (B) Sep. 26, 1875, (BD) Dec. 28, 1875, (S) Wm. G. and Mrs. Susan M. McCausland, (MG) Rev. J. W. Dunn.

Lillian Maud Kidwell, (PRTS) Chas. H. and Carrie Kidwell, (B) Nov. 16, 1875, (BD) Feb. 13, 1876, (S) Alberth Bothman, Mrs. Mary Farrar, (MG) Rev. J. W. Dunn.

William Thomas Wood, (PRTS) Chalmers T. and Ella F. Wood, (B) Aug. 1, 1868, (BD) Dec. 28, 1875, (S) George Wilson, (MG) Rev. J. W. Dunn.

Chalmers Pemberton Wood, (PRTS) Chalmers T. and Ella F. Wood, (B) Nov. 23, ????, (BD) Dec. 28m 1875, (MG) Rev. J. W. Dunn.

Conn Mildred Belt, (PRTS) Thos. S. and Mary Eliza Belt, (B) Oct. 13, 1873, (BD) May 12, 1876, (S) Lizzie W. Dunn, Wm. Howard, (MG) Rev. J. W. Dunn.

William Morris Belt, (PRTS) Thos. S. and Mary Eliza Beltm (B) Dec. 15, 1875, (BD) May 12, 1876, (S) Lizzie W. Dunn, Wm. Howard, (MG) Rev. J. W. Dunn.

Carrie Eliza Hines, (PRTS) Jonah and Mrs. Hines, (BD) May 14, 1876, (MG) Rev. J. W. Dunn.

Anna Louisa Hines, (PRTS) Jonah and Mrs. Hines, (B) Jun. 14, 1869, (BD) May 14, 1876, (MG) Rev. J. W. Dunn.

George Sparks, colored, adult, (BD) Jul. 25, 1876, (MG) Rev. J. W. Dunn.

Cornelia Bradell Purnell, (PRTS) Isaac B. and Mary A. Purnell, (B) Jul. 16, 1876, (BD) Nov. 11, 1876, (MG) Rev. J. W. Dunn.

Miss Nina Limrick, (BD) Mar. 11, 1877, (MG) Rev. J. W. Dunn.

Mrs. Rebecca Limrick, (BD) Mar. 11, 1877, (MG) Rev. J. W. Dunn.

Anna Winsor Chew, (PRTS) Francis T, and Mary W. Chew, (B) Feb. 19, 1876, (BD) Apr. 29, 1877, (S) J. O. and A. Lesueur, (MG) J. W. Dunn.

William Trigg Lesueur, (PRTS) Jos. O. and Annie Lesueur, (B) Nov. 4, 1876, (BD) Apr. 29, 1877, (S) Francis Chew, (MG) Rev. J. W. Dunn.

Richard Shewalter Standish, (PRTS) Thos. and Adelia Standish, (B) Feb. 8, 1877, (BD) Jun. 3, 1877, (S) Rufner Smith, Mrs. Geo. K. Smith, (MG) Rev. J. W. Dunn.

Martha Prettie Powell, (PRTS) John and Mary Ann Powell, (B) Nov. 30, 1876, (BD) Jul. 22, 1877, (S) Miss Matilda Powell, (MG) J. W. Dunn.

Kate May Farrow, (PRTS) Geo. and Mary Ann Farrow, (B) Apr. 27, 1877, (BD) Aug. 26, 1877, (S) Wm. and Mary Boothman, (MG) Rev. J. W. Dunn.

Samuel Harrison Reams, (PRTS) Bartlett and Rebecca Reams, (B) Aug. 1, 1868, (BD) Aug. 26, 1877, (S) Mrs. Lizzie Wilds, Albert Boothman, (MG) Rev. J. W. Dunn.

Rosa Ann Harrison, (PRTS) Bartlett and Rebecca Reams, (B) Dec. 25, 1870, (BD) Aug. 26, 1877, (S) Mrs. Lizzie Wilds, Albert Boothman, (MG) Rev. J. W. Dunn.

William Albert Reams, (PRTS) Bartlett and Rebecca Reams, (B) Jun. 19, 1873, (BD) Aug. 26, 1877, (S) Mrs. Lizzie Wilds, Albert Boothman, (MG) Rev. J. W. Dunn.

Edward Charles Reams, (PRTS) Bartlett and Rebecca Reams, (B) Feb. 28, 1875, (BD) Aug. 26, 1877, (S) Mrs. Lizzie Wilds, Albert Boothman, (MG)

Rev. J. W. Dunn.

Farrar Franklin, (BD) Mar. 22, 1878, (MG) Rev. J. W. Dunn.

Agnes Wilson, (PRTS) Hugh T. and Mary C. Wilson, (B) Apr. 9, 1877, (BD) Jun. 23, 1877, (S) Mrs. S. S. A. McCausland, (MG) Rev. J. W. Dunn.

Florence Trigg Lesueur, (PRTS) A. A. and Florence Lesueur, (B) Apr. 14, 1877, (BD) Jun. 24, 1878, (S) Mrs. Annie Lesueur, (MG) Rev. J. W. Dunn.

Allen Trigg Howard, (PRTS) Wm. Henry and Amanda Howard, (B) Nov. 14, 1877, (BD) Jul. 4, 1878, (S) Rev. J. W. Dunn, A. M. Dunn, (MG) Rev. J. W. Dunn.

Thomas Peter Akers, (PRTS) Mrs. Kate Akers, (B) Jul. 20, 1876, (BD) Aug. 11, 1878, (MG) Rev. J. W. Dunn.

Caroline May Wild, (PRTS) John and Elizabeth Wild, (B) Apr. 5, 1873, (BD) Sep. 2, 1878, (S) Chas. and Caroline Kidwell, (MG) Rev. J. W. Dunn.

Emily Rebecca Wild, (PRTS) John and Elizabeth Wild, (B) Jan. 31, 1875, (BD) Sep. 2, 1878, (S) Chas. and Caroline Kidwell, (MG) Rev. J. W. Dunn.

Miss Fannie Porter Bayliss, (BD) Dec. 1, 1878, (MG) Rev. J. W. Dunn.

John Reid Moreland, (BD) Dec. 1, 1878, (MG) Rev. J. W. Dunn.

George Farrar Kidwell, (PRTS) Chas. Carrie Kidwell, (B) Feb. 22, 1878, (BD) Jan. 5, 1879, (S) Geo. and Mary A. Farrar, (MG) Rev. J. W. Dunn.

Anna Beck Thomas, (PRTS) Jos. and Elizabeth M. Thomas, (B) Feb. 18, 1878, (BD) Mar. 28, 1879, (S) Mr. and Mrs. Mansfield, Mrs. Reid, (MG) Rev. J. W. Dunn.

Reid Moreland Hicklin, (PRTS) Robert A. and Anna Hicklin, (B) Oct. 4, 1878, (BD) Jul. 8, 1879, (MG) Rev. J. W. Moreland.

Louisa Farrar, (PRTS) George and Mary Farrar, (B) Oct. 27, 1879, (BD) Jan. 4, 1880, (S) Charles and Carrie Kidwell, (MG) Rev. J. W. Dunn.

Lizzie Hickman Lesueur, (PRTS) A. A. and Florence Lesueur, (B) Jul. 22, 1879, (BD) Mar. 22, 1880, (S) Mrs. Susan Trigg, Mrs. Annie L. and A. A. Lesueur, (MG) Rev. A. T. Sharpe.

Adelia Dritt Standish, (PRTS) Thos. and Adelia Standish, (B) Jan. 26, 1879, (BD) Mar. 25, 1880, (S) Mrs. Virginia Ferguson, Mrs. Mary Kowusler, John Langford Standish, (MG) Rev. A. T. Sharpe.

Emmet Morris, (PRTS) Wirt and Mary L. Morris, (B) Oct. 6, 1876, (BD) Mar. 25, 1880, (S) Capt. A. A. Lesueurm Mrs. Reid, (MG) Rev. A. T. Sharpe.

Emma Bradley Moreland, (PRTS) Jos. and Bettie Moreland, (BD) Mar. 25, 1880, (MG) Rev. A. T. Sharpe.

Sarah Bay McClelland, (PRTS) M. V. L. and Sarah McClelland, (B) Aug. 12, 1874, (S) Mary McClelland, (MG) Rev. A. T. Sharpe.

Jessie Maude Edelen, (PRTS) James and M. J. Edelen, (B) Oct. 17, 1879, (BD) Jun. 21, 1880, (S) Mary McClelland, (MG) Rev. A. T. Sharpe.

Helen Blackhurst, (PRTS) John and Helen Blackhurst, (BD) Aug. 10, 1880, (W) Mrs. Elizabeth Thomas and Mrs. Ella Wentworth, (MG) Rev. A. T. Sharpe.

Nina Edna Kidwell, (PRTS) Charles N. and Carrie Kidwell, (B) Jul. 19, 1880, (BD) Aug. 15, 1880, (S) John N. and E. L. Kidwell by proxy, Bartlett and Rebecca Reams, (MG) Rev. A. T. Sharpe.

Nellie Anna Tebbs, (PRTS) Thomas and Emma T. Tebbs, (B) Jun. 6, 1880, (S) Mrs. Mary Kriehn, (MG) Rev. A. T. Sharpe.

Mary Elizabeth Tebbs, (PRTS) Thomas and Emma T. Tebbs (B) Jun. 6, 1880, (BD) Aug. 22, 1880, (S) Mrs. Mary Kreihn, (MG) Rev. A. T. Sharpe.

Carry Nason Sharpe, (PRTS) Chas. N. and Sophie Sharp, (B) Aug., 1880, (BD) Oct. 3, 1880, (S) Sophie N. Barre, A. T. Sharpe, (MG) Rev. A. T. Sharpe.

Elizabeth Sybil Thomas, (PRTS) Jos. L. and Elizabeth M. Thomas, (BD) Nov. 14, 1880, (S) Mrs. Anna D. Mansfield, Mrs. Ella Wentworth, (MG) Rev. A. T. Sharpe.

Saline County, Missouri, Zoar Baptist Church, Napton, MO, Abstract of W.P.A. Church Survey, Center for Baptist Historical Studies, Wm. Jewell College, Liberty, MO.

Per Mary Marguerite Gault, August 9, 1939:

Church was organized in 1827 with nine charter members. The church burned in 1867 along with the church records.

Rev. Payton Nowlin was the first pastor serving the congregation from 1827 - 1835. He was born in Virginia, May 4, 1764. At age 21 he went to Georgia where he married Miss Lucy Townsend in 1792. He came to Missouri in 1818 and settled near Arrow Rock. He died April 1, 1837. He weighed 225 pounds and was 5 ft., 10 in. tall.

Rev. Thomas Fristoe served 1835 - 1847. He died Mar. 2, 1872, age 76.

Rev. David Anderson was the third pastor. He was born in Kentucky in 1806 and died in Barry, MO, July 5, 1870.

Other pastors serving the church were Thornton Rucker, William Gentry, J. D. Murphy, Thomas Hudson, J. C. Hammar, Wm. Cleveland, J. L. Tichenor, C. L. McDaniel, I. B. Dotson, J. S. Nordyke, G. W. Stroud, J. B. Stark, D. C. Bolton, Orlo Jeffrey, L. M. White.

Rev. J. L. Tiechnor was born in Kentucy in 1830. He was baptized at age 16 and became licensed to preach in 1858. He lived with Rev. J. S. Coleman for two years. He died in 1897, age 67.

Rev. L. M. White resigned in 1908 and was succeeded by Rev. P. P. Hummell, M. E. Broadus, N. E. McCoy, Edwin Nowell, L. T. Osborne, J. G. Barker, Marshall Renno.

Walter J. Clark was ordained at Zoar Baptist Church. He attended Wm. Jewell College in 1935 and Southwest Baptist College, Bolivar in 1936-1939.

Some of the oldest graves at the church cemetery are Mollie Eastham, d. Jan. 15, 1875; Rebecca Kennedy, wife of S. H. Kennedy, d. Mar. 2, 1876; Margie Jones, wife of B. H. L. Jones, d. Dec. 2, 1877.

Bethel United Baptist Association, Farmington, St. Francis County, Missouri, "St. Louis Free Press," Oct. 24, 1833.

Name	Congregation
Jesse Bound	New Hope Church
John Blanton	New Hope Church
John Carter	New Hope Church
William Champion	Franklin Association
James Cundiff	Franklin Association
Stephen Colyer	Wolf Creek Church
Thomas P. Green	Cape Girardeau County
Elder James Halbert	Pendleton Church
Joel Hammer	Hepzibah Church
Noe Hunt	Hepzibah Church
Wingate Jackson	Hepzibah Church
Joshua Kimworthy	Pendleton Church
Elijah O'Banion	Providence Church
William Polk	In Attendance
James Ritter	Pendleton Church
John Strickland	Bethany Church
Samuel Vance	Wolf Creek

Macedonia Methodist Church, Macedonia, Ripley County, Missouri.
Classbook, May 1, 1881

Name	Comments
Permelia J. Thompson	Widow
William Thompson	Married
Letty Thompson	Married
Thomas Thompson	Married
Mary J. Thompson	Married
Martha R. McKinney	Married
Thomas McKinney	Married
Martha C. McKinney	Married
Amy Jordan	Widow, d. Apr. 25, 1883
George J. Jordan	Married
Martha J. Jordan	Married
Frank Walker	Married, Steward 1880-81
Emil Lassin (Lassen)	Married
Rebecca Lassin (Lassen)	Married
Mary J. Payne	Married
John Myers	Married, Church Leader 1880-81
Julia Myers	Married
Kitty A. Reeves	Married
Mary A. McKagh	Married
William Steel	Married, Joined theCampbellites
E. Jane Bowshear	Married, d. Feb. 15, 1882
Margaret L. McKinney	Married
Sarah Brooks	Single
Oma A. Thompson	Single
Amanda Patterson	Married, d. Nov. 17, 1881
George McKinney	Widow
Mary F. Grant	Married
Louisa Steel	Married
William R. McKinney	Married
Eliza J. Brooks	Single
John C. Reeves	Married
Susie E. Thompson	Single
Thos. E. McKinney	Married, d. Sep. 15, 1882
Martha McKinney	Married
William Steel	Single
Mary E. Myers	Single
Emma J. Lassen	Single
Frances E. Hopkins	Single

133

Name	Comments
Rosa Pattieson	Single
Sarah A. Mills	Married
Margaret M. Hooper	Single, Gone to the Baptists
Rodney Besheer	Married. Reports are against him for drunkness and dancing.
Missouri C. McKinney	Single
Tilmon Mills	---
Hugh S. Jordan	Married
Isaac A. Payne	Married
Martha C. Thompson	Single
Joseph A. Jordan	Single
Sol W. Brooks	Single
Thos. A. McKinney	Married

Renewed 1883

Name	Comments
Permelia J. Thompson	Widow
Wm. Thompson	Married
Letty Thompson	Married
Thos. Thompson	Married
Mary J. Thompson	Married
Martha R. McKinney	Married
Martha C. McKinney	Married
Emil Lassen	Married
Rebecca J. Lassen	Married
Mary J. Payne	Married
Kitty A. Reeves	Married
Mary A. McKugh	Married
George J. Jordan	Married
Mary J. Jordan	Married
John Myers	Married
Julia Myers	Married
Margaret L. McKinney	Married
Sarah Smeltser	Married
Chas. A. McDowell	Married
George McKinney	Married
Mary F. Grant	Married
Wm. R. McKinney	Married
Eliza J. Brooks	Single
John C. Reeves	Married
Susie E. Brooks	Married
Martha McKinney	Married
Wm. Steel	Single
Amy J. Lassen	Single
Mary E. Lassen	Married
Mo. C. McKinney	Single
Hugh S. Jordan	Married
Isaac A. Payne	Married

134

Name	Comments
Martha C. Thompson	Single
Joseph A. Jordan	Single
Sol W. Brooks	Married
Thomas A. McKinney	Married
Alfred S. Lassen	Married
Frank Walker	Married
Sarah J. Walker	Married
Nathan Mattox	Married
L. J. Mattox	Married

Renewed August, 1884

Name	Comments
Permelia J. Thompson	Widow
William Thompson	Married
Letty Thompson	Married
Thomas Thompson	Married
Mary J. Thompson	Married
Thomas McKinney	Married
Martha C. McKinney	Married
Martha R. McKinney	Married
Emil Lassen	Married
Rebecca J. Lassen	Married
Isaac A. Payne	Married
Mary J. Payne	Married
John R. Reeves	Married
Kitty A. Reeves	Married
Mary A. McKugh	Married
George J. Jordan	Married
Martha J. Jordan	Married
John Myers	Married
Julia Myers	Married
Margaret L. Hassel	Married
Sarah Smeltser	Married
Oma A. McDowell	Married
George McKinney	Married
Mary F. Grant	Married
Wm. R. McKinney	Married
Elisa J. Brooks	Single
Sol W. Brooks	Married
Susie E. Brooks	Married
Martha McKinney	Married
William Steel	Single
Emma J. Lassen	Single
Alfred S. Lassen	Married
Mary E. Lassen	Married
Mo. C. McKinney	Single
Hugh S. Jordan	Married
Martha C. Thompson	Single
Joseph A. Jordan	Single

Name	Comments
Thomas A. McKinney	Married
Frank Walker	Married
Sarah J. Walker	Married
Nathan Maddox	Married
L. J. Maddox	Married
Estella Myers	Single
Schuyler H. Myers	Single
Ora A. Lassen	---
Harrison Davis	Transferred from Flat Creek
Burney Davis	Transferred from Flat Creek
Mary L. Myrick	---

Renewed July, 1885

Name	Comments
Peremlia J. Thompson	Widow
William Thompson	Married
Letty Thompson	Married
Thomas Thompson	Married
Mary J. Thompson	Married
Thomas McKinney	Married
Martha C. McKinney	Married
Martha R. McKinney	Married
Emil Lassen	Married
Rebecca Jane Lassen	Married
Isaac A. Payne	Married
Mary J. Payne	Married
John R. Reeves	Married
Kitty A. Reeves	Married
Mary A. McKague	Married
George J. Jordan	Married
Martha J. Jordan	Married
John Myers	Married
Julia Myers	Married
Margarite L. Hassel	Married
Sarah Smelser	Married
Oma A. McDowell	Married
George McKinney	Married
William R. McKinney	Married
Eliza J. Brooks	Single
Sol W. Brooks	Married
Susan E. Brooks	Married
Martha McKinney	Married
William Steel	Single
Amy J. Lassen	Single
Alfred S. Lassen	Married

Name	Comments
Mary E. Lassen	Married
Martha C. Thompson	Single
Joseph A. Jordan	Single
Nathan Maddox	Married
L. J. Maddox	Married
Ora A. Lassen	Single
Harrison Davis	Married
Burney Davis	Married
Mary L. Myrick	Married
Thomas A. Mckinney	Married

Permanent Register, Jan. 4, 1886

Listed members without comments: Mrs. Permelia J. Thompson, Wm. Thompson, Mrs. Letty Thompson, Thomas Thompson, Mrs. Mary J. Thompson, Miss Mary C. Thompson, Thomas McKinney, Mrs. Martha C. McKinney, William R. McKinney, Emil Lassen, Mrs. Rebecca J. Lassen, Miss Amy J. Lassen (McDowell), Alfred T. Lassen, Mrs. Mary E. Lassen, Miss Ora A. Lassen, Isaac A. Payne, Mrs. Mary J. Payne, John R. Reeves, Mrs. Kitty A. Reeves, Mrs. Mary A. McKague, George J. Jordan, Mrs. Martha J. Jordan, John Myers, Mrs. Julia Myers, Mrs. Margaret Hassel, Mrs. Sarah Smeltser, Oma A. McDowell, Miss Eliza J. Brooks, Solomon W. Brooks, Mrs. Susan E. Brooks, William Steel, Nathan Maddox, Mrs. L. J. Maddox, Harrison, Davis, Burney Davis, Mrs. Mary L. Myrick, Elizabeth Sullivan, Sarah Sullivan, Rebecca Barton, Sam. Sullivan, Miss Minnie Myrack, Miss Calodonia Myrack, Katy Lassen.

Listed members with comments:

Name	Comments
Channcey (Janson) W. Root	Adm. Aug. 2, 1886, by Rev. W. D. Overton.
Mrs. Martha B. Root	Adm. Aug. 2, 1886, by Rev. W. D. Overton
J. W. Myrack	Adm. Aug. 4, 1886, by Rev. W. D. Overton
John A. Harbison	Adm. Aug. 4, 1884, by Rev. W. D. Overton
Miss Mary Miller	Adm. Aug. 4, 1884, by Rev. W. D. Overton
Miss Rhonda Thompson	Adm. Aug. 4, 1884, by Rev. W. D. Overton
Thomas A. McKinney	Adm. Aug. 4, 1886, by Rev. W. D. Overton
Mary Drysdale	Adm. by Rev. W. D. Overton, Transferred from Flat Creek

Name	Comments
Mrs. Cara Jane Brooks	Adm. by Rev. W. D. verton
John Grimes	Transferred to Flat Creek
Missouri C. Grimes	Transferred to Flat Creek
Miss Stella Myers	Adm. Aug. 14, 18??, by Rev. W. H. Pashall
Ennis Thompson	Adm. Aug. 14, 18??, by Rev. W. H. Pashall
Bennie Thompson	Adm. Aug. 14, 18??, by Rev. W. H. Pashall
Miss Jennie Stratton	Adm. Aug. 14, 18??, by Rev. W. H. Pashall
Ganam (sic) McDowell	Adm. Aug. 14, 18??, by Rev. W. H. Pashall

Membership Register, 1888

Permelia J. Thompson, William Thompson, Letty Thompson, Thomas Thompson, Mary J. Thompson, Martha C. Thompson Brooks, Thomas McKinney, Martha C. McKinney, Martha R. McKinney, George M. McKinney, Martha S. McKinney, William R. McKinney, Emil Lassen, Rebecca J. Lassen, Amy J. McDowell, Alfred S. Lassen, Mary J. Lassen, Ora A. Lassen, Isaac A. Payne, Mary J. Payne, John R. Reeves, Kitty A. Reeves, Mary A. McKague, Mary J. Jordan, John Myers, Julia Myers, Sarah Smelzer, Oma A. McDowell, Eliza J. Brooks, Solomon W. Brooks, Susan E. Brooks, Nathan Maddox, L. J. Maddox, Mary L. Myrick, J. W. Myrick, John A. McKinney, Rhoda Thompson Brooks, Clara J. Brooks, Thomas A. McKinney, Elizabeth Sullivan, Monroe Hickson, Minnie Mrick McDowell, Caledonia Payne Evans, Ennis Thompson, G. J. Grews, Stella Myers (Dis. Feb., 1891), Bennie Thompson, Ganam A. McDowell, Katie Lassen, Jennie Stratton, John Grimes, Missouri Grimes, Harry Grant, Mary grant, J. M. McDowell (Dis. Feb., 1891), Tilda Ann Mckinney, Sarah J. Thompson, Charles Thompson, Levi Hackworth, Wm. Lacey, Linda Lacey.

Register of Infant Baptisms

Nellie Genveva Wright, (PRTS) Thomas L. and Minnie Wright, (BD) Mar. 18, 1886, (MG) Br. Batten.

Thomas Franklin Wright, (PRTS) Thomas L. and Minnie Wright, (BD) Mar. 18, 1886, (MG) Br. Batten.

John Wesley Brooks, (PRTS) Solomon and Susan Brooks, (BD) Aug., 1887, (MG) W. H. Pasahll

Members Renewed, 1892

Permelia Thompson, William Thompson, Letty
Thompson, Thomas Thompson, Mary Thompson, Martha C.
Brooks, Thomas McKinney, Martha C. McKinney, Thomas
McKinney, Martha C. McKinney, Martha R. McKinney,
George McKinney, Martha S. McKinney, William R.
McKinney, Emil Lassen, Rebecca Jane Lassen, Amy J.
McDowell, Alfred S. Lassen, Ora A. Lassen, Katie
Lassen, Isaac A. Payne, Mary J. Payne, John R.
Reeves, Kitty A. Reeves, Mary A. McKague, Martha J.
Jordan, John Myers, Eliza J. Brooks, Solomon W.
Brooks, Nathan Maddox, Mary L. Maddox, Mary L.
Myrick, Rhoda Brooks, Thomas A. McKinney, Clara J.
Brooks, Elizabeth Sullivan, Callie Evans, Ennis
Thomspon, Bennie Thompson, Ganam A. McDowell, John
Grimes, Henry Grant, Mary Grant, Charles Thompson,
Tilda A. McKinney, Levi Hackworth, William Lacy,
Linda Lacy, Elias Brannam, Manerva A. McKinney,
Nancy Jane McDowell.

Register of Adult Baptisms

Name	Date	Minister
John A. Harbison	Aug. 5, 1886	H. D. Overton
Mary Miller	Aug. 5, 1886	H. D. Overton
Minnie Myrick	Aug., 1887	W. H. Pascall
Calie Payne	Aug., 1887	W. H. Pascall
Stella Myers	Aug., 1887	W. H. Pascall
Bennie Thompson	Aug., 1887	W. H. Pascall
Ennis Thompson	Aug., 1887	W. H. Pascall
Jennie Stratton	Aug., 1887	W. H. Pascall
Ganam McDowell	Aug., 1887	W. H. Pascall

Membership Register, 1892

Elias Brannan (preacher), William M. Thompson
(church leader), Thomas D. Thompson (steward and
supt. of Sunday School), Permelia J. Thompson,
Letty Thompson, Mary Jane Thompson, Martha C.
Brooks, Martha R. McKinney, George Mckinney, Martha
S. McKinney, William R. McKinney, Emil Lassen,
Rebecca Jane Lassen, Amy Jane McDowell, Ora A.
Lassen McDowell, Alfred S. Lassen, Katie Lassen,
Isaac A. Payne, Mary J. Payne, John R. Reeves,
Kitty A. Reeves, Mary A. McKague, John Myers, Eliza
Brooks, Solomon W. Brooks, Susan E. Brooks, Mary L.
Myrick, Nathan Maddox, Eliza J. Maddox, Rhoda
Brooks, Thomas A. McKinney, Clara J. Brooks,
Elizabeth Sullivan, Callie Evans, Ennis Thompson,
Bennie Thompson, Ganam M. McDowell, John Grimes,
Henry Grant, Mary Grant, Charles Thompson, Thomas
McKinney, Wm. Lacy, Levi Hackworth, Tilda A.
McKinney, Manerva A. Mckinney, Nancy Jane McDowell,
Elizabeth Reeves Jordan, Amy Thompson Jordan, Wm.

O. H. Brooks, Nancy Brannan Thompson, Birdie Brannan, Addie Brannan, Jerry Payne, Mary Azelie McKinney (Joined the Baptists), Missouri Thompson, Missouri Thompson (Joined the Baptists), Willie McKinney, Jane McKinney, Sphronia Hixson, Lurinda McKinney, Viola Reeves, I. J. Foweler, John Polk, Emily McKinney.

Resgister of Pasters

Name	Appointment Date
Henry D. Overton	Sep. 29, 1885
W. H. Pashall	1887

Macedonia Class Book - 1897 -1953

The following information was recorded on the inside front cover:

On Apr. 16, 1886 Thos. A. McKinney and wife, Minervia Jane McKinney, to Gus Rife, D. B. Young and W. H. Allen, trustees of the M. E. Church and their successors. The legal description of the land was given.

Register of Pastors

Name of Bishop	Name of P.E.	Name of P.C.	Date
A. W. Wilson	H. M. Euer	R. D. Steward	1897
W. A. Candler	H. M. Euer	R. D. Steward	1898
W. A. Candler	H. M. Euer	J. C. Simpson	1899
J. C. Grandburg	J. R. Eddleman	C. L. Denis	1900
W. A. Candler	J. C. L. Bohem	C. L. Denis	1901
A. M. Wilson	J. C. L. Bohem	John Cox	1902
---	J. C. L. Bohem	E. Carlile	1903
---	S. W. Emory	C. M. Bramlet	1904
---	S. W. Emory	B. L. Wright	1905
---	T. M. Jackson	Geo. M. Brooks	1906
---	T. M. Jackson	J. M. England	1907
---	---	Thomas Lord	1908
W. A. Chandler	W. A. Humphreys	Ed. Tetley	1909
			1910

Register of Marriages

Willoughby Brooks and Martha C. Thompson, (MD) Sep. 4, 1887, (JP) Emil Lassen.

Joseph Brooks and Rhoda A. Thompson, (MD) Oct. 18, 1891, (JP) Emil Lassen.

John Jordan and Amy A. Thompson, (MD) Jul. 28, 1895, (MG) Elias Brannum.

Charles Thompson and Vickie Leroux, (MD) Apr. 5,

1896, (MG) Elias Brannum.
    Will Hopkins and Sarah J. Thompson, (MD) Jun.
18, 1896, (JP) Emil Lassen.
    Alfred S. Lassen and Missouri Thompson, (MD)
Oct. 31, 1897, (JP) Emil Lassen.
    Jake Stanley and Jennett McCloud, (MD) Apr. 5,
1899, (MG) R. D. Steward.
    Thomas McKinney and Laura Johns, (MD) Jun. 10,
1900, (MG) J. C. Simpson.
    Thomas Joplin and Jane Johns, (MD) Mar. 3, 1901,
(MG) C. L. Dennis.
    James Hood and Jane Mckinney, (MD) May 28,
19000, (MG) J. C. Simpson.
    Alonzo Hood and Alma Lassen, (MD) Mar. 8, 1903,
(JP) Emil Lassen.
    Willie Jordan and Callie Evans, (MD) May 30,
1903, (JP) Emil Lassen.
    W. H. Thompson and Margaret McKinney, (MD) Feb.
21, 1904, (JP) Emil Lassen.
    Robert McKinney and Golden Johns, (MD) Mar. 18,
1904, (MG) T. D. Thompson.
    Alonzo Skaggs and Paulina Sullivan, (MD) Mar.
22, 1906, (MG) Geo. M. Brooks
    Chas. C. Estes and Emma Brooks, (MD) Jun. 2,
1906, (MG) Geo. M.
Brooks.
    Churchman Bible (?) and Phoeba Reeves, (MD)
Dec., 1911, (JP) John McKinney.
    Earnest McDowell and Clara Brooks, (MD) Jan.,
1912, (MG) T. D. Thompson.
    Arch Beschers and Lizzie Franklin, (MD) Sep. 6,
1914, (MG) ?.
    Jack Johnson and Mary Raymer, (MD) Mar. 21,
1915, (MG) T. D. Tompson.
    W. H. Thompson and Lettie Doyle McKinney, (MD)
Sep. 11, 1918, (MG) T. D. Thompson.
             Register of Members, 1897
    Permelia Thompson, Wm. R. McKinney, Thos. D.
Thompson, Thos. McKinney, Wm. M. Thompson, Letty
Thompson, Mary J. Thompson, Marcus E. Brooks, Rhoda
Brooks, Chas. Thompson, Amy Jorden, Missouri
Thompson, Martha R. McKinney, Ella Lassen, Katie
Greene, Alfred S. Lassen, Ora A. McDowell, Bennie
Thompson, Birdie Thompson, Isaac A. Payne, Mary J.
Payne, Collie Evans, John R. Reeves, Viola Reeves,
Kittie A. Reeves, Mary A. McKague, Eliza Brooks,
Susie Brooks, Mary L. Myrick, Eliz. Sullivan, Wm.
A. Lacy, Linda Lacy, Henry Grant, Mary Grant, Lucy
McDowell, Willie McKinney, Jane McKinney, Lurinda

McKinney, Saphronia Hixson, I. J. Fowler, Emily
McKinney, Thilda A. Bacon, Vickie Thompson, J. D.
McKinney, Monroe Hixon, M. C. Hixon, Oma J.
Thompson, Emil Lassen, Emma Brooks.

Bonhomme Presbyterian Church, St. Louis County, Missouri

Register of Membership

Name	Comments
Rev. J. N. Gilbreath	Adm. May 15, 1842
Daniel Potterfield	Adm. May 15, 1842
Elizabeth Potterfield	Adm. May 15, 1842
Thomas K. Humphreys	Adm. May 15, 1842
Helen A. Humphreys	Adm. May 15, 1842
Eleanor Ann Garrott, Sr.	Adm. May 15, 1842
Eleanor Ann Garrott, Jr. (Hogg)	Adm. May 15, 1842
Nancy Bacon	Adm. May 15, 1842, d. Sep. 20, 1843
Benjamin P. VanCourt	Adm. May 15, 1842
Andrew Gunning	Adm. May 15, 1842
Joseh Conway	Adm. May 15, 1842
Virginia Conway	Adm. May 15, 1842
Samuel Shepherd	Adm. May 15, 1842
Andrew Ross	Adm. May 15, 1842
Amelia Cordell	Adm. May 15, 1842
Elizabeth Hagar	Adm. May 15, 1842
Sarah Ann Garrott	Adm. May 15, 1842
Sarah King	Adm. May 15, 1842
William Hamilton	Adm. Jan., 1845, d. Jan. 7, 1846
Frederick Albrecht	Adm. Jan., 1845, Dis. Sep., 1847
Benjamin Carter	Adm. Feb. 2, 1845, Dis. Sep., 1847
Daniel Albert Eaches	Adm. Feb. 1, 1845
Charles Bennett Eaches	Adm. Feb. 1, 1845
Mrs. Eliza Ross, wife of Washington Ross	Adm. Feb. 1, 1845, By letter from Paris Presbyterian Church, KY
Mrs. Elizabeth Chase	Adm. July, 1845, By letter from Presby. Church, Jefferson City, MO
Thomas, serv. of M. M. Bussard	Adm. Jan., 1846
John Bruce	Adm. Mar., 1846
Edy Bruce	Adm. Mar., 1846

Name	Comments
Daniel Albert Eaches	Dis. Mar., 1846, Letter forwarded to Virginia
Louisa Ann Clark	Adm. May 8, 1847, Dis. to Second Presbyterian Church, St. Louis, MO
Milton M. Bussard	Adm. May 8, 1847, Dis. to Dr. Pott's Church St. Louis
Mary Ann Bussard	Dis. May 8, 1847, to Dr. Pott's Church
Margaret R. Potterfield	Adm. May 26, 1847, Dis. to Maryland Church.
Anna Matthews	Adm. Aug. 8, 1847, By letter Salem, PA
Letitia Duncan	Adm. Aug. 8, 1847, By letter from Second Presbyterian Church, St. Louis, MO
Missouri Ann Stevens	Adm. Sep., 1847
Joshua Boston	Adm. Mar. 14, 1848
James Sappington	Adm. Mar. 14, 1848, Dis. to Central Church, St. Louis
Elizabeth Sappington	Adm. Mar. 14, 1848, Dis. to Central Church, St. Louis
Mrs. Sarah A. Boston	Adm. Jun. 10, 1848
Elizabeth Shelby	Adm. Jun. 10, 1848
Eliza J. Wiseman	Adm. Jun. 10, 1848
Eliza A. Kinkead	Adm. Jun. 10, 1848
Edward Harrison	Adm. Jun. 25, 1848
Mrs. Mary Massey	Adm. Aug. 6, 1848
Mrs. Mary Eliz. Albright	Adm. Nov. 10, 1848
George Wiseman	Adm. Nov. 10, 1848
Letitia Duncan	Dis. Mar. 10, 1850
Mrs. Eliza Potterfield	Dis. Mar. 10, 1850
Miss K. Elizabeth Garrett	Dis. Mar. 10, 1850
Mrs. Anna Matthews	Dis. Sep. 1, 1850
Mrs. Mary J. Turner	Dis. Sep. 1, 1850
V. Burns	Dis. Sep. 1, 1850
Silas Kinkead	Adm. Sep. 20, 1851
Dulcina Conway	Adm. Sep. 20, 1851
Lucinda Conway	Adm. Sep. 20, 1851

Name	Comments
John M. Clarkson	Adm. Sep. 20, 1851
Mrs. Eliza Clarkson	Adm. Sep. 20, 1851
Fredrick Albright	Adm. Sep. 20, 1851, By letter from Dr. Pott's Church, St. Louis
Mrs. Nancy Brown	Dis. Sep. 21, 1851 to St. Louis Church
Mrs. Mary Shumate	Dis. Mar. 25, 1852 to Fee Fee Church
Miss Laura Meynard	Adm. Oct. 9, 1852, By letter from W. Pottsdam, MA, Dis. May, 1854 to IN.
John Hartshorn	Adm. Oct. 10, 1852
Miss Harriet A. Hartshorn	Adm. Oct. 10, 1852
Mary E. Boteler	Adm. Oct. 10, 1852
Susan K. Wiseman	Adm. Oct. 10, 1852
Rebecca Woods	Adm. Oct. 10, 1852
Alton M. Hibler	Adm. Oct. 30, 1852
Mary Ann Hibler	Adm. Oct. 30, 1852
Virginia Conway	Adm. Oct. 30, 1852
Eleanor Conway	Adm. Oct. 30, 1852
Emmaville Blackwell	Adm. Oct. 30, 1852
Katherine Humphreys	Adm. Oct. 30, 1852
Mary Ann Hibler, Jr.	Adm. Oct. 30, 1852
Anna Campbell	Adm. Oct. 30, 1852
Rachel Campbell	Adm. Oct. 30, 1852
Martha J. McElhinney	Adm. Oct. 30, 1852
Alexander McElhinney	Adm. Oct. 30, 1852
Miss Harriet Baker	Adm. Oct. 30, 1852, By letter from Alton, IL
Squire Fitzgerald	Adm. Jan. 29, 1853
Mrs. Sarah Wilson	Adm. Sep. 29, 1853, By letter from Presby. Church Kanawha Co., VA
Harriet Baker	Dis. Oct. 25, 1853, to Ohio
Robert A. Walton	Adm. Oct. 25, 1853, By letter from Dardenne Church, St. Charles Co., MO
Mrs. Emily Walton	Adm. Oct. 25, 1853, By letter from Dardenne Church, St. Charles Co., MO

Name	Comments
William J. Hibler	Adm. Jan. 28, 1854
Ann Hibbler	Adm. Jan. 28, 1854
Mary Ellen Wiseman	Adm. Jan. 28, 1854
Amarinda Kinkead	Adm. Jan. 28, 1854
Sophronia Woods	Adm. Jan. 28, 1854, d. May 10, 1859
Samuel J. Wilson	Adm. Aug., 1854
Mrs. Clarissa J. Boothe	Adm. Nov. 11, 1854, By letter from Des Peres Church
Mrs. Eliza C. Ross	Dis. May, 1855 to Fee Fee Church, Dis. Sep. 8th to a Mississippi Church
John Hartshorn	Dis. Aug. 26, 1855 to Des Peres Church
Thomas J. Mason	Dis. Jul. 27, 1856 to Knobnoster Church
Sarah Ann Mason	Dis. Jul. 27, 1856 to Knobnoster Church
Adam Lamb	Adm. Dec. 14, 1856, By letter from Maline Creek Church, St. Louis CO..
Mrs. Ann Fitzgerald	Adm. Dec. 19, 1856
Susan Smith	Adm. Dec. 19, 1856
Susan C. Yokel	Adm. Dec. 19, 1856
America McElroy	Adm. Dec. 19, 1856
Oce Ann Hibler	Adm. Dec. 19, 1856
Janet Humphreys	Adm. Dec. 19, 1856
Sophronia Davenport	Adm. Dec. 19, 1856
Minerva Cordell	Adm. Dec. 19, 1856
Mary Campbell	Adm. Dec. 19, 1856
Mary Ann Conway	Adm. Dec. 19, 1856
Emily Boston	Adm. Dec. 19, 1856
Mary Ann Deffebach	Adm. Dec. 19, 1856
Henry Yokel	Adm. Dec. 19, 1856
Stephen D. Hibler	Adm. Dec. 19, 1856
William Phelps	Adm. Dec. 19, 1856
Daniel W. Turner	Adm. Dec. 19, 1856
Gustavus R. Simmons	Adm. Dec. 19, 1856
William Smith	Adm. Dec. 19, 1856
William J. Smith	Adm. Dec. 19, 1856
Thomas J. Kinkead	Adm. Dec. 19, 1856
Green B. Kinkead	Adm. Dec. 19, 1856
Charles E. Smith	Adm. Dec. 19, 1856
James A. McElroy	Adm. Dec. 19, 1856
Henry J. McElroy	Adm. Dec. 20, 1856

Name	Comments
Robert McElroy	Adm. Dec. 20, 1856
William Campbell	Adm. Dec. 20, 1856
Edward Fitzgerald	Adm. Dec. 20, 1856
Elwood Humphreys	Adm. Dec. 20, 1856
Susan A. Myers	Adm. Dec. 20, 1856
Emma R. Manning	Adm. Dec. 20, 1856
Mary P. Walton	Adm. Dec. 20, 1856
Jane Payne	Adm. Dec. 20, 1856
Mrs. Almarinda Henderson	Dis. Jan. 25, 1857 to Pine St. Church St. Louis
Alexander Kinkead, Jr.	Adm. Feb. 27, 1857, Letter from Fulton, Callaway Co.
John M. Clarkson	Dis. Apr. 26, 1857, St. Louis Church
Eliza B. Clarkson	Dis. Apr. 26, 1857, St. Louis Church
Lucius A. Walton	Adm. May 31, 1857
Frederick B. Walton	Adm. Aug. 9, 1857
Mrs. Mary Ann Strickland	Dis. Sep. 20, 1857 to Washington Church, Franklin Co., MO
Mrs. Virginia Hardy	Adm. Oct. 10, 1857, By letter from Lexington, VA
Robert A. Walton	Dis. Oct. 10, 1857 to St. Charles Church
James Sappington	Adm. Feb., 1858, By letter from Central Church
Elizabeth Sappington	Adm. Feb., 1858, By letter from Central Church
Mrs. Helen Humphreys	Dis. Aug. 21, 1858 to Fulton, Calloway Co., MO
Alexander Kinkead	Dis. Oct. 3, 1858 to Creve Coeur Ch.
Missouri E. Hibler	Adm. Nov. 27, 1858
Mrs. Julia A. Baker	Adm. Feb. 26, 1859 from Methodist Episcopal Church, Irving, IL
John B. Ruby	Adm. Feb. 26, 1859
Narcissa Byrd	Adm. Feb. 26, 1859

Name	Comments
Emavilla Blackwell	Dis. May 29, 1859 to Savanna Church
Joshua Boston	Dis. Jun. 5, 1859 to Franklin Co., MO
Emily Boston	Dis. Jun. 5, 1859 to Franklin Co., MO
Squire Fitzgerald	Dis. Jun. 5, 1859 to Franklin Co., MO
Eliza Fitzgerald	Dis. Jun. 5, 1859 to Franklin Co., MO
Edward Fitzgerald	Dis. Jun. 5, 1859 to Franklin Co., MO
Mary Fitzgerald	Dis. Jun. 5, 1859 to Franklin Co., MO
Mrs. Ann Fitzgerald	Dis. Jun. 5, 1859 to Franklin Co., MO
Julia A. Baker	Dis. Sep. 10, 1859
William H. Huckstep	Dis. Jan. 6, 1860 to Manchester Church
Elizabeth Huckstep	Dis. Jan. 6, 1860 to Manchester Church
Dr. Joseph T. Brown	Adm. Feb. 26, 1860 from Des Peres Church
Joseph Shepherd	Adm. Apr. 6, 1862
William Enders	Adm. 1864
Mrs. Louisa Walton	Dis. Jul., 1865 to St. Charles Church
Elwood Humphreys	Adm. Jan. 21, 1866, By letter from Fulton, MO
Lizzie Humphreys	Adm. Jan. 21, 1866, By letter from Fulton, MO
Mrs. Pamela Long	Dis. Jan. 21, 1866 to 16th St. Church
James Wilson	Adm. May 14, 1866
James Woods	Adm. May 14, 1866
James C. Hempstead	Adm. May 14, 1866
Ella Conway	Adm. May 14, 1866
Joseph Lanham Conway	Adm. May 14, 1866
Anne Albright	Adm. May 14, 1866
Jesse Conway	Adm. May 14, 1866
Goodrich Wilson	Adm. May 14, 1866
Nicholas Shaw	Adm. May 14, 1866
Annett Conway	Adm. May 14, 1866, By letter from Dardenne Church

Name	Comments
Mary Humphreys	Adm. May 14, 1866 from Fulton, MO
Garrett Humphreys	Adm. May 14, 1866 from Fulton, MO
Helen Humphreys	Adm. May 14, 1866 from Fulton, MO
Richard Humphreys	Adm. May 14, 1866 from Fulton, MO
Alexander Kinkead, Sr.	Adm. May 14, 1866
Edward Fitzgerald	Adm. May 14, 1866 from Boeuff Church, Franklin Co., MO
Mary Ellen Fitzgerald	Adm. May 14, 1866 from Boeuff Church, Franklin Co., MO
Elizabeth A. Booth	Adm. May 20, 1866
Catherine V. Shawl	Adm. May 20, 1866
Dora Ann Hosey	Adm. May 20, 1866
Mary C. Slaughter	Adm. May 20, 1866
Ann Meredith Trent	Adm. May 20, 1866
Mary Wilson Trent	Adm. May 20, 1866
Jesse W. Hogg	Adm. May 20, 1866
Enis Hogg	Adm. May 20, 1866
Edward A. Boteler	Adm. May 20, 1866
Joseph Lyon Conway	Adm. May 20, 1866
James Richard Byrd	Adm. May 20, 1866
Isaac Woods, Jr.	Adm. May 20, 1866
Samuel Wilson, Jr.	Adm. May 20, 1866
Charles W. Gerhart	Adm. May 20, 1866
Thomas J. Kinkead	Adm. May 20, 1866
Charles Mason Lock	Adm. May 20, 1866
Hiram Lewis	Adm. May 20, 1866
Nelson Wiseman	Adm. May 20, 1866
Henry Shawl	Adm. Jun. 24, 1866
Edward Boteler	Dis. Oct. 28, 1866 to Fee Fee Church
William Enders	Dis. May 25, 1867 to Potosi Church
Mrs. Louisa Bates	Adm. Dec. 8, 1857
Mrs. Sophronia B. Booth	Adm. Early 1868 by letter form Carondelet Church
Walker Payne	Adm. Early 1868, Former Methodist
Miss S. C. Hogg	Adm. Jan. 30, 1869, By letter from Mt. Zion Church, St. Charles

Name	Comments
Virginia Hogg	Adm. Apr. 3, 1869
S. J. WIlson, Jr.	Adm. Aug. 6, 1870
Mrs. Robert King	Adm. Nov. 5, 1870, By letter from Dardenne Church
Mrs. Catherine Hosey	Adm. Jan. 8, 1871
Mrs. Mary Kinkead	Adm. Aug. 5, 1871
Miss Sallie Trent	Dis. Feb. 18, 1872 to Old School PresbyterianChurch, Brunswick, MO
* Mrs. Virginia Conway, Jr. *(Formerly Miss Hogg)	Dis. Jun. 23, 1873 Old School PresbyterianChurch, Kansas City, MO
Alice Payne	Adm. Nov. 22, 1873
Mrs. L. M. Conway, wife of Joseph S. Conway	Adm. Nov. 15, 1874, from M. E. Church in Fulton, MO
Mrs. Lavina M. Kinney	Dis. Nov. 15, 1874 to church that whorships in Hibler's School House St. Louis Co., MO
Arthur Conway	Adm. Feb. 14, 1875
Richard Llewellyn	Adm. Feb. 19, 1876
Mrs. Elizabeth Clarkson	Adm. Dec. 15, 1877
Miss Annie H. Clarkson	Adm. Dec. 15, 1877, By letter from St. Charles Church
Frederick Andrae	Adm. Dec. 21, 1877
Richard Boteler	Adm. Dec. 21, 1877
Conway Bates	Adm. Dec. 21, 1877
Joseph H. Kinkead	Adm. Dec. 21, 1877
William Albright	Adm. Dec. 21, 1877
William Conway	Adm. Dec. 21, 1877
John Tutty	Adm. Dec. 21, 1877
Mrs. F. J. Kinkead	Adm. Dec. 21, 1877
Fenton Hempstead	Adm. Dec. 21, 1877
Mrs. Anna Bird	Adm. Dec. 21, 1877
Miss Mary Baxter	Adm. Dec. 21, 1877
Miss Jemima Baxter	Adm. Dec. 21, 1877
Isaac Woods, Jr.	Adm. Dec. 23, 1877
John F. Bird	Adm. Dec. 23, 1877
Mrs. Pamela Hogg	Dis. May 12, 1878
Mrs. Servella Albright	Dis. May 12, 1878
Ellen Catherine Llewellyn	Adm. May 12, 1878,

Name	Comments
	By letter from Lexington, MO Church
Miss Anna Clarkson	Dis. Oct., 1878 to Kirkwood Church
W. B. P. Fenn	Adm. Oct., 1880, By letter from Wakeman Congregational Church, Ohio
Mary L. Yokel	Adm. May 8, 1881
Virginia Yokel	Adm. May 8, 1881
Jessie M. Yokel	Adm. May 8, 1881
Thomas Humphreys	Adm. May 8, 1881
Chalmers Humphreys	Adm. May 8, 1881
Joseph Lanham Conway	Dis. Oct. 2, 1881 to Brownsville, MO Presbyterian Church
Lillian M. Conway	Dis. Oct. 2, 1881 to Brownsville, MO
Mrs. Jessie Snider	Dis. Nov. 27, 1881 to Des Peres Church
Laura Mary Kinkead, dau. of Thomas J. and Mary	Adm. May 12, 1882
Willis Conway	Dis. Jul., 1884 to Lamonte Church, Pettis Co., MO
Miss Myra Ware, (Lucius)	Adm. Jan. 1, 1885, By Hibler letter from Lafayette Park Presbyterian Church
Mrs. Ella Boteler	Dis. Jan. 1, 1885 to Lamonte Church, Pettis Co., MO
Joseph Conway, Sr.	Adm. Apr. 5, 1885
Mrs. Mary A. Hibler and son	Dis. Apr. 26, 1885
Elihu Nettie Conway	Dis. May 7, 1885
William Albright	Dis. May 7, 1885
Mrs. Henry C. Payne	Adm. Jul. 5, 1885, By letter from Presby. Church, Washington Co., MO
Dr. R. L. Boteler	Dis. Jul. 5, 1885
Thomas K. Humphreys	Dis. May 1, 1887 to Springfield Church
Virginia Humphreys	Dis. May 1, 1887 to

Name	Comments
	Springfield Church
Mrs. John King	Dis. May 1, 1887
Mrs. Simon Brewster	Dis. May 1, 1887
J. W. Hogg, wife Pamela,	Dis. Nov. 2, 1889
daughter Mary and sister Sarah	
Ida May Stephens, dau. of	Dis. Oct. 5, 1890
James and Elvira	

Register of Deaths

Name	Death Date
Green B. Conway	Jan. 23, 1857
Mary Campbell	Mar. 20, 1859
America McElroy	Aug. 24, 1861
Alton H. Hibler	Dec. 9, 1861

Marriage Register

Bride's Name	Groom's Name
Miss Elizabeth Schultz	B. Johnston
Eliza J. Wiseman	S. Fitzgerald
Susan Wiseman	J. Beck
Mary Ellen Wiseman	E. Fitzgerald
Amerinda Kinkead	F. Henderson
Louisa Conway	F. Walton
Mary Ann Conway	--- Strickland

Register of Infant Baptisms

Name	Type	Date
Virginia Conway	B	Jun. 11, 1838
Mary E. Conway	B	Jan. 20, 1840
Ann Conway	B	Nov. 26, 1841
Mary Ann Conway	B	Dec. 4, 1830
Dulcena Conway	B	???? 18, 1832
Lucinda Conway	B	Oct. 29, 1834
Eleanor Conway	B	???? 4, 1836
Louisa Conway	B	Apr. 24, 1840
Edmund Virgil Conway	B	May 11, 1842
James Andrew Ross	B	May 26, 1846
Stephen D. Smith	B	Feb. 15, 1846
Ange Perry Farris	BD	Sep. 20, 1851
Louisa G. Clarkson	BD	Sep. 20, 1851
Joseph L. Conway	BD	Sep. 20, 1851
Samuel W. Conway	BD	Sep. 20, 1851
Ella Conway	BD	Oct. 10, 1852
Annette Conway	BD	Oct. 10, 1852
Joseph Conway	BD	Oct. 10, 1852
Jesse Conway	BD	Oct. 10, 1852
Julia A. Conway	BD	Aug. 13, 1854
Alfred Walton	BD	Oct. 10, 1852
Andrew J. Smith	B	Feb. 24, 1849
Missouri E. Boston	BD	Oct. 10, 1852
Name	Type	Date

Name	Type	Date
John Boston	BD	Oct. 10, 1852
Thomas P. Wiseman	BD	Oct. 10, 1852
Nelson Wiseman	BD	Oct. 10, 1852
Mary A. Wiseman	BD	Oct. 10, 1852
John W. Huckstep	BD	May 30, 1852
Lucy A. Huckstep	BD	May 30, 1852
Edwin Huckstep	BD	May 30, 1852
William Mason	BD	May 30, 1852
Lemel Hibler	B	Jun. 30, 1850
Madora Hibler	B	Jun. 21, 1852
Ann E. Albright	B	Sep. 23, 1852
Richard E. Albright	B	Jun. 3, 1851
Joseph H. Kinkead	BD	May 27, 1854
Samuel Wilson	BD	Nov. 11, 1854
Robert F. Wilson	BD	Nov. 11, 1854
Charles H. Boothe	B	Oct. 13, 1853
Joseph C. Hempstead	BD	May 13, 1855
Mary Ann Hibler	B	Jan. 21, 1839
Elisha Hibler	B	May 9, 1843
Lucius Hibler	B	Feb. 15, 184?
Elihu Hibler	B	Jul. 26, 1846
Leora Hibler	B	Sep. 12, 1847
Isidora Hibler	B	Dec. 31, 1848
Pamelia Hibler	B	Feb. 6, 1854
Huldah Hibler	B	Jan. 26, 1855
Susan C. Wiseman	BD	1857
Mary E. Wiseman	BD	1857
Fieldon M. Wiseman	BD	1857
Susan W. Walton	BD	Aug. 8, 1857
Mary E. Walton	BD	Aug. 8, 1857
Everett Walton	BD	Aug. 8, 1857
William Conway	BD	May 24, 1858
Andrew B. Boothe	BD	May 24, 1858
Conway Bates	BD	Jul. 4, 1858
Zachary T. Hibler	B	Jul. 20, 1847
Albert F. Hibler	B	Dec. 23, 1849
John W. Hibler	B	Feb. 20, 1854
Richard H. Hibler	B	Aug. 14, 1856
Mary S. Sappington	B	Mar. 5, 1858
Laura Sappington	B	Dec. 6, 1853
Nancy M. Wilson (age 3y)	BD	Dec. 17, 1858
Benjamin Wilson (age 1y)	BD	Dec. 17, 1858
Sarah E. Trent (age 7y)	BD	Dec. 19, 1858
John M. Trent (age 4y)	BD	Dec. 19, 1858
Nancy A. Trent (age 2y)	BD	Dec. 19, 1858
Ellen Trent	B	Mar., 1861
Hetty Wilson	B	Mar. 6, 1861
Samuel Conrad Andreas	BD	Jun. 2, 1862

Name	Type	Date		
Elizabeth Andreas	BD	Jun.	2,	1862
Arthur Conway	BD	Jun.	2,	1862
Laura Brown	BD	Jun.	2,	1862
Alva Norman Hibler	BD	Jun.	2,	1862
Edward Everett Hibler	BD	Jun.	2,	1862
Martha Spencer Trent	BD	Jun.	2,	1862
John McKnight Boothe	BD	Jun.	2,	1862
Virginia C. Brown	B	May	14,	1866
Joseph C. Brown	B	1868		
Lucia Lee Bates	BD	1868		
Meredith Conway	B	Nov.	4,	1869
Beverly H. Brown	B	Dec.	11,	1869
Mary Ann Fitzgerald	B	Dec.	29,	1866
Oscar Washington	B	Sep.	25,	1869
Eugene Albright	BD	Jan.	7,	1871
John Loper Albright	BD	Jan.	7,	1871
Arthur Albright	BD	Jan.	7,	1871
Lewellen Humphreys	B	Sep.	16,	1867
Helen Humphreys	B	Sep.	16,	1867
Allen Humphreys	B	Mar.	16,	1869
Marion Humphreys	B	Mar.	16,	1869
Howard Walton	B	Oct.	31,	1869
Grace Walton	B	Sep.	10,	1871
Margaret Virginia Conway	BD	Feb.	20,	1876
Elwood Humphreys	BD	187?		
Paul Boteler	BD	Dec.	15,	1877
Conway Boteler	BD	Dec.	15,	1877
Laura Mary Kinkead	BD	Dec.	15,	1877
Mary Emma Kinkead	BD	Dec.	15,	1877
Maied (?) Audrey Kinkead	BD	Apr.	28,	1878
Ida Conway	BD	Oct.	6,	1878
Mary Eleanor Hogg	B	Aug.	31,	1875
Garrett Hogg	B	Feb.	15,	1878
Bertram Kerr Humphreys	BD	Oct.	31,	1880
Nettie Boteler	BD	May	13,	1882
Lanham Boteler	BD	May	13,	1882
Donald Boteler	BD	Aug.	31,	1884
Mary Baxter Humphreys	BD	Sep.	5,	1886
Matilda Alice Linss	BD	Jan.	2,	1887
Edward Linss	BD	Apr.	1,	1888

Register of Adult Baptisms

Name	Date		
Sarah Ann Garrett	May	25,	1842
Milton M. Bussard	Oct.	2,	1842
James J. Sappington	Oct.	2,	1842
Elizabeth Conway	Oct.	2,	1842
Nancy E. Lanham	Oct.	2,	1842
Martha Ann Powell	Oct.	2,	1842

Name	Date
Mary Ann Bussard	Apr. 2, 1843
Mary Ellen Botteler	Apr. 2, 1843
Katherine E. Garrett	Apr. 2, 1843
Mary Jane Kinkead	Apr. 2, 1843
Green B. Conway	Apr. 2, 1843
Hudson B. Powell	Apr. 2, 1843
Mary Osborne Huckstep	Sep., 1843
Amanda Wiseman	Sep., 1843
--- Hogg, Jr.	Sep., 1843
Uriel B. Burrous	Jan. 25, 1845
Andrew J. Hibler	Jan. 25, 1845
Mary Ester Kinkead	Jan. 25, 1845
Margaret R. Potterfield	Jan. 25, 1845
Lucinda Kinkead	Jan. 25, 1845
George W. Smith	Jan. 25, 1845
Winifred Freeman	Jan. 25, 1845

St. Louis County, Missouri, Antioch Baptist Church, Chesterfield.
Register of White Membership

Name	Comments
James Wright and wife Mary	Adm. May 29, 1841, James d. Apr. 5, 1872
Wm. Jacobs and wife Sarah	Adm. May 29, 1841, Wm. d. 1846
Virginia A. Lipscomb	Adm. May 29, 1841
Marie C. Lipscomb	Adm. May 29, 1841
Benj. F. Lipscomb and wife Ann R.	Adm. May 29, 1841
Mary A. Boxley	d. 1841
Margaret Chiles	---
Lucinda Taylor	d. Sep. 25, 1866
Margaret Chiles	---
Sarah A. Jacobs	---
Abner Blize	d. May 4, 1857
John Wright	d. Jan. 11, 1843
Richd. Faulconer and wife Julia	---
Mary A. Wright	d. Jun. 15, 1843
Ann F. Locker	---
John Post & wife	Adm. 1842, BD. Oct. 9, 1842
Adams Bates & wife	Adm. 1842
Mrs. Sarah Kelly	Adm. 1842
Miss C. Wright	Adm. 1844, BD. Jun. 7, 1844
Wm. H. Coleman & wife	Adm. 1844

Name	Comments
Hardenia B. Coleman	Adm. 1844
Robert G. Coleman	Adm. 1845
Thomas Wright	Adm. 1845
Caroline R. J. G. Munroe	Adm. 1861
Huldah A. Nickerson	Adm. 1862
Anna H. Hardenia Coleman	Adm. 1862
Anne Locke	Adm. 1862
Lizzie Coleman	Adm. 1862
Lucinda Bacon	Adm. 1863
Spencer Tyler	Adm. 1863
Edward Bacon	Adm. 1863
John Hockensmith & wife Salina	Adm. 1864
Lucy Mary Ferguson	Adm. 1865
Sarah Lewis Coleman	Adm. 1865
Arabella Harris Coelman	Adm. 1865
Ellen Coleman	Adm. 1865
Mrs. Margaret Brown	Adm. 1867
Mary Harris Coleman	Adm. 1867
Jennie H. Coleman	Adm. 1867
Mrs. Sarah Ann Howell	Adm. 1867
Mrs. Lucy Ann Grafford	Adm. 1867
Andrew J. Cummings	Adm. 1868
Elizabeth T. Warfield	Adm. 1880
Lee E. Monroe	Adm. 1880
Nanny Terry	Adm. 1880
Frank D. Terry	Adm. 1880
Lillie Coleman	Adm. 1880
Arthur J. Keller	Adm. 1886
Jennie Kellar	Adm. 1890
Maggie Kellar	Adm. 1890
Lillia Pleasants	Adm. 1891
Alice Ferguson	Adm. 1891
Nellie Pleasants	Adm. 1891

Reorganization of Coloured Membership, Oct. 18, 1868

Richard Hughs & wife Sally, David Taylor & wife Martha, Elijah Maderson & wife Jun, John Graves (d. Jul. 18, 1871) & wife Silva, Lindsay Robinson, Charles Anderson, Lewis Brown, Pauline Grauls, Winston and Clara Jefferson, Joe Smith, Mary Jefferson, Barrett Layton, Moses White & wife Catherine, Patsy Anderson, Watt and Isabella Hughs, John Layton, Carrie Bailey, Lizzie Bailey, Nelson Lewis, Susan (?), Jacob Robertson, William Dickerson, Anderson Dickerson, Cicy Yancy, Cloe Sandridge, George Brown, Killy Hamilton.

July 4, 1841

The following coloured brethren were admitted to the church:
1. Elijah, Henry, and Linsey, the property of Robert G. Coleman.
2. Lewis, Jeff, Malinda and Rose, the property of John M. Coleman.
3. Merry, Dick and Sally, the property of William H. Coleman.
4. Jack, Primus, Mike, Tom and Mima, the property of Capt. William Tyler.
5. Sally, the property of Benj. F. Lipscomb.

1842

Hannah, the property of W. C. was baptized Oct. 9, 1842.

Kitty was baptized Oct. 9, 1842, Louisa on May 9, 1842 and Anna in 1842. They were the property of R. C.

1844

Eliza, the property of W. B., was baptized Jun. 9, 1844.

Sep. 9, 1844

1. Sam, the property of John Wright, was received by letter.
2. Mary and Richmond, the property of Wm. Henry Tyler were admitted.
3. Lucy, Huldah and Betsy, the property of the estate of Jeff Coleman, dec. were admitted.
4. Patrick and Isabel, the property of R. G. Coleman were admitted.

1859

1. Dinah, Malinda, Jack, James, the property of A. J. S. Stevens' estate, were admitted.
2. Jacob Bailey, George Williams, and Mahailey Bailey were admitted.
3. Louisiana Ferguson was dismissed.

Phelps County, Missouri, Maramec Iron Workers' Cemetery, St. James
Maria G. Bartley: b. Germany; d. 1883, Germany; Member of the Southern Baptist Church for 55 years.

156

Cape Girardeau County, Missouri, "Missouri Intelligencer," October 5, 1833, Appointments at the Missouri Methodist Episcopal Church Conference.

Name	District
J. Greene, P. E.	Missouri
W. A. H. Spratt	Lexington
A. W. Arrington	Boon's Lick
W. W. Redman	Cedar Creek
J. Glanville	St. Louis
G. W. Bewley	Bowling Green
Thomas Randol	New Madrid
John H. Rubel	White River
Lemuel Wakely	Greenville
A. Pearce	Bellvieu
Henry Cornelius	Washita
John H. Rives	Arkansas
J. McMahan	No. Grand River Mission
Thomas Johnson	Indian Mission District
William Johnson	Shawnee Mission
E. T. Peery	Delaware Mission
J. C. Berryman	Kickapoo Mission
N. M. Talbott	Peori Mission
A. Smith, P. E.	Little Rock
Wm. Keenon, P. E.	Cape Girardeau
M. Wells, P. E.	Arkansas
Richard Overby	Mount Prairie
M. B. Denton	Mount Prairie
J. K. Lacey	Lamoine
R. M. Lee	Richmond
J. H. Slavens	Chariton
A. Monroe, P. E.	St. Louis
J. M. Jameson	Palmyra
R. H. Jordan, N. R.	St. Charles
C. Eaker	West Prairie
Valentine P. Fink	Spring River
J. V. Watson	Farmington
John Neill	Helena
Fountain Brown	Hot Springs
Alvan Baird	Washington
W. G. Duke	Little Rock
Urial Haw	Cape Girardeau
P. Tackett	Creek Mission
L. B. Statler	Creek Mission
J. M. Hamill	South Arkansas
P. Berryhill	Creek Mission
John Harrell	Cherokee Mission
T. Berthelf	Cherokee Mission
R. W. Wells	Cherokee Mission
J. Brewton	Kings River Mission

157

----, Charlotte 121
   Thomas 142
---LLER, 77
ABSLIN, 95
ADAIR, 9 10 14
ADAMS, 39 58-60 86-88 94
  95 100
ADDAMS, 96
ADDINGTON, 62 64 66-68
  72
ADKINS, 93
AGARD, 107
AGEE, 101
AKERS, 98 130
ALBRECHT, 142
ALBRIGHT, 116 143 144
  147 149 150 152 153
ALDERIDGE, 92
ALDRIDGE, 92 93
ALEXANDER, 39 98 118
ALLDTADT, 128
ALLEE, 107
ALLEN, 1 2 10 21 24 29
  39 56 63 64 86 95 99
  104 107 140
ALLISON, 29
ALSPAW, 24
ALSUP, 39
ALVERSON, 58 59
AMICK, 28
AMRINE, 24
AMSBERRY, 24
AMSBERY, 22
ANDERSON, 22 39 70 75
  101 104 132 155
ANDRAE, 114 149
ANDREAS, 152 153
ANDREW, 7 17
ANDREWS, 93 119
ANGLE, 79

APPEL, 117
APPLEGATE, 72
ARMSTRONG, 31 32 39
ARNOLD, 10 39 90 120 121
  123 124 126
ARRINGTON, 157
ASBURY, 120
ASHBURN, 104
ASHLEY, 1 2 118
ASKEW, 10
ASSELMEYER, 24
ATTERBURY, 21 22 39
AULGER, 39
AUSTIN, 39 122
AVITT, 39
AYRES, 104
B, 156
BABB, 104
BACON, 69 118 142 155
BAILEY, 6 7 10 15-18 93-
  96 103 155 156
BAIRD, 157
BAKER, 8 16 22 39-41 58
  61 80 83 101 104 118
  144 146 147
BALDWIN, 119
BALL, 17 41 100 108 114
  118 125
BALLARD, 21 22
BANKLAGE, 3
BARBEE, 104 118
BARKER, 7 8 10 11 17 79
  132
BARKSDALE, 40 50 56
BARNABY, 41
BARNES, 91 108
BARNETT, 101 102
BARNHART, 62-64 67-70 72
BARNHURST, 104
BARNS, 108

BARR, 18
BARRAGAR, 15
BARRAGER, 6 14 15
BARRE, 131
BARRETT, 104
BARTLEY, 156
BARTON, 137
BASHAW, 1
BATCHELOR, 96
BATES, 3 148 149 152-154
BATTEN, 138
BATTERON, 104
BAXTER, 149
BAYER, 117
BAYLEY, 92
BAYLISS, 130
BEAN, 92
BEARD, 119
BEATY, 8 9 18
BEAUCHAMP, 104
BECK, 121 124 125 127
    151
BECKER, 42
BECKHAM, 99
BEDINGER, 120
BEETS, 94
BEHRENS, 4
BELL, 33 57 104
BELLAMY, 39-41
BELT, 123 124 128 129
BELTM, 129
BELTON, 83
BEMIS, 6 14
BENBOW, 24
BENEDICT, 39 40 56
BENNETT, 40 79 117 118
BENNZETTE, 10
BENZ, 4
BERGE, 123
BERGER, 3 10
BERGESCH, 4
BERRY, 40 41 56 118
BERRYHILL, 157
BERRYMAN, 2 157
BERTHELF, 157
BERTRAM, 40
BESCHERS, 141
BESHEER, 134
BETTS, 99
BEVERLY, 39
BEWLEY, 157

BIBB, 104
BIBLE, 141
BIDWELL, 40
BIESER, 18
BIGELOW, 21
BIGGS, 103
BILLICK, 73
BIRD, 22 90 149
BLACK, 40 41 104
BLACKBURN, 40
BLACKHURST, 131
BLACKWELL, 144 147
BLADES, 87
BLAKELY, 104 114
BLANCHARD, 40
BLANKET, 82
BLANTON, 102 132
BLEIL, 10
BLEVINS, 40
BLIZE, 154
BLOOMER, 83
BLOUNT, 82 83
BOBBETT, 22
BOCTING, 22
BOGARD, 77
BOGGS, 124
BOHEM, 140
BOLEY, 108
BOLING, 5 14
BOLTON, 132
BOLTZER, 83
BOND, 6 14 120
BOONE, 10
BOOTH, 148
BOOTHE, 145 152 153
BOOTHMAN, 121 122 125
    129
BOOTING, 39
BOPP, 117
BOSTON, 143 145 147 151
    152
BOTELER, 144 148-150 153
BOTHMAN, 128
BOTTELER, 154
BOULDING, 38
BOULTON, 40 41
BOUND, 102 132
BOWEN, 95
BOWERS, 66 102
BOWLES, 2 104
BOWMAN, 63 67 69

BOWSHEAR, 133
BOXLEY, 154
BOYLE, 118
BRADDEN, 101
BRADEN, 102
BRADIN, 101
BRADLEY, 8 18 40 56 104
  119
BRADNEY, 20 21
BRADSHAW, 7 16 17 101
BRADY, 87
BRAMLET, 140
BRANARD, 68
BRANNAM, 139
BRANNAN, 139 140
BRANNUM, 9 140 141
BRAUT, 4
BREON, 18
BREUSCH, 60
BREWSTER, 151
BREWTON, 157
BRIDEWELL, 104
BRIDGES, 40 45
BRIM, 101 102
BROADUS, 132
BROCK, 57
BROCKWAY, 22 24
BROILES, 108
BRONAUGH, 14 17
BROOK, 32 33 118
BROOKING, 87 100
BROOKINGS, 99
BROOKS, 3 12 31 32 38
  115 117 118 133-142
BROUAGH, 9
BROWN, 3 5 10 13 22 24
  29 39-41 51 56 62-64
  67 69 70 72 73 82 83
  86 101-104 108 144 147
  153 155 157
BROWNE, 79
BROWNING, 30 31 33-36 64
  71 72 118
BROYLES, 72 108
BROZLES, 68
BRUCE, 142
BRUNNER, 4
BRUSCIE, 88
BRUSH, 60
BRYSON, 10 40
BUCHANAN, 32 57 58

BUCK, 65
BUCKINGHAM, 123 126-128
BUCKNER, 104
BUFORD, 114 115 117
BULER, 82
BULKLY, 125 126
BULLOCK, 78-80 108
BUNBERRY, 118
BURCH, 76
BURDELL, 22
BURGES, 12
BURGESS, 5 95
BURGSTRASSER, 19
BURGSTRESSOR, 21
BURGSTUSSER, 21
BURKS, 24 118
BURNETT, 21 22
BURNS, 65 143
BURROUS, 154
BURRUSS, 86
BURTON, 21 22 24 80 86
BUSBY, 104
BUSCHMANN, 4
BUSH, 108 114
BUSHMAN, 41
BUSHNELL, 40
BUSHON, 63
BUSHONG, 69
BUSSARD, 142 143 153 154
BUTLER, 10 40 101
BUTT, 81
BUTTS, 95
BYBEE, 40
BYERS, 41 56 119
BYRD, 40 146 148
C, 156
CAKE, 104
CALDWELL, 10 12 31 32 34
  36 82 83 87 104
CALDWILL, 37
CALE, 6 14
CALLAHAN, 41 42
CALLAWAY, 110
CALOWAY, 93
CALVERT, 60 108-110
CAMERON, 17 41 42
CAMPBELL, 32 41 62 64 65
  67-69 71 81 88 91 96
  97 100 144-146 151
CANDLER, 140
CARDWELL, 98

CAREY, 104
CARLILE, 140
CARNEAL, 95
CARNEY, 20
CARPENTER, 10 122
CARR, 2
CARROL, 42
CARROLL, 41 42
CARTER, 10 42 73 78-80
  102 127 132 142
CARTHEE, 98
CASEBOLT, 97
CASEY, 5-12 14-16 21
CASSADY, 33
CASSY, 4
CATES, 2
CEICIL, 10
CHAMPION, 132
CHANDLER, 22 140
CHANEY, 104
CHAPEL, 95
CHAPMAN, 58 59
CHASE, 142
CHEW, 129
CHEWNING, 101
CHILDS, 42
CHILES, 76 154
CHISIM, 87
CHISM, 100 104
CHRISMAN, 100
CHRIST, 42 56
CHRISTIAN, 101
CLAGETT, 5 12 119
CLARK, 15 18 32 34 35 37
  63 70 72 103 104 121
  132 143
CLARKSON, 144 146 149-
  151
CLAY, 91
CLEMONS, 98
CLEVELAND, 132
CLEVENGER, 71
CLEVINGER, 104
CLIFFORD, 41 56
CLODFELTER, 62 63 69 70
COATS, 97
COBB, 103
CODY, 42
COFFEY, 104
COGSWELL, 41
COKER, 104

COLE, 10 41
COLEMAN, 132 154-156
COLGIN, 87 100
COLLEY, 109
COLLINS, 21 41 95
COLMAN, 98 118
COLSTON, 109
COLVIN, 98
COLYER, 103 132
COMER, 6 7 10 14 17 18
COMMER, 7 14
COMMINS, 100
COMPTON, 41 56
CONNER, 103
CONWAY, 142-145 147-154
COOK, 6 14 22 25 41 83
  84 101
COONS, 41
COONTZ, 101
COOPER, 41
COORLANE, 66
COOTERS, 117
COPPAGE, 10
CORDELL, 142 145
CORDER, 31 32 37 38
CORNELIUS, 157
CORNET, 100
COURTNEY, 100
COVINGTON, 10
COWAN, 21 22
COX, 3 60 99 100 140
CRABTREE, 4 11
CRAIG, 21 22 24 25 30 64
CRAMER, 42
CRANDALL, 18
CRANE, 73
CRAUCH, 108
CRAVEN, 19 21
CRAWFORD, 41 42
CREEL, 109 110
CRENSHAW, 101
CRESSEY, 10
CRIM, 30-39
CRISMAN, 86
CROCKER, 109
CROCKETT, 66
CROMELL, 104
CROOKS, 4 7-13 16 17
CROSS, 23 62 67
CROW, 16
CULBERTSON, 32 38 103

CULLEY, 10
CULP, 79 80
CUMMINGS, 155
CUMMINS, 94
CUNDIFF, 132
CUNNINGHAM, 57 96 97 120
CURTIS, 10
DACOMB, 8
DAILEY, 92
DAILY, 94
DALTON, 32 34 35
DANFORTH, 70
DANIEL, 104
DANIELS, 96
DARLING, 8
DARNEALE, 91
DAULTON, 32 37 38
DAVENPORT, 93 94 104 145
DAVIDSON, 21 22 25 74
DAVIS, 3 8 12 22 25 26
    63 69 81 95 96 98 99
    119 128 136 137
DAY, 42 56
DEAN, 62 68 70 72 110
DECKER, 42 56
DEFFEBACH, 145
DEFORE, 116 117
DEIBEL, 4
DEIS, 43
DELANO, 119
DELONG, 43
DEMPSEY, 74 75
DENHAM, 97 98
DENIS, 140
DENNIS, 141
DENTON, 157
DESAVOM, 98
DESCOMBS, 7 10 14 15 18
DESKIN, 60
DESKINS, 58 60
DEVALL, 31
DEVENPORT, 87
DEVORE, 58 60
DEWEESE, 1 2
DEWLY, 95
DICKERSON, 42 87 155
DICKHOENER, 4
DICKSON, 25 43
DILLARD, 42 56
DILLINER, 33
DILLON, 88

DIRNEL, 65
DISERT, 58
DIXON, 22 42
DOBBINS, 43
DOBSON, 43
DODSON, 43
DOERGEA, 4
DOLAN, 94
DOLTON, 34
DONOHOE, 43
DONOHUE, 42
DOOLEY, 1
DORY, 75
DOTSON, 132
DOTY, 110
DOYLE, 103 104
DRANE, 127
DRESHEE, 33
DRISCOLL, 42
DRUMELLER, 22
DRYSDALE, 137
DUCKWORTH, 75
DUDSWORTH, 92
DUKE, 157
DULANEY, 42 56
DULIN, 86 91 104
DUNAWAY, 16 18
DUNBAR, 103
DUNCAN, 22 26 43 68 69
    81 104 143
DUNHAM, 64
DUNLAP, 72 78-80
DUNLOP, 119 120-122
DUNN, 7 16 123-130
DUNWOODY, 64 71
DURFEY, 87 104
DURHAM, 71
DURNIL, 110
DURRETT, 29
DUSTON, 3
DUTTEN, 60
DUVALL, 31 86 95 103 104
DWLY, 95
DYSART, 25 26 42
EACHES, 142 143
EAGER, 8 14
EAGLESON, 5 6 8 9 12-14
EAKER, 157
EARL, 128
EARLE, 86
EARLY, 120

EASLEY, 87
EASTHAM, 132
EASTRIDGE, 64 65 67-69
   71 73
EATHERTON, 117
EATON, 80
EBERTING, 77
EBERWEIN, 117 118
EBERWIN, 118
EBRICHT, 115
ECHOLDS, 95
ECKERT, 4
EDDINGTON, 64
EDDLEMAN, 140
EDDY, 87
EDELEN, 131
EDMASON, 93
EDMONDS, 38
EDMUNDS, 32 37
EDSON, 28
EDWARDS, 43 72 94
EHLICH, 4
EICHMAN, 43
ELDER, 12 43 82
ELEDGE, 94
ELGIN, 43
ELIS, 95 120
ELISTON, 75
ELLIOTT, 5-7 9 12-14 16-
   18 43
ELMORE, 43
ELTHEL, 14
ELY, 11 114
EMBREY, 10
EMERSON, 21
EMERY, 32 38
EMORY, 140
ENDERS, 147 148
ENGLAND, 140
ENGLER, 117
ENTRICKIN, 43
EPPRIGHT, 87
ESKERN, 11
ESRA, 57
ESRY, 57-61
ESTES, 89 104 141
EUBANK, 44 56
EUBANKS, 29 43
EUER, 140
EVANS, 8 16 21 87 100
   101 138 139 141

EVERMAN, 22
EVERMANN, 21
EVERSMAN, 22
EVERSMANN, 21
EWING, 122
FABING, 121
FAIRCHILD, 119
FAIRES, 2
FALES, 83
FARMER, 86 100 104 105
FARNS, 101
FARR, 10
FARRAR, 121 122 128 130
FARRIS, 151
FARROW, 129
FAUBIAN, 32 33
FAULCONER, 154
FEATHERSTON, 44
FEATHERSTONE, 44 56
FEIS, 44
FENLEY, 17
FENN, 150
FENWICK, 26
FENWOCK, 18
FEREL, 10
FERGUSON, 66 68 105 116
   155 156
FERIE, 3
FERRELL, 19 97 103
FICKLE, 87
FIELAND, 11
FIELDEN, 12
FIELDS, 44
FIGGINS, 22 26
FIKE, 76
FILE, 83
FINCH, 110
FINGLE, 10
FINK, 157
FINKS, 74
FINLAY, 117
FINLY, 3
FINNEY, 118
FIRMAN, 32
FISHBECK, 43 44 56
FISHER, 77 83 100
FITZGERALD, 144-148 151
   153
FITZINGER, 117
FITZWATER, 9 10 11
FLANERY, 100

FLEENOR, 91
FLETCHER, 119
FLINT, 126
FLOOD, 105
FLYN, 28
FORD, 16
FORMAN, 31 33-36
FOSKET, 65
FOSTER, 10 101
FOWELER, 140
FOWLER, 142
FOX, 44 100
FRAME, 82 83
FRANCE, 110
FRANCIS, 44 56
FRANK, 4
FRANKLIN, 86 101 105 130
  141
FRAZER, 60
FRAZIER, 22 26 57-60
FREELAND, 10
FREEMAN, 93 154
FREIL, 44
FRELDEN, 5
FRENCH, 110
FRISTO, 90
FRISTOE, 87 100 105 110
  132
FRITACHLE, 3
FRITSCH, 44
FRITSCHLE, 3
FROGG, 33
FRYE, 3 4
FUNK, 44
FUQUA, 105
FURGESON, 62 65
GABRIEL, 110
GAINES, 73 74 77
GAINS, 7 17 66
GALBRAITH, 74
GANO, 90 91
GARIUS, 22
GARNER, 86
GARNETT, 18
GARRET, 89
GARRETT, 22 101 143 153
  154
GARROTT, 142
GARST, 62 65 66 70 72
GARTH, 10
GARTON, 101

GARY, 101 102
GASKELL, 78
GATES, 3
GAULT, 131
GAY, 119
GEELE, 64
GEHART, 101
GEISLER, 22
GENTRY, 105 132
GEORGE, 44 100
GERGORY, 22
GERHART, 148
GERMAN, 88
GIBBON, 87
GIBBS, 44
GIBSON, 26
GIEGER, 117
GIESLER, 26
GILBERT, 10 45
GILBREATH, 142
GILLAM, 10 11 74
GILLENWATER, 95 96
GILLESPIE, 8 110
GILLHAM, 117
GILLIAM, 44 74
GILMORE, 103
GIPSON, 105
GIVENS, 57
GLANVILLE, 157
GLASGOW, 4 11-13
GLASS, 94
GLENN, 22
GODSEY, 111
GOEN, 105
GOINGS, 11
GOLDSMITH, 10
GOOD, 62 65-73
GOODEN, 122 123
GOODING, 61
GOODRICH, 105
GOODSN, 52
GOODSON, 45 105 114
GOODWIN, 63 64 70-73 105
GOOSE, 65
GORKER, 44 45 56
GOTT, 105
GOULDING, 119
GOWENS, 4
GOWINGS, 61
GRAFFORD, 35 37 155
GRAHAM, 96 98

GRANDBURG, 140
GRANT, 45 105 135 138
  139 141
GRATIOT, 119
GRAULS, 155
GRAVES, 61 105 155
GRAY, 86 88 105
GREEN, 105 132
GREENBERG, 13
GREENE, 30 157
GREGG, 114-117
GREGORY, 22 105
GREWS, 138
GREY, 4 8 10 11 83
GRIER, 105
GRIFFIN, 31 32 36 37 86 105
GRIGG, 121
GRIM, 110
GRIMES, 138 139
GRIMSLEY, 45
GROCE, 44 45 56
GROOMS, 22
GROSS, 119
GROTHPETER, 115
GRUBER, 44
GUIAN, 4
GUILE, 45
GUIMPLE, 45
GUINER, 98
GUINN, 32
GUION, 5 10 14
GUNNING, 142
GURGESS, 86
GUTHERY, 83
GWINN, 44 45 56 101
HACKETT, 120 122 123
HACKWORTH, 138 139
HAGANS, 94
HAGAR, 142
HAGEN, 78
HAGGARD, 22
HAINER, 38
HAINS, 46 69
HAISER, 33
HALBERT, 102 132
HALE, 65 69 71
HALES, 63
HALEY, 21 22
HALHAN, 100
HALL, 3 26-28 46 47 62
  64-66 72 73 118

HALLER, 119
HALSY, 111
HAM, 45 46 56
HAMBY, 47
HAMILL, 157
HAMILTON, 46 142 155
HAMMAR, 17 102 132
HAMMEL, 4
HAMMER, 132
HAMMES, 33
HAMMETT, 19 21
HAMMON, 77
HAMMOND, 76 88
HAMMONS, 15
HAMNER, 38
HAMTON, 100
HAND, 10 46
HANKINS, 15
HANNAN, 63 64 68
HANNON, 64 71
HARBISON, 137 139
HARDEN, 101
HARDIN, 46
HARDING, 22 88
HARDISTER, 58
HARDY, 146
HARING, 22 26 27
HARL, 97
HARMAN, 80 111
HARPER, 46 47
HARRELL, 157
HARRIGER, 10
HARRING, 22 23
HARRIS, 2 33 37 38 58 59
  61 63 69 70 92-94 100
  105
HARRISON, 46 65 90 129
  137 143
HARTLEY, 22
HARTMAN, 19 21
HARTSELL, 88
HARTSHORN, 144 145
HARVEY, 26 29
HARWOOD, 10 97
HASELIP, 93
HASKINS, 93
HASSEL, 135-137
HATHAWAY, 7 18
HATTAWAY, 18
HATTIE, 19
HATTON, 119

HAUGN, 1
HAUN, 4
HAVENS, 74
HAW, 157
HAWKINS, 6 89 103 111
HAWLEY, 46 65 105
HAY, 27 65
HAYCRAFT, 105
HAYDEN, 31-38
HAYES, 115
HAYNES, 57
HAYNIE, 45-47 56 96-99
HAYS, 2 4 8 11 22 62-65
  70 71 73 117 125
HAYSLER, 10
HAYTER, 82 83
HEAND, 57
HEATH, 2
HEATHAM, 120
HEATHMAN, 120 124 126
HEAUSSLER, 105
HECKTER, 7 17
HECKTOR, 17
HECTOR, 82 83
HEDGES, 103
HEDINGTON, 95
HEIBNER, 47
HEITMER, 3
HELAGE, 3
HELFENSTEIN, 4
HELM, 10 12
HELMAN, 67 69
HELMRICHS, 4
HEMPSTEAD, 147 149 152
HENDERICK, 100
HENDERSON, 86 146 151
HENSICK, 3 23 26
HENSON, 51
HERIDER, 45-47
HERKETT, 10
HERNDON, 127
HERRON, 65
HERRYMAN, 86
HERSENFLOW, 1
HERZIG, 115
HESSENFLOW, 1
HEUMAN, 22 26
HEWITT, 111 117
HIBBLER, 145
HIBLER, 144-146 150-154
HICKE, 117

HICKERSON, 5 12 13
HICKINSON, 5
HICKLEN, 83
HICKLIN, 97-99 130
HICKMAN, 30 45 46 105
  121
HICKS, 7 16 93 94
HICKSON, 138
HIGGINS, 18 122
HIGGNS, 122
HIGHBARGER, 22 23
HIGHLOWER, 86
HILDEBRAND, 117
HILL, 46 83 88 111 117
  119-121
HINCHER, 6 16
HINES, 86 129
HINKLE, 5 13
HINSHAW, 3
HINTON, 5 8-11 16 17 47
HIRT, 4
HITCH, 32
HITCHBORN, 46
HITE, 105
HIXON, 123 125 142
HIXSON, 140 142
HOAGE, 95
HOBSON, 46
HOCKADAY, 46 47 56
HODGES, 65 86
HOECKER, 4
HOEH, 116
HOGARD, 105
HOGG, 142 148 149 151
  153 154
HOLLIS, 105
HOLLOWAY, 86 88 93
HOLMAN, 46
HOLMES, 46 88
HOLT, 6 10 14 105
HOLTON, 17
HOOD, 6 15 46 93 141
HOOPER, 134
HOOVER, 3 57 77 78 95
HOPKINS, 133 141
HOPSON, 46
HORN, 32 35 65 68 88
HORNBACK, 77
HORNBECK, 73 75 98
HORNBUCK, 86
HORNBUCKLE, 86

HORNE, 105
HORTON, 111
HOSA, 61
HOSEY, 148 149
HOTCHKISS, 32
HOTTELL, 47
HOUCHIN, 26
HOUGH, 95
HOUGHT, 95
HOUSE, 100
HOUTS, 98
HOWARD, 20 91 111 123
124 126 128-130
HOWE, 98
HOWEL, 26 27 34
HOWELL, 22 23 35 46 155
HOWLETT, 72
HUBARD, 22
HUBBARD, 5 13 103 111
HUBBEL, 91
HUBBELL, 90 91
HUBBRAND, 118
HUCKSTEP, 147 152 154
HUDSON, 22 26 65 86 111
114 132
HUDSPETH, 2 3
HUEMAN, 27
HUFF, 10 98 102
HUFMAN, 97
HUGHES, 14 63 105
HUGHS, 64 65 69 72 155
HULL, 72
HUMBLE, 32 37 38 79
HUMMELL, 132
HUMPHREYS, 140 142 144-
148 150 153
HUNT, 87 102 132
HUNTER, 35 101
HUNTLEY, 116
HURLEY, 96
HURST, 101
HUSTON, 123
HUTCHINSON, 46 47
HUTTON, 1 73 75
HYCKS, 47
IGO, 47
ILES, 95 96
IMAN, 27
INGOLD, 3
INLOW, 105
IRVIN, 82

IRWIN, 75 83 84
ISH, 47 56
ISLE, 95
IVEY, 121
JACK, 19-21
JACKOBY, 58 60
JACKSON, 21 23 47 92-94
102 132 140
JACOB, 87
JACOBS, 154
JACOBY, 58
JAMES, 38 88
JAMESON, 157
JANSON, 137
JAQUES, 47
JARVIS, 23 47 48 56
JAYNE, 83
JAYNES, 83
JEFFERSON, 155
JEFFREY, 132
JEMISON, 76
JENKINS, 1 47 57-60 89
JENNINGS, 105
JOHANNIGMEIER, 18
JOHNS, 3 141
JOHNSON, 10 12 21 27 28
47 48 63 69 70 77 80
86 88 93 97 101 103
105 111 117 141 157
JOHNSTON, 48 86 151
JONES, 2 5 13 21 23 30
31 32 47 62 66-68 86
93-96 99 100 115 118
132
JONSON, 27
JOPLIN, 141
JORDAN, 133-141 157
JORDEN, 141
JUDGE, 10
JULIAN, 47 48
JUNKER, 59
KAPELLE, 4
KAVANAUGH, 87
KAYLER, 105
KAYSER, 3
KEACH, 105
KEELE, 72
KEEN, 114
KEENON, 157
KEETON, 21
KEISER, 3

KEITH, 27 48
KELLER, 80 155
KELLEY, 79 80 87 111
KELLY, 154
KEMP, 10 107
KEMPER, 87 88
KENDALL, 119
KENDEL, 95
KENNEDY, 88 89 132
KENNEY, 105
KENSINGER, 7-9 14 15
KERDOLFF, 126-128
KESSLER, 117
KESTERSON, 87
KETON, 94
KEY, 78-81 116 117
KEYTON, 27 48
KIDD, 18
KIDWEEL, 127
KIDWELL, 48 62 127 128
    130 131
KILE, 97
KIMBROUGH, 77
KIMSAY, 10
KIMSEY, 4 8 10-12
KIMWORTHY, 132
KINAMON, 94
KINCAID, 94 118
KING, 8 23 63 70 101 105
    142 149 151
KINKEAD, 23 143 145 146
    148-154
KINNARD, 105 114
KINNEY, 149
KINSINGER, 14 17
KINWORTHY, 102
KIRBY, 48
KIRKPATRICK, 19 21
KIRTLEY, 87
KISER, 36 39
KLING, 4
KNOX, 31 36
KOOTS, 94
KRAMER, 48
KREIHN, 127
KRENNING, 3
KRIBS, 58
KRIEHN, 125 131
KRONING, 118
KUEHNER, 3
LACEY, 105 138 157

LACKARD, 66
LACY, 118 139 141
LAFAIVER, 25
LAFFOON, 94-96
LAFORCE, 23
LAKIN, 27
LAMAR, 10
LAMB, 145
LAMBERT, 10 13
LAMBETH, 117
LAMBORN, 123
LAND, 10 13
LANDON, 18
LANDRUM, 103 106
LANE, 48 65 126 127
LANGSTON, 101
LANHAM, 118 153
LANKFORD, 87
LANTON, 3
LARRICK, 125
LASH, 117 118
LASSEN, 133-142
LASSIN, 133
LATIMER, 99
LAUGHLIN, 23 27
LAWLER, 49
LAWSON, 67 69 70
LAYCOCK, 16 18
LAYTON, 155
LEACH, 106
LEAKE, 106
LEAR, 31-33 36 38
LEE, 23 34 48 49 68 76
    157
LEETON, 112 114
LEIGHTON, 32
LEINBERRY, 49
LENT, 98
LEROUX, 140
LESUEUR, 124-130
LESUEURM, 130
LEWIS, 8 10 18 96 98 99
    148 155
LIEMKUELER, 27
LIGGET, 95
LIGGETT, 23 48 49
LIGHTNER, 93
LIGON, 48 92 106
LILLARD, 106
LIMRICK, 123 124 129
LINDEMANN, 4

LINDSEY, 10 92
LINDSLEY, 67
LINK, 106
LINSS, 117 153
LINSTONE, 13
LINVILL, 111 112
LINVILLE, 112
LIPSCOMB, 154 156
LITTLE, 49 111 112 120 121
LLEWELLYN, 149
LOCK, 148
LOCKE, 155
LOCKER, 118 154
LOCKETT, 105
LOCKWOOD, 49
LONG, 48 147
LONGGREAR, 116
LORD, 140
LOUDY, 23
LOUES, 82
LOUIS, 84
LOWES, 95
LOWRANCE, 31
LOWRY, 19-21
LOYD, 10 27
LUCAS, 25
LUCIUS, 150
LUCK, 106
LURME, 106
LUTHER, 106
LUTZ, 65 73
LYCOOK, 6
LYKENS, 106
LYNCH, 92-94 101
M'MILLION, 64
MADDOCK, 82
MADDOX, 136-139
MADERSON, 155
MAGERS, 93 94
MAGILL, 95
MAHAFFEY, 123
MAIN, 15
MAITLAND, 126
MAIZE, 5 6 8 9 11-13
MAIZO, 14
MAJOR, 89 90 106
MAJORS, 94
MALLARD, 50
MALLORY, 3
MALONE, 19-21 93
MANN, 67

MANNING, 19-21 57 146
MANNS, 72
MANSFIELD, 53 106 130 131
MAPLE, 106
MARKSBERRY, 50
MARLY, 88
MARPIN, 95
MARRS, 66
MARSHALL, 22 50
MARTIN, 1 4 8 26 30 49
    50 62 70 73 82 87 88
    97 98 106 120 122 127
MASON, 10 145 152
MASSEY, 92 94 143
MASSY, 92
MASTON, 30 35
MATHERLY, 65
MATHES, 74
MATHEW, 114
MATTHEWS, 67 143
MATTIX, 27 50
MATTOX, 23 84 135
MAUPIN, 85
MAXWELL, 31 38
MAY, 1 2 49 50 106
MAYFIELD, 49
MAYS, 4
MAZE, 4
MCADAM, 106
MCADAMS, 66 67
MCAFEE, 23
MCALRAVY, 62
MCAMIS, 49 50
MCCABE, 23
MCCALL, 5 13
MCCAN, 8
MCCANN, 6 10 14 15
MCCARTY, 23 90
MCCASULAND, 122
MCCAUSLAND, 122 123 128
    130
MCCLAIN, 28 49 112
MCCLELLAND, 127
MCCLOUD, 32 34 141
MCCLURE, 1
MCCOLLINS, 10
MCCOLLOUGH, 58
MCCORKLE, 91
MCCOUN, 74
MCCOWEN, 78
MCCOWN, 74-76

MCCOY, 132
MCCULLANAH, 58
MCCULLOUGH, 59 60 61
MCCULLY, 86
MCCURDY, 28
MCDADE, 49
MCDANIEL, 132
MCDONALD, 103
MCDORMAN, 16
MCDOWELL, 134-139 141
MCELHINNEY, 144
MCELROY, 145 146 151
MCELVOY, 117
MCFARLAND, 10 63 64 71
MCFORTUNE, 38
MCGEE, 49 50
MCGILL, 94
MCGLOTHLEN, 84
MCGLOTHLIN, 82
MCGREW, 103
MCILRAVY, 72
MCILRAVZ, 63
MCILROY, 68
MCINTIRE, 32 33 34 38
MCINTOSH, 49
MCINTRE, 32
MCINTYE, 32
MCINTYRE, 36 38
MCKAGH, 133
MCKAGUE, 136-139
MCKINNEY, 133-142
MCKINSEY, 76
MCKUGH, 134 135
MCLAIN, 112
MCLANE, 1
MCLATHLUE, 82
MCLAUGHLIN, 19 20
MCLAUHLIN, 20
MCLELLAND, 106 131
MCLEOD, 63 72
MCMAHAN, 12 40 98 157
MCMAHON, 97
MCNEAL, 62 64 66-68 70
MCNUTTS, 93
MCPHERSON, 20
MCQUIE, 106
MCWILLIAMS, 112
MEADE, 100
MEADOR, 95
MEADOW, 87 88 94
MEANS, 49 50

MEDCALF, 84
MEDDER, 96
MEDLIN, 112
MEEK, 94
MELHADO, 119
MELLIGAN, 49
MELOND, 34
MELTON, 75
MELVIN, 80
MENDENHALL, 49 56
MERCER, 74
MERRELL, 28
MERRICK, 3
MERS, 3
MESKENDORF, 4
MESTEMACHER, 3
METCALF, 49 50 83
METHERS, 94
MEYER, 118
MEYERS, 49
MEYNARD, 144
MICHEL, 3
MICKLES, 82
MICKLSON, 76
MIKE, 156
MILLAKEN, 84
MILLER, 10 14 28 39 49
   50 58 60 68 73 74 76
   77 83 99 101 112 116
   125 137 139
MILLIGAN, 50
MILLS, 3 5 14 75 125 134
MILSAPS, 97
MIMMS, 106
MINER, 96
MINKS, 49
MINOR, 97
MITCHEL, 2 67 82 112
MITCHELL, 2 33 37 84 94
   103 106
MIZNER, 112
MOCK, 103
MOCKBEE, 93
MODISETT, 106
MOGART, 18
MOHRHARDT, 3
MONROE, 155 157
MONTGOMERY, 49 50
MOORE, 3-11 13-16 23 27
   49 63-65 68 71 76 103
   119

MOORLAND, 67
MORE, 87
MOREE, 18
MORELAND, 121 125 130 131
MORGAN, 62 63 65 67-73
MORGART, 8 15 18
MORNEY, 112
MORRIS, 2 15 27 29 49 60
  61 87 106 126 130
MORROW, 65-67
MORTON, 70
MOSLEY, 23 24
MOSS, 30-36 38 103
MOSSELL, 93
MUELLER, 4
MUFFLEY, 119
MUIR, 100
MULIGAN, 93
MULLENS, 97 98
MULLINS, 98 99
MUNKER, 82 83
MUNKERS, 82
MUNROE, 155
MURDOCK, 28
MURPHY, 9 106 132
MURRAY, 6 8 10 11 16
MURRY, 88
MUSICK, 106
MYERS, 50 119 133-139
  146
MYRACK, 137
MYRICK, 136-139 141
NASH, 14
NCILROY, 66
NEAL, 8 50 118
NEFF, 21-23 25 28 50
NEGRO, Adam 97 Agniss 98
  Clowey 93 John 97
  Lestha 99 Martha 93
  Mary 97 99 Patten 97
  Rosin 93 Simon 97
  Sophia 99 Tinkney 93
NEIL, 10 70
NEILL, 157
NETHERTON, 50
NEUMINSTER, 68
NEW, 87
NEWGENT, 88
NEWKIRD, 93
NEWMAN, 50 51 65 119
NEWSOM, 112 114

NICHOLS, 9 17 50 74 75
  106 117
NICKERSON, 155
NICKLESON, 5 13
NICKOLS, 77
NIDEFER, 51
NIES, 4
NIEUIMISTER, 69
NILLER, 59
NIVIN, 118
NIX, 65
NOBLE, 64 65 71
NOEL, 92
NOELS, 65 73
NOLAND, 106
NOLTE, 3
NORDYKE, 132
NORRIS, 10
NOWELL, 132
NOWLIN, 106 131
NOX, 73
NUCKOLS, 82
NUGENT, 50 51
NUNIES, 50
NUTTER, 50
O'BANION, 102 132
O'BIEN, 119
O'BRIEN, 119
O'BRYAN, 106
O'NEAL, 45
OCHTERBACK, 4
ODELL, 24 28 66 68
OFFICER, 40 51
OLDHAM, 88
OLIPHANT, 121 124 126
OLIVER, 106
OLMSTEAD, 106
OOTS, 51 56
ORKINS, 5
ORR, 8 9 15-17 117 118
OSBORNE, 132
OSBURN, 83
OSKINS, 13
OVERBY, 57 157
OVERTON, 139 140
OWEN, 58 59 106
PADGETT, 1
PAGE, 51 52 56 57 83
PAINIS, 77
PARAMOUR, 106
PARKS, 51 52 73-78

PARRIS, 2
PARSON, 96
PARSONS, 99
PASAHLL, 138
PASCALL, 139
PASHALL, 138 140
PATTERSON, 38 88
PATTIESON, 134
PATTON, 84 101
PAUL, 10 94
PAULL, 52
PAULY, 1
PAVY, 1
PAYNE, 31 33 34 36 133-
141 146 148-150
PEACOCK, 63 64 71
PEARCE, 157
PEARSON, 23 28
PEAY, 103
PEEL, 51 52
PEERY, 157
PELL, 2
PELLIN, 2 3
PENDLETON, 96 97
PENN, 3 18
PENNOCK, 51 52
PEPE, 3
PEPER, 82
PERRY, 97
PETERSON, 95
PETTY, 86
PHELPS, 145
PHILIPS, 96 112
PHILLIPPS, 52
PHILLIPS, 51 52 56 95
PICKER, 4
PICKERINE, 28
PICKETT, 65 73
PIERCE, 21
PIGOT, 124
PILKERTON, 57
PILKINGTON, 58 59
PILLIAM, 51
PILLKINGTON, 125
PIPER, 21 23 28 52 82-84
PITMAN, 94
PLASTERS, 66
PLEASANTS, 155
PLEDGE, 52
POERS, 86
POINDEXTER, 2 3 23 28

POLK, 103 132 140
POLLARD, 89
POLSTON, 61
POOL, 31-33 57 87
POPE, 51
PORTER, 52 94 95
POST, 154
POTT, 143
POTTERFIELD, 30-34 36-38
142 143
POWEL, 94 96
POWELL, 1 52 81 93-96
116 129 153 154
POWER, 92
POWERS, 4 7-11 16 17 65
66 82 86 106
PRATHER, 73
PREISS, 115
PRENTICE, 106
PRESTON, 88 92 93
PRETTYMAN, 94
PREWITT, 23
PRICE, 21 23 28 39 86 88
90 94 96 106 115
PRIDDY, 2 3
PRIOR, 19 20
PROCTOR, 86
PROSSER, 12
PULLIAM, 51 52
PURNELL, 124 129
PURVIS, 29
PURVIUS, 24
QUARREL, 10
QUICK, 74 76 77
QUIGG, 28
QUISENBERRY, 52 100
RAGLAND, 10 16
RAIS, 61
RALEIGH, 73
RALSTON, 52
RAMBAUT, 90
RAMSEY, 59 61
RANDOL, 157
RANDOLPH, 3 96
RAUBAUT, 90
RAVENSCRAFT, 37
RAVENSCROFT, 32
RAY, 88
RAYMER, 141
READ, 74 77
REAMS, 125 129 131

REARIDON, 29
RECKEWAG, 3
REDFORD, 16
REDMAN, 157
REED, 75 77 125
REEDE, 58 60
REEVES, 62-64 66 69-71
  133-135 137-141
REID, 121 130
REINHARD, 3 4 117 121-123
RENFRO, 76
RENFROW, 3
RENNO, 132
REYNOLDS, 28 52 98 99 112
RHOADES, 106
RHODES, 32 63 64 66 70 71
RICE, 5 13 52 87 90 95 96
RICHESON, 35
RICKMAN, 98 99
RIDDLE, 77
RIEDS, 103
RIEHL, 10
RIFE, 114 140
RIGGS, 103
RIGHT, 106
RILEY, 52 56 61
RIMBY, 52
RINGO, 119
RIPPETOE, 112 114
RITTER, 28 102 132
RIVE, 88
RIVES, 157
RO, 52
ROACH, 31 36 62 63
ROAN, 106
ROBERTS, 10 23 29 55 77
  78 91 101 106
ROBERTSON, 52 97 106 118
  155
ROBEY, 106
ROBINS, 13
ROBINSON, 52 70 72 87
  100 106 155
ROBUCK, 60
RODDY, 93
RODGERS, 103 106
RODNEY, 127
ROEHRY, 119
ROGERS, 10 93 106
ROLAND, 21
ROLLINS, 88 89

ROMINES, 23
RONDEL, 15
ROOT, 137
ROSE, 120 121
ROSER, 6 15
ROSS, 23 52 68 69 100
  142 145 151
ROTH, 87 107
ROUT, 58
ROUTT, 58
ROUTTE, 61
ROY, 8
RUARK, 112
RUBEL, 157
RUBLE, 64 71
RUBY, 146
RUCKER, 107 132
RUCKERT, 3
RUDD, 52 54
RUDDER, 118
RUFNER, 88
RUMMERFIELD, 68 71
RUMMONS, 23
RUNNELS, 96
RUNNER, 6 15
RUNYAN, 91
RUSSELL, 4 9-11 80
RUTTE, 60
RUWWE, 118
SACHLEBEN, 3
SAINES, 71
SALE, 85
SALINA, 155
SALMON, 10
SANBURN, 102
SANDER, 4
SANDRIDGE, 155
SAPPINGTON, 29 118 143
  146 152 153
SAVAGE, 94
SCHABERG, 3
SCHABURG, 3
SCHAFER, 115
SCHEFFING, 115
SCHOLLMEYER, 4
SCHRADER, 4
SCHROEDER, 117
SCHULTZ, 39 151
SCIPES, 46 53
SCOTT, 2 3 7 18 23 29 85
  96 97 112 113 127

SCRADER, 118
SCRY, 116
SCWENKER, 4
SEARCY, 91
SEARS, 96
SEAY, 98
SEMSON, 5
SERCY, 113
SETTLE, 53
SHANDY, 64 65 72
SHANKS, 53 82 85
SHANNON, 53 103
SHARP, 5 8-13 42 53 57
    85 113 131
SHARPE, 57 58 130 131
SHAVER, 89
SHAW, 21 35 59 61 123
    124 147
SHAWL, 148
SHEARON, 85
SHEETS, 88
SHELBY, 119 143
SHELTON, 53 100
SHEPARD, 53
SHEPHERD, 29 142 147
SHEPPARD, 96
SHERON, 60
SHEWALTER, 125
SHIELDS, 119-121
SHIFLETT, 61
SHILDS, 119
SHILFETT, 61
SHINN, 113
SHINT, 85
SHIPLEY, 93
SHOAN, 53
SHOCKLEY, 53 54
SHOEMAKER, 18
SHOPE, 29
SHORT, 53 57 95
SHOTWELL, 118 119
SHRETE, 84
SHREVE, 82 85
SHRIEVES, 85
SHRITE, 85
SHULTS, 103
SHUMATE, 118 144
SHURER, 101
SHURLEY, 113
SHATZER, 53
SICHTING, 4

SIDENSTRICKER, 98
SIGNIST, 82 85
SIGRIST, 85
SILVEY, 101 102
SIMCO, 53
SIMMEN, 4
SIMMONS, 73 75 82 84 85
    95 98 145
SIMMS, 3 23
SIMPKINS, 31 36
SIMPSON, 12 140 141
SINTON, 120
SITKEN, 72
SKAGGS, 141
SKINNER, 29 53
SLADE, 82 84 85
SLANKARD, 21
SLAUGHTER, 148
SLAVE, Anna 156 Betsy
    156 Dick 156 Dinah 156
    Ed 95 Elijah 156 Eliza
    156 Emily 110 Hannah
    156 Henry 156 Huldah
    156 Isabel 156 Jack
    156 James 156 Jeff 156
    Kitty 156 Lewis 156
    Linsey 156 Lucy 156
    Malinda 156 Mary 156
    Merry 156 Mike 156
    Mima 156 Patrick 156
    Primus 156 Richmond
    156 Rose 156 Sally 156
    Sam 156 Tom 156
SLAVENS, 75 157
SLIGA, 70
SLIGER, 64 67 72
SLOAN, 53
SLOSS, 103
SMALLWOOD, 122
SMELSER, 136
SMELTSER, 134 135 137
SMELZER, 138
SMILEY, 4
SMITH, 4-6 10-14 16 17
    20 21 30 32 38 43 53
    54 63 67 71-78 87 88
    96 97 100 107 113 118
    120-123 125 126 128
    129 145 151 154 155
    157
SMIZER, 118

SMOTHERS, 57
SMYTH, 28
SNADON, 2
SNIDER, 76 150
SNODDY, 53 56
SNODGRASS, 7 10 17
SNOWDEN, 85
SNYDER, 77 89
SOLOMON, 67 69
SOPER, 23
SOPP, 4
SPANNAGEL, 3
SPARKS, 92 93 129
SPEAR, 2
SPEARS, 3 93 94
SPEER, 79
SPEERS, 2
SPELBRINK, 3
SPENCER, 28 30 53 54
SPENSE, 29
SPILMAN, 2
SPRADLEY, 53
SPRATT, 157
SPRINGER, 3 118
SPRUCE, 122 124
STAFFORD, 29 52 53
STANDISH, 124 125 128
   129
STANLEY, 141
STAPP, 23
STAR, 100
STARCK, 116
STARK, 132
STARNS, 66 67
STATLER, 157
STAYTON, 99 100
STEEL, 122 133-137
STEELS, 99
STEENBERGEN, 107
STEENSTRA, 107
STEGEMANN, 4
STELL, 122
STEPHEN, 36
STEPHENS, 31-38 64 71 92
   107 151
STEPP, 29
STERITT, 71
STERRITT, 64
STEVENS, 143 156
STEWARD, 95 140 141
STEWART, 69 107 122

STIFLE, 64 71
STILL, 2
STIVERS, 29
STOGE, 116
STOGER, 116
STONE, 10 12 22 91
STONEWALL, 124
STORCK, 114 115
STORY, 100
STOSSBERG, 3
STRATTON, 138 139
STRAUSS, 4
STRIBLING, 99
STRICKLAN, 76
STRICKLAND, 102 132 146
   151
STROTHER, 96 97
STROUD, 53 54 56 132
SUESSDORF, 4
SUGS, 93
SULLIVAN, 137-139 141
SUMMERS, 53 82 85
SUPEONA, 76
SUPPE, 4
SURBAUGH, 96 97 99
SURBER, 53
SUTTLES, 94
SUTTON, 96 117
SWANN, 98
SWINNEY, 107
SWITZLER, 91
TACKETT, 157
TALBOT, 124
TALBOTT, 119 157
TANNER, 68
TAUBMAN, 125 126
TAUL, 93
TAYLOR, 22 23 29 30 33
   54 67 71 73 87 101 102
   154 155
TEAS, 88 107
TEBBS, 131
TECKMEYER, 24
TEMME, 4
TEMPLE, 88 113
TERRELL, 20
TERRILL, 107
TERRY, 86 116 121 124
   125 155
TETER, 113
TETHRO, 82 85

176

TETLEY, 140
THARP, 65
THEBOLD, 54
THIAS, 4
THIES, 3
THISWATER, 94
THOMAS, 8 10 20 21 24 29
30 33 36 54 62 88 107
123 125 127 130 131
THOMASON, 120
THOMPSON, 13 29 30 54 88
92-95 107 133-142
THORNHILL, 64 72
THORNTO, 23
THORNTON, 21 23 24 27 29
30 101
THORP, 101
THRASHER, 10
THRESHER, 4
THRONTON, 21
THROOP, 93
TICHENOR, 132
TIECHNOR, 132
TIEKEMEYER, 4
TILFORD, 107
TILLMAN, 54
TILMAN, 6 7 15-17
TIMMONS, 32 36
TINGLE, 13
TINGLER, 13
TINLEY, 36 37
TIPPITT, 118
TIRRELL, 78
TISHLOCK, 99
TITUS, 91
TOCOLES, 98
TODD, 94
TOLLE, 107
TOMPSON, 141
TOOHEY, 54
TOONER, 90
TOWLES, 61
TOWNSEND, 10 29 30 54
131
TOWNSLER, 10
TRACEY, 54
TRADWAY, 20
TRAVIS, 86
TREAKEL, 96
TREMARY, 76
TRENARY, 75-78

TRENAY, 74
TRENT, 148 149 152 153
TRESSINRITER, 17
TRIBBLE, 101
TRIGG, 120 124 127 130
TRIMBLE, 68
TRISSEMITER, 7
TROTTER, 79 125 127
TUGGLE, 59
TULEY, 31-33 36-38
TUMBLESON, 85
TURK, 10
TURLEY, 118
TURNER, 10 57 61 62 70
85 103 107 143 145
TURPEN, 2
TURPIN, 54
TUTTLE, 8 10 12 107
TUTTY, 149
TWITTY, 95
TYLER, 155 156
UNDERWOOD, 118
UNICORE, 65
UPTON, 34
UTTERBACK, 24
VANCE, 102 132
VANCHER, 115
VANCOURT, 142
VANDERPOOL, 67
VANDERSLICE, 63 68 69 71
73
VANMETER, 96
VANNALA, 73
VANWAGNER, 57
VARDEMAN, 103
VARDIMAN, 107
VARNELL, 99
VAUGH, 58
VAUGHAM, 79
VAUGHAN, 54 79 80
VAUGHN, 60
VENABLE, 48 54
VERMILLION, 103
VERTON, 138
VICKERS, 87
VOIL, 94
VOILMAN, 94
VONSENDEN, 3
WADDELL, 86
WADE, 4 6-8 10 15-17
WADLEY, 91

WADSWORTH, 30-39
WAGGAMON, 113
WAGNER, 4
WAKELY, 157
WALDEN, 98 107
WALDENS, 114
WALDON, 113
WALDRIDGE, 7 18
WALKA, 117
WALKER, 20 21 24 33 34
   36 55 58 60 61 68 116
   133 135 136
WALKUP, 107
WALLACE, 10
WALLER, 55
WALLIS, 96 101 102
WALLS, 10 59 96
WALMSEY, 121
WALMSLEY, 120 121
WALTHAL, 107
WALTON, 124 127 144 146
   147 151-153
WAMLTON, 95
WANTLAND, 10
WARD, 2 86
WARDER, 107
WARE, 150
WARFIELD, 64 67 71 72
   155
WARNER, 93
WARREN, 34 88
WASBY, 55
WASH, 10
WASHINGTON, 153
WATKINS, 6 8-12 15 17
   119
WATS, 58 60
WATSON, 157
WATTS, 55 59 65
WAUGHTAL, 114
WAY, 55
WAYMAN, 83
WEAVER, 102 123
WEBB, 7 10 15 16 30 93
   123
WEBER, 4 116
WEBSTER, 10
WEEKLEY, 55 56
WEEKS, 10 57
WEIR, 55
WELCH, 24 57 92 107 119

WELLEN, 96
WELLS, 157
WELSH, 90
WEMP, 119
WENTWORTH, 122 131
WEST, 24 30 73 100
WESTBROOK, 116
WHARTON, 118
WHEELER, 1 2 97 99 107
WHELLER, 88
WHIDBEE, 10
WHITAKER, 12
WHITE, 30 58-60 66 77 87
   88 93 94 118 132 155
WHITEMAN, 7 18
WHITENACK, 5
WHITESIDES, 7
WHITMACK, 13
WHITSETT, 9 13 89
WHITSIDE, 6
WHITSIDES, 15 16 18
WHITTAKER, 6 15
WHITTEN, 55
WHITWORTH, 8 12 15 88
   119
WHORTON, 113 114
WI-----, 78
WICKHAM, 7 17
WIGINTON, 107
WILCOXEN, 33-35
WILCOXSEN, 101
WILCOXSON, 101
WILD, 130
WILDS, 129
WILEY, 24 125
WILHITE, 24 54 55
WILKENS, 4
WILKERSON, 24 30 79 80
WILLAIMSON, 10
WILLIAM, 20 88 101
WILLIAMS, 3 10 19-21 34
   35 55 66 75 85 93 95
   98 101 102 107 113 118
   156
WILLIAMSON, 8 10 87
WILLIS, 33 36 55 107 118
WILLOBY, 82
WILLON, 71
WILLOUGHBY, 85
WILLSON, 78
WILOUGHBY, 82

WILSHUSEN, 4
WILSON, 10 24 57 74 77
  98 117 122 124 126-128
  130 140 144 145-149
  152
WINEHOLFE, 13
WINEHOPE, 5
WINKLE, 63 71
WINN, 55
WISEMAN, 4 10 11 143-145
  148 151 152 154
WITHERSPOON, 73-78
WITT, 101
WOLF, 5 9 12 14 92
WOLFF, 6 10 12 16 17
WOLKSKILL, 97
WOOD, 19-21 24 30 54 55
  63 64 86 94 107 126
  128
WOODARD, 85 101
WOODRUFF, 24
WOODS, 55 73 103 107 144
  145 147-149
WOODSWORTH, 32
WOODWARD, 49 85
WOODY, 117
WOOLF, 7 18
WOOLFF, 9

WOOLFOLK, 10
WOOLFORK, 87
WOOLRIDGE, 107
WOOLVERTON, 114
WORD, 100
WORKMAN, 63 70
WORNAL, 86
WORRELL, 55
WRIEDEN, 4
WRIGHT, 10 16 77 118 124
  138 140 154-156
WRITE, 76
WYATT, 107
WYCOFF, 116 117
YANALL, 94
YANCY, 155
YATES, 55 58 114
YOKEL, 145 150
YORK, 65 69 72 95 96
YOUNG, 70-72 95 117 140
YOUNGMAN, 33
YOWELL, 55 56
ZARNES, 8 14
ZARRAGAR, 6
ZENG, 4
ZIMERMAN, 95
ZORK, 70
ZUPANN, 117

Other Heritage Books by Sherida K. Eddlemon:

Missouri Genealogical Records and Abstracts:
Volume 1: 1766-1839
Volume 2: 1752-1839
Volume 3: 1787-1839
Volume 4: 1741-1839
Volume 5: 1755-1839
Volume 6: 1621-1839
Volume 7: 1535-1839

Missouri Genealogical Gleanings 1840 and Beyond, Volumes 1-9

1890 Genealogical Census Reconstruction: Mississippi, Volumes 1 and 2

1890 Genealogical Census Reconstruction: Missouri, Volumes 1-3

1890 Genealogical Census Reconstruction: Ohio, Volume 1
(with Patricia P. Nelson)

1890 Genealogical Census Reconstruction: Tennessee, Volume 1

A Genealogical Collection of Kentucky Birth and Death Records

Callaway County, Missouri, Marriage Records: 1821 to 1871

Cumberland Presbyterian Church, Volume One: 1836 and Beyond

Dickson County, Tennessee Marriage Records, 1817-1879

Genealogical Abstracts from Missouri Church Records and
Other Religious Sources, Volume 1

Genealogical Abstracts from Tennessee Newspapers, 1791-1808

Genealogical Abstracts from Tennessee Newspapers, 1803-1812

Genealogical Abstracts from Tennessee Newspapers, 1821-1828

Tennessee Genealogical Records and Abstracts, Volume 1: 1787-1839

Genealogical Gleanings from New York Fraternal Organizations
Volumes 1 and 2

Index to the Arkansas General Land Office, 1820-1907
Volumes 1-10

Kentucky Genealogical Records and Abstracts, Volume 1: 1781-1839

Kentucky Genealogical Records and Abstracts, Volume 2: 1796-1839

Lewis County, Missouri Index to Circuit Court Records, Volume 1, 1833-1841

Missouri Birth and Death Records, Volumes 1-4

Morgan County, Missouri Marriage Records, 1833-1893

Our Ancestors of Albany County, New York, Volumes 1 and 2

Our Ancestors of Cuyahoga County, Ohio, Volume 1
(with Patricia P. Nelson)

Ralls County, Missouri Settlement Records, 1832-1853

Records of Randolph County, Missouri, 1833-1964

Ten Thousand Missouri Taxpayers

*The "Show-Me" Guide to Missouri: Sources for
Genealogical and Historical Research*

CD: Dickson County, Tennessee Marriage Records, 1817-1879

*CD: Index to the Arkansas General Land Office, 1820-1907
Volumes 1-10*

CD: Missouri, Volume 3

CD: Tennessee Genealogical Records

CD: Tennessee Genealogical Records, Volumes 1-3